Digital Gambling

"I am thrilled to recommend a book that is essential reading for students and scholars working across gambling and gaming studies. At last, we have a rigorous, creative and thought-provoking study to help us make sense of proliferating platforms and products that are blurring the lines between entertainment and investment in everyday life. Albarrán-Torres' concept of 'digital gamble-play' is quite literally a game-changer."
—*Fiona Nicoll, Research Chair in Gambling Policy with the Alberta Gambling Research Institute and the Department of Political Science at University of Alberta, Canada*

This book develops the concept of "gamble-play media", describing how some gambling and gambling-like practices are increasingly mediated by digital technologies. Digital gambling brings gambling closer to the practices and features of video games as audiovisual simulations structure users' experiences. By studying digital gambling from media studies, video game and cultural studies approaches, this book offers a new critical perspective on the issues raised by computer-mediated gambling while expanding our perspective on what media and gambling are. In particular, it critically analyses terrestrial, mobile and online slot machines; online poker; and stock trading apps through a selection of case studies.

César Albarrán-Torres is Lecturer in Media and Communications at Swinburne University of Technology, Australia.

Routledge Studies in New Media and Cyberculture

For a full list of titles in this series, please visit www.routledge.com.

Digital Gambling
Theorizing Gamble-Play Media

César Albarrán-Torres

Routledge
Taylor & Francis Group

LONDON AND NEW YORK

First published 2018
by Routledge

2 Park Square, Milton Park, Abingdon, Oxfordshire OX14 4RN
52 Vanderbilt Avenue, New York, NY 10017

*Routledge is an imprint of the Taylor & Francis Group, an
informa business*

First issued in paperback 2020

Library of Congress Cataloging in Publication Data
CIP data has been applied for.

ISBN: 978-1-138-30385-0 (hbk)
ISBN: 978-0-367-59172-4 (pbk)

Typeset in Sabon
by codeMantra

For Gabriella, David and Isabel: home

To my academic mentors,

Chris Chesher, Gerard Goggin and Peter John Chen (University of Sydney)

Fiona Jean Nicoll (University of Alberta)

Tom Apperley (Deakin University)

Contents

List of Figures and Table

Figures

Table

Preface
The VIP Lounge

This is how I became interested in exploring digital gambling as a media form. The first time I walked into an Australian pub in 2010, something caught my eye: a room framed by neon lights and suggestively called the "VIP Lounge". Two golden Chinese dragons framed the red sign. This space, in Sydney's Chinatown, was clearly demarcated from the rest of the venue, and patrons entered the room discreetly. I assumed something illegal or of an erotic nature was taking place in that room. Needless to say, I did not enter the VIP Lounge that first time, worried that it might somehow jeopardise my reputation.

However, after noticing similar spaces in almost every pub I walked past or visited, I finally pushed the door into the enigmatic VIP Lounge. I was not expecting what greeted my eyes: a series of animated slot machines in perfect rows, displaying video game-like imagery and showcasing high-tech 3D graphics and animations. It was unlike anything I had seen before. Up until 2009, slot machines had been uncommon in Mexico, my home country, and the gaming machine industry turned out to have a very short honeymoon with the authorities. In late 2013, President Enrique Peña Nieto increased scrutiny on slot machines. The country, riven by drug-related violence, had seen an increase in slot machine gambling since 2010, with many casinos being rumoured to be running as money laundering sites for the cartels (Animal Político, 2013; El Universal, 2017). However, stricter rules on the gaming machine industry haven't prevented it from running up to 90,000 devices in the country as per the latest counts (Ziolkowski, 2017).

A fully regulated space related to gambling, such as the Australian VIP Lounge, was, for me, foreign and fascinating.

The space resembled the game arcades of my childhood, and the devices reminded me of titles such as *Donkey Kong* (first released by Nintendo in 1981), the first iterations of *Mario Bros* (developed by Nintendo in 1983) or *Street Fighter* (launched by Capcom in 1987). The VIP Lounge triggered a feeling of nostalgia. The devices themselves demanded physical actions similar to the ones involved in other forms of interactive entertainment, such as pinball machine playing: the slot machine player pushes a button, activates a mechanism and waits for an outcome determined by chance. Smith and Abt have written about the "gambling roots in pinball" (1984, p. 130) and how in this game, "the contest seems to be human against machine – or computer – surely an archetypal confrontation in twentieth-century America" (1984, p. 131). Outcomes in a pinball game are triggered by chance events and then determined by the player's level of skill, just like in some forms of gambling, such as poker. Smith and Abt's appraisal of the cultural meaning of pinball machines reveals how gaming devices are able to synthesise history and culture. Where pinball is an expression of the human vs. machine "archetypical confrontation" (Smith & Abt, 1984, p. 131), gambling devices such as slot machines distil this confrontation into a pure and fun ritual of chance.

I would later find out that slot machines are known as 'pokies' in Australia and New Zealand, and that they are networked, complex devices that look deceptively archaic. Two leading Australian scholars on gambling cultures, policy and gaming machine addiction, Richard Wooley and Charles Livingstone wittily describe contemporary slots as "a 1960s Volkswagen equipped with a Ferrari motor" (Woolley & Livingstone, 2010, p. 46). In the VIP Lounge, gamblers sat quietly in front of these machines, pushing a series of buttons time after time. Animated reels rolled. Gamblers celebrated or silently cursed their fate, mumbling swear words ("Bugger!"). Others stood there, motionless, sipping their pints of beer. The screens showcased fantastic characters and strange, kitsch versions of mystical environments that included the North Pole, ancient Egypt, the Australian outback and the Aztec empire as well as John Wayne, a kangaroo, Cleopatra, buffalos, polar bears, a Native American chief and a moustached Mexican revolutionary (a clichéd representation that I was certainly troubled by!). Titles such as *More Chilli* and *Queen of the Nile*, both manufactured by Aristocrat, and even a Dolly Parton-themed machine, were available in the venue (ironically, one of the country star's hits is a duet with Kenny Rogers titled "The Gambler"). Even though the gameplay itself could be judged as quite simple and even boring (insert a note, choose your bet, push the button and hope for the best), the intense engagement that the punters established with the machine seemed to reveal a deeper meaning. Some even appeared to be undergoing a transcendental, transformative experience. Something else caught my eye: money seemed to be losing its real-life value and becoming a sort of gaming token, the price gamblers had to pay for entering a 'zone' with its own spatial and temporal rules.

Additionally, all around the pub, there were screens showing rugby games, horse and greyhound races and sports scores. Patrons had the opportunity to gamble on all of these. A sign hung over the slot machines, flashing the word 'PROSPERITY'. The pub itself was a cultural space framed and constructed by gambling and, more precisely, by the digital and networked technologies that brought together different locations and practices as well as financial and informational infrastructures and participants from all over the country and quite possibly the world. Patrons were physically co-present in the pub, but they were also co-present in digital spaces built around gambling and entertainment. Some played a slot machine connected to other slot machines in the venue and elsewhere. Others bet on a rugby match or on a greyhound race alongside thousands of other punters collectively defining the odds. Gambling technologies configured the spatial and temporal dynamics of the cultural space of the pub.

Digital gambling in Australia and other Global North countries extends far beyond the pub and slot machines. Many contemporary forms of gambling are, in fact, inconspicuously digital as they imply the generation of random events through algorithmic means, namely, Random Number Generators or RNGs. How truly random the outcomes are is still a matter of debate among mathematicians (Pironio et al., 2010). Even in physical venues such as casinos (venues in Las Vegas or Macau, Native American casinos in the United States and Canada, The Star in Sydney or Crown Casino in Melbourne, for example), games that are traditionally analogue/mechanical are now also staged through digital means. We can think, for example, of the Novo Unity II Roulette, which is played on an electronic terminal, and which is linked to both a live roulette table and an automated wheel game. The Novo Unity II Roulette uses haptic technology as its play demands that bets be placed via a touch screen on your own individual player terminal (New South Wales Independent Liquor and Gaming Authority, 2016). The material qualities of this device are more closely related to those of social gaming apps played on a tablet than to traditional gambling artefacts.

Roulette is the game infamously portrayed in the great Russian novelist Fyodor Dostoyevsky's arguably autobiographical novella *The Gambler*, originally published in 1867. The roulette wheel is described as an artefact that exercises a strong hold over gamblers. *The Gambler* provides an accurate representation of how gambling disrupts spatiotemporal regimes. The following passage describes the main character's state of mind by the roulette table, a gambling technology that is different from poker and slots but that also produces a sense of what cultural theorist of games Roger Caillois defined as *ilinx*, a sense of physical disorientation or *vertigo* that is the defining element of some gambling games (2001). Dostoyevsky describes his character's trance as follows:

> Of course, I live in constant anxiety, I play for the smallest stakes and wait for something; I make calculations, I stand for days on end by the gaming table and *observe* the play, I even see them playing in my sleep, but all that not withstanding I seem to have become numb, as it were, as if I'd become mired in some sort of mud.
>
> (Dostoyevsky, 2010, p. 265)

This passage relates to a drive to learn the nuances of the game and the inability to do so, which is an experience shared by slot machine players. In this literary text, the mechanical actions involved in the gameplay represent a defining characteristic of a chance event. The roulette wheel is particularly revealing as it produces a binary outcome out of mechanical actions. The main character, Alexei Ivanovich, further exclaims, "Is it really impossible to come into contact with the gaming table without at once becoming infected with superstition?" (Dostoyevsky, 2010, p. 137). Ivanovich, a compulsive gambler, also questions the social stigma placed upon gambling as opposed to other economic activities in which luck might play a part:

> For why is gambling a whit worse than any other method of acquiring money? How, for instance, is it worse than trade? True, out of a hundred persons, only one can win; yet what business is that of yours or mine?
>
> (2010, p. 134)

As in Dostoyevsky's novel, contemporary forms of digital gambling are defined by negotiations between individual autonomy and institutional control, between user agency and state regulation. It is also worth noting that Ivanovich lists gambling and trade as uncertain methods of capital accumulation. Even in late nineteenth-century Russia, the gambling roots in finance, and the moral dilemmas generated by this relationship, became evident.

This book is an exploration of the gambling "zones" (Schüll, 2012) created in spaces such as the VIP Lounge and in a multifarious array of digital media, as well as of the expansion of the cultural logic of gambling into other arenas, such as global finance. Digital gambling is a prominent and extensive digital cultural practice not only in Australia but also in most Western media-saturated markets, such as the United States and Western Europe. In Australia, the sociotechnical networks present in the cultural space of the pub exist in parallel to others, such as online casinos and racetracks. More recently, 'freemium' social casino apps allow users to play with no money at stake but nevertheless often demand payment and labour for continuous engagement.

These types of spaces and their social and media dynamics are quite fascinating as they represent an unexplored set of cultural forms that consists of overlapping assemblages of fixed and mobile devices. This provides this book with an opportunity to make a significant contribution in the fields of gambling and media studies by describing and conceptualising the effects of media change in gambling cultures. Gambling is enmeshed with informational networks. Digital gambling practices, which I group under the term 'gamble-play', extend rapidly, forming a set of overlapping media assemblages. This book is about both the intimate human-machine couplings that form these assemblages and the wider transformation in markets and cultures of gambling, media, finance and play.

Melbourne, Australia, February 2018

References

Animal Político (2013, October 24). Gobernación prohíbe (casi) todas las máquinas tragamonedas. *Animal Político*. Retrieved from www.animalpolitico. com/2013/10/gobernacion-prohibe-casi-todas-las-maquinas-tragamonedas/# axzz31SY30sVA

Caillois, R. (2001). *Man, play and games*. Urbana, IL: University of Illinois Press.

Dostoyevsky, F. (2010). The gambler and other stories. New York, NY: Penguin Classics.

El Universal (2017, December 12). Atacan fuentes financieras de los grupos criminales en Tamaulipas. *El Universal*. Retrieved from www.eluniversal. com.mx/estados/atacan-fuentes-financieras-de-los-grupos-criminales

New South Wales Independent Liquour and Gaming Authority (2016). *Novo Unity II Electronic Gaming Table*. Retrieved from www.liquorandgaming. nsw.gov.au/Documents/casino/novo-unity-ii-electronic-table-game-2-june-2016.pdf

Pironio, S., Acín, A., Massar, S., de La Giroday, A. B., Matsukevich, D. N., Maunz, P., & Monroe, C. (2010). Random numbers certified by Bell's theorem. *Nature, 464*(7291), 1021–1024.

Schüll, N. D. (2012). *Addiction by design: Machine gambling in Las Vegas*. Princeton, NJ: Princeton University Press.

Smith, J., & Abt, V. (1984). Gambling as play. *Annals of the American Academy of Political and Social Sciences, 474*, 122–132.

Woolley, R., & Livingstone, C. (2010). Into the zone: Innovating in the Australian poker machine industry. In S. F. Kingma (Ed.), *Global gambling: Cultural perspectives on gambling organizations* (pp. 38–63). New York and London: Routledge.

Ziolkowski, S. (2017). The World Count of Gaming Machines 2016. *Gaming Technologies Association*. Retrieved from http://gamingta.com/wp-content/ uploads/2017/05/World_Count_2016.pdf

Acknowledgements

Thanks to Dr Robbie Fordyce for his editorial assistance in the preparation of the manuscript. Thanks to the Routledge and codeMantra teams for their expertise throughout the book production process.

Introduction
Digital Gambling as Media

> Games are one cultural form which requires algorithm-like behaviour from the players.
>
> —Lev Manovich (2000, p. 180)

Are digital gambling platforms a media form?

In short, the answer, although far from intuitive, is a resounding yes.

This book explores the media changes associated with the digitisation of gambling platforms as well as the cultural practices and new markets associated with this technological development. I introduce the concept of gamble-play to describe current forms of digital gambling media in which gambling situations are staged through digital means and chance events are produced through algorithms. In one dimension of gamble-play, the fun aspects of gambling are privileged over winning or losing, establishing new dynamics of seduction and control. In another dimension, gambling practices are staged in ways that resemble digital games. In the last chapter, I argue that the cultural dynamics of gamble-play extend into other spheres of contemporary capitalism, such as amateur stock trading through apps.

Gamble-play media are hybrid in that they incorporate the affordances of other media forms, such as traditional gambling platforms, social networking sites (SNSs) and digital games. The development of digital gamble-play is a major – and as yet under-researched – techno-social shift in the gambling, gaming and entertainment industries as well as in broader cultural notions concerning risk, money and leisure in capitalist societies. It is also part of larger media trends, such as convergence and the rise of participatory culture.

I deal with three forms of digital gamble-play that are representative of different media dynamics:

i   traditional slot machines,
ii poker in online casinos and
iii slot machine apps, mainly for Facebook, Android and iOS platforms.

I additionally argue that a different type of media, stock trading apps, which exemplify the close relationship between gambling and capitalist financial systems, follows the logic of gamble-play. As DeGoede (2005) argues, the roots of many financial institutions, cultures and practices can be found in games of chance. The trading of future options, for example, is heavily reliant on chance and the risk that investors/players are willing to take.

The negotiation between chance and skill is key in understanding gamble-play media. Physical poker has traditionally been seen as a game that involves both chance and skill (Mahmoon, 2006), while slots are seen as a game of pure chance. However, the balance between chance and skill is reconfigured by the digitisation of these gambling forms and their convergence with other media, primarily digital games and SNSs. For example, free bonuses are given in social casino apps when users share their results on SNSs such as Facebook.

The digitisation of gambling generates new practices and subjectivities. As novel platforms expand, they involve a new set of media literacies and demand "the ability to access, analyze, evaluate, and communicate messages in a wide variety of forms" (Hobbs, 1998, p. 16). This means that users need to learn how to interact through digital media, which can potentially generate relationships based on unequal terms because some players are more literate in digital media than others. The "wide variety of forms" through which users engage with digital gambling products borrow from other media, most saliently digital games, which has wide implications for gambling markets in terms of product design, consumption, regulation and notions of problem gambling.

Online poker and traditional slot machines involve gambling for real money, while slot apps entail digital currency or play money. I group these gambling media under the umbrella term 'gamble-play', which I will expand upon in the following paragraphs and throughout this book, particularly in Chapter 1, "Towards a theory of gamble-play".

An important part of my contribution to the field of gambling studies is treating symmetrically the cultural practices of real-money gambling and those that are purely play. In between gamble-play and gameplay are services in which players pay for heightened game experiences. By treating these gambling and gambling-like media on equal terms, the preponderance of gameplay is more easily prone to scrutiny. This approach represents a significant departure from previous gambling studies, which focus on the effects rather than the dynamics of games of chance or the platforms on which they are carried out.

Gambling is a powerful cultural and social phenomenon that has been for the most part neglected by scholarly traditions of media studies. Gambling has wide social and cultural implications for, as Abt and McGurrin point out, it "provides a collective means by which human beings deal with risk" (1992, p. 415). For James Cosgrave, the proliferation of casinos is "illustrative of the transformation of economic ethics, cultural values, and socialization processes in the shift from industrial to postindustrial consumer societies" (2010, p. 116). Gambling is a window into history and culture, into how people deal with risk, hope, fun and aspiration.

For decades, various forms of gambling, particularly those more closely related to chance, such as slots, have been a salient area in disciplines including psychology or law studies. But, as Cosgrave and Klassen have also pointed out, "much of the social scientific research undertaken on gambling activities in Western countries has focussed on the economic and tax implications of different forms of gambling, the motivation of individuals to gamble, and the phenomenon of problem gambling" (2001, p. 1). Sociological or cultural-symbolic issues are rarely the source of academic work, even though gambling practices are constantly shifting and expanding to adapt to consumer taste and regulation. Studies in this field could engage in richer discussions around the commoditisation of contemporary life or the pervasiveness of risk as the raison d'être of market economies (Calhoun, 2006). They could also shed light on the cultural transformations inspired by digital, online and mobile media. This is where this book is situated.

Media and cultural studies scholars have generally overlooked gambling. There are very notable exceptions, of course, particularly from sociology, cultural studies and political science. We can think, for example, of Fiona Nicoll's work on the cultural spaces of gambling (2011) and the intersections of finance, gambling and power, or what she calls 'finopower' (2013); Gerda Reith's thorough cultural history *The Age of Chance: Gambling in Western culture* (published in 1999 before digital gambling became a widespread phenomenon); Thomas Malaby's work on the cultural dynamics of gambling and play in Greece (1999, 2003) as well as his analysis of economic dynamics in virtual environments (2006); James Cosgrave's work on gambling and the state (2001) as well as his 2006 collection *The Sociology of Risk and Gambling Reader*; or Rebecca Cassidy, Andrea Pisac and Claire Loussouarn's 2013 book *Qualitative Research in Gambling: Exploring the Production and Consumption of Risk*, which begins to explore the negotiations between traditional forms of gambling and new game delivery models, such as social casino gaming. Holly Kruse's work is also noteworthy. In her 2016 monograph *Off-Track and Online: The Networked Spaces of Horse Racing*, she writes about how horse racing has witnessed developments in computer networks, first with mechanic totalisator machines, followed by electronic, then digital and mobile technology, supporting the calculation of odds and taking of bets. I reference this valuable body of literature throughout this book.

A group of social scientists including Charles Livingstone, Reith and Natasha Dow Schüll, many of whom are referenced in this book, recently published the article "On gambling research, social science and the consequences of commercial gambling" (2017), defending a humanities approach to the study of gambling. They contend that "as social scientists, we choose to focus our research on the social processes and formations that lead to the production of risky gambling environments" because "a series of social, political and economic changes have resulted in the proliferation of commercial gambling opportunities" (Livingstone et al., 2017, p. 7). Scholars outside the Anglosphere have also identified the need to go beyond a psychological approach to gambling issues (Vacchiano & Mejía Reyes, 2017). This book contributes to this vast interdisciplinary and transnational field.

The field of media studies of digital gambling, where this monograph is situated, is, however, evolving and still largely uncharted. Dow Schüll's outstanding book *Addiction by Design: Machine Gambling in Las Vegas* (2012) is an exception and is widely referenced here. Schüll analyses slot machines in Las Vegas as both a media form designed to trigger addiction and a telling cultural phenomenon that reveals new forms of interaction between people and digital technology. As she puts it,

> In a historical moment when transactions between humans and machines unfold "at an even greater level of intimacy and on an even greater scale" (as the sociologist Bruno Latour has written), computers, video games, mobile phones, iPods, and the like have become a means through which individuals can manage their affective states and create a personal buffer zone against the uncertainties and worries of their world.
>
> (Schüll, 2012, p. 13)

Gamble-play media provide some of these "personal buffer zones" (Schüll, 2012, p. 13) and generate particular material and expressive transactions between humans and machines. Gamble-play media also modulate affective states by providing environments where users invest hope, creativity, emotional capital and disappointment. Schüll argues that slot machine and casino operators encourage repetitive consumption. This pattern is sustained in other forms of gaming delivery, such as online casinos and social casino apps.

The study of digital gamble-play is a gateway into the under-researched gambling-related cultural trends in transnational and convergent digital media. Schüll's book is the exception in studies of gambling platforms as media, even though digital gamble-play represents a growing subset of interactive screen cultures and networked communications. As Farnsworth and Austrin argue, discussing poker,

> poker enthusiasts have access to an immense spectrum of media, ranging from popular television series to games played on mobile,

handheld devices... The interaction of these technologies and their human participants constantly changes how the game is reported, played or watched.

(Farnsworth & Austrin, 2010, p. 1121)

By being incorporated into media ecologies, gambling is experienced as an increasingly normalised form of entertainment. The emergence of digital media into popular culture is widespread. In 2011, new media scholar Larissa Hjorth wrote in regard to digital games and their cultural normalisation,

The haunting and persistent image of smoky, dark rooms filled with males sitting like mushrooms in front of their computers playing online games for hours on end is beginning to subside as games become increasingly part of global popular culture.

(Hjorth, 2011, p. 56)

Digital gamble-play media have also become normalised and assimilated into popular culture worldwide. The intersections between digital screen-based gambling and other forms of digital communication, mainly digital games, are increasingly evident in terms of textual and visual discourses, practices and markets. These intersections call for a reframing of what we think of as the cultural practices of gambling.

In her widely referenced cultural history of gambling in Western culture *The Age of Chance*, Gerda Reith describes gambling as "the commoditization of chance" (1999, p. 89) and as

a ritual which is strictly demarcated from the everyday world around it and within which chance is deliberately courted as a mechanism which governs a redistribution of wealth among players as well as a commercial interest or 'house'.

(Reith, 1999, p. 1)

This definition needs to be revisited because gamble-play is no longer separate from other spheres of everyday life. Recent cultural and technological developments, such as the networked infrastructures and ubiquitous devices through which digital gambling is carried out, allow wagering to infiltrate the everyday. Digital gamble-play is carried out on both desktop and mobile platforms. Hardware has distinct affordances, such as portability, that shape gambling and gaming cultures in particular ways.

The "redistribution of wealth" (Reith, 1999, p. 1) also acquires a new dimension. In current forms of digital gambling, users pay with a mixture of money, labour, time and access to digital social networks. Thus, recent forms of digital gambling have new implications. They institute new economic dynamics as operators increasingly rely not only on the traditional consumption of gambling but also "on the exploitation of communications" (Dean, 2010, p. 4) to maintain and expand their networks and increase profit. Digital gambling platforms have built-in affordances that allow users to engage in digital media practices, such as sharing and archiving, that align with the dynamics of, for instance, social networking. The loss of money, labour and time is gradually camouflaged through the play and social aspects of gambling.

Digital gamble-play media have structural features similar to those that make mainstream video games alluring to players. These characteristics, as identified by researchers of video game and gambling addiction Daniel King, Paul Delfabbro and Mark Griffiths in their 2010 article "Video Game Structural Characteristics: A New Psychological Taxonomy", are grouped according to their social features, modes of manipulation and control, narrative and identity features, reward and punishment features, and presentation features. They include social features, such as chats and leader boards. Control features manage multiple resources that give players a false sense of mastery over the game and the outcome. They support avatar creation for narrative and identity. They provide reward and punishment features, such as bonuses and increased difficulty. They include presentation features, such as branding and logos. King, Delfabbro and Griffiths's work highlights concerns about gaming addiction in what they term "excessive video game playing" (2010, p. 90), but their taxonomy remains useful in studying gamble-play. As I will show throughout this book, digital gamble-play media presents diverse combinations of these features, generating particular configurations of play. I use this taxonomy in Chapter 5, "Gamble-play as *Second Life*: the case of *PKR*", in which I analyse an early and now shut down online casino that mixed real-money gambling with a sophisticated virtual environment similar to the pioneering virtual world *Second Life*, which also has complex economies and value systems (Malaby, 2006, 2011).

The transition from an analogue to a digital production of random events is a significant example of media change. Digital events happen within what the French sociologist Bruno Latour calls a 'black box' (2005), a device that requires inputs and generates outputs but whose inner workings are, for the most part, unknown to the lay user, who generally has an illusion of control over the outcomes (Griffiths, 1993). As digital media in which content is "accessible or transmissible" (Couldry, 2012, p. 35), gamble-play platforms consist of different elements that produce and maintain flows and loops of information, with strategic levels of access defined, for the most part, by user expertise.

The flow of information in digital gamble-play is much more complex than the analogue staging of a bet at, for instance, a casino poker table. At an online poker table, such as the pioneering *PKR*, the data is entered from different places in the world. The processing engine is generally located in an offshore server due to regulatory constrictions (Albarrán-Torres, 2017; Gainsbury, Russell, Hing, & Blaszczynski, 2017). The interface is displayed in a variety of platforms, and the users are a multifarious group that can potentially consist of humans and non-humans. Non-human agents include software known as pokerbots; on cyber fraud in online poker, see Miller (2006) and McMullan and Kervin (2012).

Pioneering video game theorist Espen Aarseth identified four elements of a games platform when discussing video games such as *Doom*: "the data, the processing engines, the front-end medium (interface), and the users" (1997, p. 104). Digital gamble-play complicates the interplay of these four elements, something that can be seen in a recent example related to online poker. In April 2014, a fire in Gibraltar's main power station rendered several online betting sites unable to operate for several hours, much to the desperation of punters and online casino operators. Among those affected were the UK firms William Hill, Ladbrokes, Betfred, Stan James and Betfair (Russell, 2014). This case is significant as it exemplifies some of the complications that arise with media changes in gambling. Technological infrastructures are put in place to allow for the co-presence of players. Often, these infrastructures bridge the user's location to servers in jurisdictions with lax regulations and generous tax regimes as changes in tributary laws have a significant impact in the gambling sector (Lyall, 2013). Infrastructures become evident when there are significant problems, as was the case with the fire in Gibraltar. Gamble-play is staged in digitally produced environments but relies on physical infrastructures for the processing of information and the transmission of content.

Researching Gamble-Play

An academic investigation of gamble-play is significant mainly for two reasons. First, it responds to major changes in the gambling industry. These changes are indicative of common patterns and trends in entertainment industries at large, such as user participation and media convergence. Second, gambling is being shaped as a normalised form of entertainment that has ample political implications. By studying digital gambling from media studies, video game and cultural studies approaches, this book offers a new critical perspective on the issues raised by computer-mediated gambling while expanding our perspective on what media and gambling are.

Because digital gambling is a multifaceted new media and cultural phenomenon, I take a pluralistic approach, moving across a variety of theoretical frameworks. I transverse critical theory, video game studies, new media studies and cultural studies of gambling to understand contemporary forms of digital gambling as well as the political implications of the intersections between gambling and entertainment industries. Work in philosophy; sociology; and social theory, cultural theory and cultural studies, such as that of Jean Baudrillard, Guy Debord and Walter Benjamin, helps to explain some of the cultural dynamics of gamble-play. I also draw from video game theorists, such as Ian Bogost and Michael Nitsche, to analyse digital gambling interfaces and the ways in which they exercise seduction and control. New media theorists, such as Jay David Bolter and Richard Grusin, Henry Jenkins, Larissa Hjorth and Nick Couldry, among others, also help explain how digital gambling relates to other forms of new media.

Among theoretical approaches that provide a critique of media ontological phenomena is Manuel DeLanda's assemblage theory, as explained in his book *A New Philosophy of Society: Assemblage Theory and Social Complexity* (2006). I use DeLanda's work to explain how gamble-play platforms are generated and how markets and media interact. For DeLanda, assemblages are networked formations that counter totalising notions that dictate that social groupings are monolithic structures resistant to change. Assemblages, on the other hand, are "wholes whose properties emerge from the interactions between parts" (DeLanda, 2006, p. 5). I argue that digital gamble-play markets follow these productive dynamics and that their somewhat unstructured expansion is best grasped through the concept of assemblages. Assemblage theory allows me to abstract and theorise gamble-play.

Even though DeLanda's theory is on a grand scale and deals with sizeable social formations, such as nations and markets, the concepts through which he explains the malleability of assemblages, such as 're-lations of exteriority' (how component parts of assemblages are introduced in other assemblages) and 'deterritorialisation' (processes that destabilise the identity of social formations), are useful in understanding particular technocultural formations related to gamble-play. This understanding appears on both an intimate and larger scale, resulting from the interaction between humans and technology.

The French philosophers Gilles Deleuze and Félix Guattari heavily influence DeLanda's sociological theory. I mobilise some of their concepts to analyse particular cultural forms derived from gamble-play. These include 'procedure-images' and 'gambling-machines', concepts through which I analyse the images in digital gambling platforms and human-machine couplings in gamble-play, respectively.

Deleuze and Guattari are often referenced in discussions around the relationship between humans and technology, mainly through the notion of assemblages and desiring-machines elaborated on *Anti-Oedipus*. Their world view emphasises the coexistence of multiplicities in terms of identity, ideologies and social structures. For them, machines are the generators of some of these multiplicities. As Deleuzian scholars David Savat and Mark Poster argue, Deleuze "was at times directly engaged in considering specific technologies and the effect of their usage as a component or function within larger assemblages" (2009, p. 1). I analyse specific human-machine assemblages generated in gamble-play, such as the gambler-slot coupling that I term 'gambling-machine'.

Deleuze's philosophical engagement with technology is particularly evident in two of the texts that I discuss in this book. First, in his book *Cinema 1. The movement-image* (1986) – originally published in 1983 – he reflects on the technical and cultural innovation of cinema and how it alters our engagement with images and ultimately with the world. Second, he argues in the essay "Postscript on the Societies of Control" (1992) – first published in *L'Autre Journal* in 1990 – that modern technologies afford the formation of flowing individuals and social groupings.

DeLanda and Deleuze and Guattari offer productive theoretical frameworks to understand malleable, ductile media. Their understanding of society as a system that is fluid, and within which elements can play interchangeable roles, counters totalising theories that see society as a stable system. Digital gamble-play assemblages are networks of machines, content (sound, images, cross-platform narratives and global brands) and subjects that establish connections and generate complex gamble-play assemblages.

Gamble-Play Markets: Cultural and Industrial Significance

Digital gambling is a multimillion-dollar industry that in recent years has seen many instances of industry convergence and consolidation. The change is so dramatic that even industry insiders have coined terms such as "the new poker", referring to a different set of practices that are in tune with values and practices of networked digital communication (McDonald, 2005).

In the early 2010s, social casino apps, a salient example of what I call 'gamble-play', were mere curiosities, not the groundbreaking phenomenon that they became in 2011–2014 (Morgan Stanley, 2012) and consolidated during the next three years. Social networking and mobile platforms have further complicated the market transformations in the digitisation of gambling as new forms of online and offline socialisation alter the relationships among gamblers and between consumers and service providers. In 2012, an industry insider was reported as saying, "When online gambling is legalized, Facebook will be a $100 billion company" (Blodget, 2012). It is relevant to note that since then, Facebook's value has surpassed that figure. In August 2013, Jamie Odell, CEO of the Australian company Aristocrat, one of the world's largest slot machine manufacturers and a significant source of tax revenue for the Australian government, told *The Wall Street Journal*,

> But we're most excited about social media. We just bought a company called Product Madness, a gaming platform for Facebook that

competes with the likes of Zynga. Consider games like *Farmville* where you can actually buy animals or treats with Facebook credits. We're learning that people are prepared to pay small amounts to play slot machines without a win.

(Odell cited in Kelly, 2013)

Technosocial transformations associated with gambling affect a diverse range of stakeholders. As Gainsbury and Wood state in relation to on-line gaming platforms,

Internet gambling has presented governments, politicians, regulators, operators and consumers with a whole host of challenges and opportunities, and represents an important and real change to the provision of gambling services.

(Gainsbury & Wood, 2011, p. 320)

Since 2010, the practice of playing the slots through social media platforms without the possibility of hitting a real jackpot has emerged as a viable revenue model (Cowie, 2013; Duryee, 2013; Griffiths, 2013; Kelly, 2013). This runs counter to previous understandings of gambling, which have based the design and promotion of products on offering big wins and perks to lure players (Gibson & Sanbonmatsu, 2004). Classic gambling studies argue that in order for a game to be gambling, money needs to be at stake (Reith, 1999). However, current forms of social casino games stage transactions without mediating an actual bet among the gamblers and the house. If there are significant changes in legislation to loosen regulation, though, actual gambling through social networks could have wide-ranging industrial and cultural repercussions. The path for the legalisation of gambling through SNSs, however, has been hazardous.

Digital gambling is gathering strength as a cultural and economic force in informational networks and gaming and mobile markets. As these technocultural networks become increasingly multifaceted in terms of platforms, devices and evolving consumer desires, the variety of gambling products will only grow in number and become more intertwined. For as Farnsworth & Austrin state, digital gambling practices such as online poker typify "common patterns of interaction across traditional and new media, as well as mass and personal media forms" (2010, p. 112). In these patterns of interaction, "mass media actors no longer have a monopoly as mediators and constructers of factual and fictional reality" but "are increasingly aware of the value of user-generated content within a mass media setting" (Lüders, 2008, p. 696).

In the introduction to *Qualitative Research in Gambling: Exploring the Production and Consumption of Risk*, long-time researcher of gambling economies Rebecca Cassidy has called the relationship between real-money gambling and social casino games a "partial convergence" (2013, p. 157), arguing that

> the courtship between social gaming and real-money online gambling is based on the reach of the former, its low costs and 'fit' with digital forms of distribution and cloud technology, and the profitability of the latter.
>
> (Cassidy et al., 2013, p. 161)

Digital gambling operators adapt to contemporary entertainment assemblages by configuring their products according to the cultural and economic dynamics of their target and potential markets, such as those of social media and social gaming users.

Mergers and acquisitions involving gambling and play, as well as other entertainment companies, continue to influence the morphology of this market. Even though the gambling industry extends across the world, gamble-play has been most widespread in Europe, the United States and Australia (Morgan Stanley, 2012).

As mentioned, in this book, I deal with three forms of gaming delivery: poker in online casinos; slot machines in their land-based form (cabinet); and slot machines in app forms, mainly Facebook, Android and iOS platforms. I will now describe the markets of the digital gambling media that I analyse in this book.

Electronic Gaming Machines

Traditional slot machines are the oldest form of digital gamble-play media. In their traditional form, outcomes are generated purely by chance. They evolved from mechanical slot machines and are now complex digital devices akin to computer and arcade games, which is why I consider them digital gamble-play.

Slot machines, or 'pokies' in the Australian context, are part of the Electronic Gaming Machine (EGM) market segment, which is a multibillion-dollar industry. As of 2016, there were an estimated 7,870,643 EGMs in the world, including slot machines, video lottery terminals, amusements with payouts, the Japanese varieties *pachinko* and *pachislot*, and electronic table games (Ziolkowski, 2017). Slot machines are mainly located in casinos, clubs and pubs and on cruise ships (Ziolkowski, 2017).

The biggest manufacturers are the companies Aristocrat, Bally Technologies and International Game Technology (IGT), which was bought by Italy's GTECH – the world's largest provider of lottery systems – for USD $6.4 billion (Palmeri, Lepido & Rahn, 2014). The jurisdictions (territories subject to the same gaming laws) with the most gambling machines in the world as of 2016 are Japan, Italy, Germany, Spain, Nevada (the United States), the United Kingdom, Argentina, New South Wales

(Australia), Mexico and Peru (Ziolkowski, 2017). This list provides insight into how there can be a high density of machines in particular localities, influencing local culture and social life.

Online Poker

Although it is hard to assess the size and reach of the online poker industry, it is clear that it involves large numbers of players. According to the results of a pioneering audit of online poker operators conducted by researchers from the University of Hamburg, in 2010 alone, six million people engaged in online poker, giving a USD $3.61 billion rake to the operators. These figures speak both of a greatly profitable industry and a vast network of users (Fiedler & Wilcke, 2011). Fiedler and Wilcke (2011) describe the structure of online poker sites: "large player pools and the corresponding network effects have helped the game to grow to a size not to be matched in the offline world" (Fiedler & Wilcke, 2011). Fiedler and Wilcke's study remains the only publicly available survey of its kind, but it is safe to assume that the online poker sector has since then enjoyed a steady growth.

As of July 2017, the ten most popular online poker websites, according to the online poker traffic rank published by PokerScout, are PokerStars, IDNPoker, *888 Poker, Party Poker*, PaiWangLuo (Bodog), Winning, Winamax.fr (France), GGNetwork, iPoker and PokerStars.it (Italy).

Online poker is particularly popular in countries such as Austria, Canada, Finland, France, Italy, Spain, Sweden, the United States and the United Kingdom (PokerScout, 2017), even though not all these jurisdictions are fully regulated.

Most online poker servers are located in jurisdictions with lax regulations, such as Costa Rica (Albarrán-Torres, 2017), Malta, the Isle of Man, Gibraltar, Antigua and Alderney (the small European island where the 3D online casino *PKR*, which I explore in Chapter 5, was based; on the online gambling industry on the island, see also Bowers, 2012). Laws and taxation regimes complicate the legal framework of online poker. Owens exposes the jurisdictional complexities posed by online poker for real money:

> five men are playing poker. But they are all in different locations, for they are playing on the Internet. One player is from Tokyo, another lives in Los Angeles (United States), the third is in London (United Kingdom), the fourth in Cape Town (South Africa), and the last in Sydney. The website they are all using locates its server in Antigua. Now, which country has jurisdiction over that poker game?
> (Owens, 2008, p. 93)

The development of online poker assemblages is highly reliant on changes in regulation. Now and again, online poker makes an appearance on mainstream news, such as on April 15, 2011, known by industry insiders in the United States as the "Black Friday of online poker", when the owners of some of the biggest sites – *Full Tilt Poker, PokerStars* and *Absolute Poker* – were arrested and the casinos shut down after the FBI alleged that the sites "laundered money and defrauded banks to get around gambling laws" (Rovell, 2011). The shutting down of these casinos has had far-reaching effects on the industry in the US market and has, according to industry analysts, damaged the profitable links between online gambling and televised poker, further expanding the effects of the media change associated with the digitisation of gambling and its network configuration.

The legalisation of online gambling in jurisdictions such as the US state of New Jersey has opened the doors for traditional, long-standing gambling companies to enter the digital market, particularly online poker. In New Jersey alone, brick-and-mortar casinos, including Tropicana, Borgata Hotel Casino & Spa, the Golden Nugget Atlantic City, Trump Plaza Hotel and Casino and the Trump Taj Mahal Casino Resort, have already entered this arena (Parry, 2013). However, the state has tried to enforce stringent laws to make sure that everyone who gambles online under its jurisdiction is physically within the state (Parry, 2013). It remains to be seen if the Donald Trump presidency will bring substantial changes to online gambling regulation.

Some industry power players have compared recent regulations surrounding online poker to the Prohibition era. In late 2013, casino mogul Steve Wynn told reporters that "playing poker is America, and outlawing poker is like the Volstead Act where they outlawed beer" (Sieroty, 2013). Some political personalities in the United States have taken a surprising stance in favour of online poker. Texas Representative Joe Barton, for example, exclaimed during a congressional hearing on the Poker Freedom Act in December 2013 that God is in favour of online poker (Weber, 2013). Other US politicians have stated a complete aversion to online gambling, exercising cultural regulation. In 2014, amidst moves to legalise online wagering in his state, New York Governor George Pataki stated that online gambling would allow terrorists and organised criminals to launder money more easily (Morganteen, 2014). In August 2014, the highly influential *Newsweek* magazine published a cover story, "How Washington Opened the Floodgates to Online Poker, Dealing Parents a Bad Hand", condemning the moves to legalise online gambling in the United States by emphasising potential harm to digital natives (McGrath Goodman, 2014).

Social Casino Apps

Social casino apps are the clearest example of 'gamble-play'. They are platforms that incorporate the visual tropes and basic gameplay of traditional gambling forms but also structural characteristics of video games, such as avatar creation, leader boards, and reward and punishment features.

The social casino apps market, which includes mainly slot and poker platforms, is also a vast industry that has gained currency since 2011 as it experienced a large expansion (Morgan Stanley, 2012). Social casino games generally operate on a 'freemium' model. Play is free, but "players have the ability to use real money to purchase additional 'credits' or features that would otherwise be earned through extended gameplay" (Dayanim, 2014, p. 31). However, only about 5 per cent of players buy extra credits (Dayanim, 2014, p. 31).

Most of the information on the social casino market comes from reports generated by consultancy firms and investment banks, which reveals vested interests in gambling research and the difficulty for academics in keeping up with industry developments. In a 2013 industry report, Nomura Equity Research found that the social gambling market far exceeds real-money online gambling in terms of number of users: 170 million users per month versus 50 million users per month (see also Morgan Stanley, 2012; Sapsted, 2013). However, there is also a big discrepancy in terms of revenue: social gambling generates USD $2 billion per month, while online gambling produces USD $36 billion. Nomura Equity Research foresees an inevitable convergence between real-money and social gambling as "ongoing industry consolidation is blurring traditional distinctions between land and online-based gambling operators and social game developers" (Nomura Equity Research, 2013, p. 18).

Most social gambling players come from North America (39 per cent) and Europe (26 per cent). It is important to note that these figures differ from the social gaming industry in general, where Asia accounts for 36 per cent of users (Morgan Stanley, 2012). This is an indication that social gambling is most alluring to users in North America (the United States and Canada) and Europe, although this practice is also highly popular in Australia, where the slots app *Slotomania* was the most downloaded product in the iTunes store in 2012 (Willingham, 2013).

Among the main stakeholders in the social gambling industry, Morgan Stanley identifies Zynga, which has a 45 per cent share of all social gambling players; slot machine manufacturer IGT, which has a very successful social gambling division, Double Down Interactive; and Caesars, which acquired Playtika, creator of the popular *Slotomania*. This consolidation has involved other key players in the gambling industry, such as WMS, which launched Lucky Cruise Social Casino, a social casino that operates on Facebook; and EGM giant Aristocrat, which acquired Product Madness, a top five operator of slot games on Facebook, with more than 500,000 daily active users. Aristocrat also acquired Big Fish, a social casino developer, in 2017 (Takahashi, 2017).

In the industry's early years, in 2013, the biggest social gaming companies formed the International Social Games Association (ISGA), which acts

> as a unified and consistent voice to represent the legal, regulatory and commercial interests of social games companies world wide, from established global operators to up-and-coming start ups, at a time when many changes in the way millions of people access, play and pay for games are taking place.
>
> (ISGA, 2014)

Members include companies from both the traditional gambling industry and the social casino industry. These are as follows: Zynga, Slingo, Plumbee, Playtika, PlayStudios, MGM, IGT, High 5 Games, Gamesys, Big Fish Games, Bally Technologies, Aristocrat, Akamon and AbZorba Games (ISGA, 2014).

In a further crossover between the entertainment and gambling industries Endemol, a Dutch media company best known for developing successful reality TV concepts such as *Big Brother, Fear Factor* and *Deal or No Deal*, has invested over USD $10 million dollars in social casino company Plumbee (Barraclough, 2013). With this acquisition, Endemol's intention was to brand social casino apps with its successful transnational concepts, a transmedia strategy that I explore further in Chapter 4. Similarly, National Geographic partnered with social casino game developer Miurka to launch *Nat Geo WILD Slots*, which features content from the Nat Geo WILD channel. The game is described by National Geographic as "a virtual journey around the world showcasing remarkable nature, history and architectural sites" (National Geographic, 2017). In 2015, Aristocrat launched a *The Big Bang Theory* slot machine. The machine was launched at San Diego Comic-Con, the biggest meeting point for Hollywood fandom cultures, and featured "more than 100 video clips from the first three seasons of the highly watched television series as part of the game's bonus rounds" (Stutz, 2015).

This market consolidation has extended to the video game industry. In early 2014, Atari, a cultural icon in its own right and a pioneering company in the video game industry that has, however, been struggling financially in recent years, announced the launch of Atari Casino games in association with virtual games company PariPlay. Atari Casino is a series of social casino games such as poker and blackjack themed after classic video games, such as *Asteroids*, *Centipede* and *Missile Command*. Atari CEO Fred Chesnais explained the move as follows: "Entering social casino gaming is a logical next step for us given its appeal across multiple generations and its natural fit with the casual audience" (quoted in Molina, 2014). Atari has also entered the real-money online gambling market with slots released by PariPlay in 2016, which resemble the retro look of the arcade games (Gaming Intelligence, 2016).

Market integration goes both ways. In similar acquisitions that point to the integration of the gaming, gambling and entertainment industries, social casino developers such as Bee Cave Games have moved into real-money gambling, adding elements of multiplayer gaming proper to other media forms, such as multiplayer online role-playing games. As Grubb explains,

> When players enter a slots game, it will match them with up to four other live gamers. The success of those people will then spill over into the other player's game, so that everyone feels more connected.
>
> (Grubb, 2013)

Aristocrat's CEO, Jamie Odell, explains the business model as follows in a 2013 interview published by *The Wall Street Journal*:

> For us, the margins are phenomenal. Once you get the cost base in place everything else is virtual, there's no hardware. If you take the player base, which through Facebook is clearly millions, and the games take in, let's say, 30 cents per player per day, the math becomes quite easy. I would be very disappointed if it's not a major profit stream for us – I'm talking tens of millions of dollars in the next two-to-three years, and one of our largest streams of profit longer term.
>
> (as quoted in Kelly, 2013)

This conscious effort by one of the gambling industry's main power players is testament to the generation of new markets, revenue models and practices. It also shows that the traditional gambling industry is willing to invest in new technologies that support the digital media practices – such as archiving, sharing and gifting – to which gamblers and players are habituated.

Australian Gambling and Gaming Markets

Most of the examples I provide in this book come from developed English-speaking countries, mainly from the United Kingdom, the United States and, most saliently, Australia. Australia provides a unique setting for studying digital gamble-play as both gambling and video games comprise widespread practices and solid, growing markets that are culturally relevant (as exemplified in the Preface, "The VIP Lounge"). Gambling is an everyday topic of conversation in Australia and a source of concern for some government bodies (see, for example, Livingstone, 2017).

Real-money gambling and social casino apps have also generated heated public disputes in Australia, where problem slot machine gambling has been a long-debated issue. For instance, some initiatives led by the hospitality industry have voted pokies out of certain pubs, offering instead the alternative "food and fun" (Han, 2013). Similarly, residents in the Australian town of Eura in New South Wales fought against the introduction of slot machines into their community, fearful of their disruptive nature (Millman, 2014).

How ubiquitous cultural spaces dedicated to gambling are in Australia is surprising to visitors, such as the American journalist Andre Murfett, who wrote,

> One of the most common observations of visitors to Australia, particularly those hailing from the US, is how much gambling has seeped into Australian cultural life.
>
> (Murfett, 2013)

Long-time gambling researcher Geoffrey Caldwell has stated that the cultural normalisation of gambling is inherent to Australian identity:

> Australians seem to take a pride in the belief that we are a nation of gamblers. Thus we do not appear to be ashamed of our gambling instincts, habits and practices. Gambling is regarded by most Australians as a normal, everyday practice in contrast to the view that gambling is a sinful activity which weakens the moral fibre of the individual and the community.
>
> (Caldwell, 1985, p. 18)

Australians bet and lose more than anyone else in the world, mainly on EGMs. As of 2016, according to *The World Count of Gaming Machine* (Ziolkowski, 2017), there are 197,122 EGMs in the country, of which 196,768 are slot machines, with the rest being electronic table games of roulette, blackjack and poker. There are 123 persons per machine in Australia. New South Wales is by far the jurisdiction with most EGMs (94,361), followed by Queensland (46,873) and Victoria (28,935) (Ziolkowski, 2017). In Australia, total gambling expenditure is "more than consumer expenditure on tobacco ($16.3 billion) and alcohol ($15.7 billion), and comparable to total expenditure on pharmaceuticals and other medications ($19.3 billion)" (Livingstone et al., 2017, p. 5).

In 2013, for example, the average Australian lost $520 on non-casino slot machines such as the ones offered in VIP Lounges (Australian Associated Press, 2014). The incidence of specific gambling problems is high in various demographic groups, including university students (Cervini, 2013), young adults prone to substance abuse problems (Hayatbakhsh, Clavarino, Williams, Bor, & Najman, 2012), migrants (Ohtsuka & Ohtsuka, 2010; Tanasornnarong, Jackson, & Thomas, 2004), pensioners (Hing & Breen, 2002), female players (Lee, 2009), aboriginal communities (McMillen & Donnelly, 2008; Young, Barnes, Stevens, Paterson, & Morris, 2007) and individuals experiencing homelessness (Holsworth, Tiyce, & Hing, 2011). Gambling is significant in Australian cultural history, and average Australian households spend at least a small amount of money on different forms of gambling, from pokies to scratch cards, every year (Worthington, Brown, Crawford, & Pickernell, 2007).

In Australia, as elsewhere, transnational gambling markets evolve in tandem with larger financial developments, such as the global financial crisis and equally transnational flows of capital, revealing wider cultural trends on how people deal with sudden wealth, hope, fun and risk. In northern Queensland, for example, the financial bonanza brought about by the mining boom has seen an increase in slot machine use, with the government suggesting that "fly-in, fly-out workers keen on gambling could be driving up the numbers" (Jacques, 2013). According to government figures, mining towns spend more per capita than urban areas with casinos, such as Brisbane or the Gold Coast (Jacques, 2013). This shows the importance of locality in the study of gamble-play assemblages.

Concerns over the omnipresence of opportunities to gamble have been exacerbated by the availability of online and mobile gambling platforms. Internet gambling has received ample attention from scholars of addiction and public health. For instance, an Australian study conducted in 2013 among 4,688 online gamblers found that 30 per cent of them experience low to moderate risks associated with gambling, compared to 15 per cent in offline bettors (Hastings, 2013). Social casino apps are also widely popular in Australia. As previously mentioned, the slots social casino app *Slotomania* was the most downloaded product in the iTunes store in 2012 (Willingham, 2013). According to the AppAnnie ranking system, as of July 2017, the top-grossing app in Australia is Product Madness' slot app *Heart of Vegas*, which makes its profit through in-game purchases. *Slotomania* holds the fifth spot on that list, and Pacific Interactive's *Slot Machines House of Fun* holds the tenth.

Interactive entertainment is also a culturally salient and economically significant everyday media practice in Australia and constitutes a set of intricate assemblages of its own. Video games have also generated controversies, such as the debate over the R18 classification rating. According to the *Digital Australia 2016* report, produced by the Interactive Games & Entertainment Association and Bond University (2016), 98 per cent of Australian households with children have at least one gaming device (personal computer or PC, console, handheld, phone or tablet), and 65 per cent of game households have three or more devices. Further results show that mobile phones are used to play games in 66 per cent of game households, with tablet computers being present in 55 per cent. In terms of age, 78 per cent of gamers are over 18; the average age of gamers is 33. Men account for 53 per cent, while 47 per cent are female. Australians also report that they have an "emotional attachment to gaming" (Battersby, 2013).

What's at Stake? Digital Gamble-Play and Recent Social Imaginaries around Gambling

Media change has long been associated with narratives about the anxieties around the expansion of gambling cultures. Until the fifteenth century, card games in Europe were an aristocratic affair due partly to the high cost of hand-painted stacks (Kelly, 2006; see also Parlett, 1991). The advent of the printing press put cards into the hands of commoners. The proliferation of gambling motivated the state and the Catholic Church to impose controls over wagering activities in Europe (Mazur, 2009, p.17).

Digital gamble-play in the 2010s not only has expanding financial reach but also is associated with age-old cultural anxieties derived from the consumption of gambling, particularly when it provides more opportunities to participate in gambling rituals and either spend, win or lose money.

Digital and mobile technologies have put digital cards and slots at the fingertips of players involved in vast and overlapping digital gamble-play assemblages. The wider availability of gamble-play products and their cultural normalisation have also inspired calls for tighter government control.

Slot machines and online poker are highly controversial devices in many countries. For example, there has been recent intense opposition in many US states to the consumption of bets, particularly to electronic slot machines, one of the earliest manifestations of gamble-play. In October 2013, opponents to the opening of seven Las Vegas-style casinos in the US state of New York placed a slot machine in front of the state capitol building and bashed it with a sledgehammer. Those who took turns pounding the vintage device, which was bought on eBay, included members of the Institute for American Values as well as associations such as Stop Predatory Gambling and the Coalition Against Gambling in New York. A journalist chronicled the protest as follows:

> The machine stubbornly held together for much of the sledge hammer poundings, though shards of glass could be seen flying in different directions with a few of the swipes.
>
> (Precious, 2013)

In parallel to volatile shifts in financial markets and the subsequent wave of unemployment, some Western European countries have also witnessed fierce opposition to the ubiquitous placement of gambling devices. In 2013, in Italy, for example, high levels of unemployment and the financial crisis led to the proliferation of slot and video poker machines in bars, petrol stations, tobacco shops and cafés in cities such as Pavia, near Milan. Italy was then one of the top ten largest gambling markets in the world (Povoledo, 2013). The proliferation of gambling devices has prompted the formation of protest movements in the country as it is estimated that one in every eight dollars spent by a local family goes towards gambling, a figure that up until 2013 had quadrupled in the past 15 years (Povoledo, 2013). In a *New York Times* report, a gambler named Roberto (he preferred to stay anonymous) stated, "You can play everywhere. There are even slot machines in the pharmacy... At least with a casino you have to travel to get there, so you only go a few times a year" (quoted in Povoledo, 2013). This quote reveals the prominent place that screen-based gambling has in some people's lives, arguably due to the wide availability of digital gambling devices. Elsewhere in Europe, concerns about the proliferation of gambling machines have been raised. In the United Kingdom, for example, former Prime Minister David Cameron pointed out that the wide availability of gambling machines has affected community life (Ramesh, 2014). Gambling machines are also a source of concern in the Global South. In Kenya, for example, the government is cracking down on illegal gambling dens with machines (Mwiraria, 2017).

Narratives about the disruptive nature of digital gambling are often manifested in mainstream journalism. Human-gambling-machine relations are framed as negotiations between human will and machine agency. In recent years, news stories from around the world, particularly from Ireland and the United Kingdom, have portrayed individuals who have succumbed to online gambling addiction. Take, for example, the story of John Carlos, a 74-year-old former schoolteacher and accountant from Dublin who defrauded his employer for a sum of €135,000. Carlos spent this money on the Paddy Power online poker website, having become a "hopeless and deeply addicted gambler" (*The Irish Times*, 2014). In Kent, England, a 40-year-old woman and "mother of three lost her home, her husband and almost lost her freedom after an online gambling obsession spiraled out of control" (Cox, 2014). Another gambler, Collette Smith, accumulated debt with payday loan companies, banks and other borrowers in her husband's name; the debt amounted to £16,000. In Fort Augustus, in the Scottish Highlands, a 55-year-old housekeeper allegedly "stole more than £18,000 from her elderly employers to fund her online gambling habit" (STV News, 2014).

Similarly, news reports often portray total immersion in video games and other virtual environments as dangerous. In 2013, for example, an American couple was accused of neglecting their daughter after being obsessed with the online video game *Second Life*. News reports about this famous incident indicated that the couple "spent so much time playing with their avatars in a life-simulation video game that they let their daughter starve" (Kemp, 2013). This case shares similarities with that of a South Korean couple who let their daughter die after becoming obsessed with *World of Warcraft*, a case that Ian Cook discusses in terms of Deleuze's concept of "the body without organs", a discussion I refer to in Chapter 4 (Cook, 2009).

Stories like these are exemplars of the ways in which online gaming and video games in general, and online gambling in particular, are culturally assessed and represented in the media as deceptive and dangerous technologies that engender anxieties and disrupt people and communities. With the recent legalisation of online gambling in some US states, such as New Jersey (November 2013), media commentators have observed that calls to gambling addiction helplines have increased (Dunn, 2014). Recovering gambling addicts see increased dangers in the carrying out of wagering activities through computers. One of them argues, "It is so easy for a teenager to find out their parents' account information and place a few bets online... That's how it [problem gambling] starts" (Dunn, 2014).

Online casino operations have been the subject of cautionary tales in popular culture. These narratives are typically framed around the risks of self-regulated markets. Two powerhouse Hollywood actors, Ben Affleck and Justin Timberlake, star in the 2013 film *Runner Runner*. Upon its release, groups in favour of the legalisation of gambling used the movie to stress the need for a comprehensive legislative framework to regulate online gambling (Dreier, 2013; Lewis, 2013). *Runner Runner* tells the story of a struggling college student who pays tuition by playing online poker and placing bets for other students, most of them from a privileged background. When he is defrauded by an online casino and discovers that a pokerbot (a computer program that passes as a regular player and establishes new relationships and codes between humans/gamblers and machines/gambling platforms) has taken his winnings, he travels to Costa Rica, where the servers are based, to confront an online casino mogul. He is lured by the glamour of the online gambling underworld and gets involved in a criminal investigation.

Gamble-Play Assemblages

This book combines close readings of gambling practices and platforms with cultural analysis and assemblage theory. In order to comprehend the cultural dynamics of gamble-play media, I use a similar approach to the one taken by Montfort and Bogost (2009) to study the Atari video game platform:

> What does a creator, historian, researcher, student, or other user do when experiencing a creative computer artefact? An encounter with such a work could involve trying to understand the social and cultural contexts in which it came to exist. It might also involve interpreting its representational qualities – what it means and how it produces that meaning. Alternatively, a study might involve looking

at the methods of this work's construction, or the code itself, or even
the hardware and physical form of the machines on which it is used.
(Montfort & Bogost, 2009, p. 1)

In this book, I delve into the "social and cultural context" (Montfort &
Bogost, 2009, p. 1) in which gamble-play platforms emerge. In order
to understand and conceptualise platforms that form gamble-play assemblages, I performed platform analysis, identifying the affordances of
these platforms, as well as common audiovisual tropes. This approach is
helpful in understanding how gamble-play platforms produce meaning,
that is to say, their "representational qualities" (Montfort & Bogost,
2009, p. 1). These representational qualities include images, text, sound
and gameplay.

This type of analysis is complemented by Nitsche's conceptualisation
of video games as media formed by five layered spaces (2008, pp. 14–16):

1   *rule-based space* is defined by algorithms and mathematical rules –
    in the case of gamble-play, this involves the Random Number Gen-
    erator (RNG) and the algorithms that produce chance outcomes as
    well as the game mechanics;
2   the *mediated space*, which Nitsche defines as "the space of the im-
    age plane and the use of this image including the cinematic form of
    presentation" (2008, p. 16);
3   the *fictional space* that lives in players' imagination as a result of
    their comprehension of the images – this is particularly important
    for this book as gamble-play platforms produce types of user en-
    gagement previously not found in gambling;
4   *play space*, which is the space of the play, meaning the player and
    the hardware, in gamble-play; this space is particularly important
    in slot machines and in social casino apps accessed through mobile
    devices; and
5   *social space*, "meaning the game space of other players affected"
    (Nitsche, 2008, p. 16); in the case of gamble-play, this is mainly
    defined by the social networking affordances of many platforms.

Based on the interplay between Nitsche's five spaces (2008), I analyse the
media and historical shifts generated by digital gambling, mainly through
assemblage theory, particularly Manuel DeLanda's (2006) rendition of
Deleuzo-Guattarian theory, as mentioned earlier. DeLanda's understanding of assemblages as wholes made from interchangeable component parts
is a useful tool for describing holistically the networks of human and
non-human agents generated around contemporary gambling practices:
networks shaped by the ways in which players consume, produce and
engage with gambling and gambling-related media. Digital gamble-play
is comprised of assemblages or networks in which both *material* and

expressive goods are exchanged (DeLanda, 2006). Gamble-play devices operate in both the material and the expressive planes.

I also mobilise DeLanda's theory to analyse the current intermeshing of digital gambling and gaming assemblages synthesised, for example, in social casino apps or in real-money gambling platforms that provide video game-like experiences. Rebecca Cassidy states, when discussing the emergence of social gambling, that

> Changes in gambling ecosystems are the result of complex inter-actions between producers, consumers, existing products and good fortune.
>
> (Cassidy et al., 2013, p. 165)

Through assemblage theory, I explain these "complex interactions" (Cassidy et al., 2013, p. 165) on a more atomic level and through partic-ular case studies.

For DeLanda, assemblages are networked formations that counter to-talising notions dictating that social groupings are monolithic structures resistant to change (think of Foucaldian institutions). Assemblages are the opposite: "wholes whose properties emerge from the interactions be-tween parts" (DeLanda, 2006, p. 5). A key concept in assemblage theory is particularly salient in understanding the products of this sort of inter-action: relations of exteriority.

Where there are 'relations of exteriority', "a component part of an assemblage may be detached from it and plugged into a different assem-blage in which its interactions are different" while also guaranteeing that "assemblages may be taken apart while at the same time allow-ing that the interaction between parts may result in a true synthesis" (DeLanda, 2006, pp. 10–11). The relations of exteriority established by individual components define the ever-shifting morphology and identity of assemblages, depending on how they link to components of other assemblages and generate meanings out of that union.

DeLanda explains that "assemblages are made up of parts which are self-subsistent and articulated by relations of exteriority, so that a part may be detached and made a component of another assem-blage" (DeLanda, 2006, p. 18). Words are a good example of individ-ual components that generate something new when inserted in another assemblage. Words are a unit of meaning in themselves but can also generate something new by being inserted into existing linguistic struc-tures. Spanglish, for instance, is an Anglicised Spanish dialect spoken by Latino communities in the United States. The Spanish word for "yard" is "patio", but when inserted in the linguistic assemblage of Spanglish speakers, it morphs into "yarda" (Ardila, 2005, p. 61).

When related to gamble-play media, relations of exteriority trigger, for instance, new acts of communication that can be exploited to generate profit. When users share their achievements in a social gambling platform with their Facebook friends (an assemblage in its own right) the operator's user network grows, and the assemblage is consolidated.

Digital gamble-play assemblages establish relations among them by making their component parts interact, generating new assemblages. For example, pokie apps, such as *Slotomania*, appropriate some of the spatial configurations of VIP Lounges and include them in the platform layout, as I will show in Chapter 6.

Digital gamble-play assemblages also incorporate component parts of other media assemblages, such as film and video games. Some slot machines, for example, structure their gameplay around Hollywood narratives, including the TV show *The Walking Dead*. In a slot machine manufactured by Aristocrat and themed after this apocalyptic drama, players have to escape a horde of zombies. In a similar way, the social casino app *Hollywood Spins*, developed by Product Madness, the Aristocrat subsidiary, invites users to "tour Tinseltown with the most amazing cinematic slot machines in the world!". The designs of the different levels are lookalikes, knock-off versions of such profitable Hollywood franchises as Lucasfilm's *Indiana Jones* and Pixar's *Monsters Inc.* – the *Lost* and *Under the Bed* titles, respectively. Other titles include *The SlotFather* (in a clear reference to *The Godfather*), *Gladiator*, *Heist* and *Rook's Revenge*, which has a design that recalls Dreamworks Animation SKG's 2000 movie *The Road to El Dorado*. Similarly, one of the levels for the social casino app *Caesars Slots* is titled *Daring Damsels* and shows cartoon characters that remind players of Disney princesses, including Snow White and Cinderella. The character design of another level, *Mammoth Moolah*, is similar to the animated Fox film franchise *Ice Age*.

DeLanda also provides an account of the two dimensions that compose assemblages. The following description can be extrapolated to digital gambling markets:

> Assemblages are characterized along two dimensions: along the first dimension are specified the variable roles which component parts may play, from a purely material role to a purely expressive one, as well as mixtures of the two. A second dimension characterizes processes in which these components are involved: processes which stabilize or destabilize the identity of the assemblage (territorialisation and deterritorialisation).
>
> (DeLanda, 2006, p. 19)

The first dimension acknowledges that component parts of the assemblage can play either a material or an expressive role. By conceptualising digital gamble-play as a set of assemblages under this notion, we can dissect its component parts and recognise that the material (hardware, monetary transactions and so on) coexists with the expressive (platform design, interactive images and the discourses exteriorised by those images). Following this logic, DeLanda defines markets as "assemblages made out of people and the material and expressive goods people exchange" (2006, p. 17). Gambling markets are assemblages under this definition, which echoes sociologist T.L. Taylor's argument in favour of understanding digital interactive entertainment products as assemblages. She points out, in relation to video games, that

> The notion of assemblage is one way to help us understand the range of actors (system, technologies, player, body, community, company, legal structures, etc.), concepts, practices, and relations that make up the play moment. Games, and their play, are constituted by the interrelations between (to name just a few) technological systems and software (including the imagined player embedded in them), the material world (including our bodies at the keyboard), the online space of the game (if any), game genre, and its histories, the social worlds that infuse the game and situate us outside of it, the emergent practices of communities, our interior lives, personal histories, and aesthetic experience, institutional structures that shape the game and our activity as players, legal structures, and indeed the broader culture around us with its conceptual frames and tropes.
>
> (Taylor, 2009, p. 332)

The second dimension of assemblages indicates that processes of *territorialisation* strengthen the cohesion of an assemblage. A second process of articulation of components that happens after territorialisation is *coding*. For DeLanda, coding "supplies a second articulation, consolidating the effect of the first and further stabilizing the identity of assemblages" (2006, p. 15).

When gambling devices such as slot machines or mobile devices are introduced, the assemblage achieves a territory. At the same time, the assemblage operates according to norms and rules, which moves the assemblage towards stabilisation. When a gamble-play assemblage falls into a jurisdiction, it gains cohesion by being institutionalised and encoded. When a new territory legalises online gambling, as in the 2013 case of the state of New Jersey in the United States, regulations fortify the cohesion of the online gambling market by allowing the maintenance of stricter controls and transaction records. Users, servers, operators and the rest of the actors forming the network of relationships are identified and accounted for. The expansion of the assemblage happens in a more orderly fashion.

On the other hand, deterritorialisation involves processes that disrupt the contours of an assemblage. The introduction of social media affordances to the realm of digital gamble-play, for example, has destabilised existing assemblages related to gambling. According to DeLanda, deterritorialisation is also a process in which the identity of an assemblage is destabilised by decreasing the degree of "sharpness of its boundaries" and its "internal homogeneity" (2006, p. 12). The modification of gambling gameplay that brings it closer to video games, for instance, is a process of deterritorialisation. When gambling images reappear in gambling-like interfaces, there is a reterritorialisation.

DeLanda recalls that Deleuze distinguished two forms of deterritorialisation: *relative* and *absolute*. Relative deterritorialisation refers to processes that "destabilize the identity of an assemblage, opening it up to transformations which may yield another identity (in a process called 'reterritorialisation')" (DeLanda, 2006, p. 123). Absolute deterritorialisation alludes to "a loss of identity altogether, but without falling into an undifferentiated chaos" (DeLanda, 2006, p. 124). As we will see, digital gamble-play is the product of both relative and absolute processes of deterritorialisation in that new identities are generated in the form of new platforms, such as social casino apps.

Assemblage theory explains the association between digital gamble-play and other assemblages. By establishing relations of exteriority with new financial flows, digital gamble-play assemblages generate new configurations. Take, for example, the case of Bitcoin, a peer-to-peer (P2P) generated cryptocurrency whose main asset "is the promise of 'doing without' intermediaries such as banks, financial institutions or political authorities dedicated to monetary exchange and regulation" (Mallard, Meádel & Musiani, 2014). Some Bitcoin-only online casinos are starting to emerge, reaffirming the elasticity and adaptability of digital gamble-play as a form of media (Levy, 2014; Rodriguez, 2013). In parallel, emerging companies, such as Bitcoin Lottery, offer apps such as *BetCoin Reels* (http://reels.betcoin.tm), "a mobile-compatible online slot machine that features an intuitive and user-friendly design that can be accessed from any mobile platform" and accepts payments in both Bitcoins and Litecoins (PRNewswire, 2014). Interestingly, two Las Vegas land-based casinos, The Golden Gate Hotel and The D Las Vegas Casino Hotel, accept Bitcoins as payment for rooms as well as in gift shops and restaurants (Reuters, 2014). An Irish site called Predictious.com offers a prediction market in which US users can bet on anything (the Oscars, sporting events, elections) using Bitcoins (Lott, 2014). In 2017, a Bitcoin gambling machine started to operate in land-based casinos (Bitcoinist, 2017). These cases exemplify the increasing intermeshing of digital and analogue economies and currencies, which is relevant to understanding the cultural dynamics of digital gambling.

The numerous ramifications of current and developing gambling markets, both legal and illegal, add a transnational and multidisciplinary scope to gambling studies. The processes of destabilisation experienced by gambling cultures as a consequence of the use of digital technologies calls for a new way of approaching the study of gambling markets with regard to the configuration and normalisation of their practices, and the destabilisation of their spatial boundaries.

Book Structure

This book is divided into two parts. Part 1, "Gamble-play theory", comprising Chapters 1–3, establishes a theoretical framework and develops concepts to understand contemporary digital gambling platforms and networks in terms of how they constitute assemblages, how they use images as rhetorical tools and what their consumption entails vis-à-vis contemporary digital media practices.

In Chapter 1, "Towards a theory of digital gamble-play", I further develop the concept of 'digital gamble-play' that permeates the rest of the book. Digital gamble-play is a set of communication practices and platforms in which gambling scenarios are staged through digital means and chance events are produced through RNGs. I argue that in digital gamble-play, users acquire a gambling or gambling-like experience that may or may not involve the chance to win real money or tangible goods. I also explain the relevance of developing new concepts that can shed light on how we understand new media forms. I then review historical definitions of 'gambling' and explain how the media changes that occur in 'digital gamble-play' across three spectrums (visual/tactile engagement, movement/stasis and homogenous/independent time) transform the spatio-temporal arrangements of play. I argue that the digitisation of gambling represents a significant departure from the experiences offered in analogue platforms.

Chapter 2, "Smoke and mirrors: procedural rhetoric in gamble-play", deals with how digital gambling platform designers produce interactive images that mobilise particular rhetorical tools that motivate constant play. Interactive images are a fundamental part of the media change brought about by the digitisation of gambling platforms. The conceptualisation of how video games operate as "procedural rhetoric" (Bogost, 2007) is also used in the analysis of audiovisual systems in digital poker. This chapter establishes a notion of interactive images that will inform the rest of the book in relation to how particular gamble-play assemblages are formed and sustained. It deals with the images involved in digitally mediated gambling in general and online poker in particular. It argues that these interfaces can be analysed by reconsidering Gilles Deleuze's movement-image and action-image categories, through which Deleuze approaches cinematic regimes of vision. Digital poker platforms are thus conceptualised as an arrangement of procedure-images where procedures convey a particular set of discourses. Through procedure-images, gambling operators strive to replicate an aura of a game of poker. Benjamin defines aura as "the unique phenomenon of a distance, however close it may be" (Benjamin, 2008, p. 222). There are five instances of procedural rhetoric in digital gamble-play: (1) Gambling is an adventure!; (2) Learn through experience, you will get better; (3) Do not feel alone, your friends and foes are here; (4) Remain loyal, the 'house' loves you; and (5) Do not miss out! There is always something to be won!

The last chapter of Part 1, Chapter 3, "Gamble-play media and practices of consumption", builds on the concepts of 'digital gamble-play' and 'procedure-image' to discuss the nature of consumption in gamble-play markets. I consider consumption to be a meaning-creating act in which both consumers and companies shape the gambler's experience. I investigate how online casino operators and social casino app developers have reacted to convergence cultures (Jenkins, 2006) by constructing corporate communications, platforms and loyalty programs around the observation that gamblers connect with one another, cooperate and generate knowledge about digital gambling. This chapter explores the patterns of gambling consumption in the online casinos *PokerStars* and *888*, as well as a variety of social casino apps, and the ways in which they are shaped by media practices derived from the use of networked applications and digital entertainment technologies. These platforms show how the industry strives to follow trends in participation-driven consumption, and adapt to contemporary digital media, in both desktop and mobile platforms. Digital interfaces extend consumption far beyond the bet, which has manifold cultural and political implications that I discuss in this chapter. I develop this critical analysis by framing the possibilities of action that casinos offer players with the varieties of digital media practices identified by Couldry (2012) – among them, searching and search-enabling (finding the tables with the best odds and making your findings searchable), showing and being shown (acquiring a reputation as a skilled gambler), *presencing* (sustaining a public presence) and commentary (participating in forums). I argue that these practices align with new modes of digital consumption that favour participation, ubiquity and blurring of the producer/consumer divide. Users can interlock their casino networks with other digital spheres, such as Facebook and Twitter.

After the initial three chapters, I explore concrete case studies in Part 2, "Gamble-play platforms", which comprises Chapters 4–7. I test my concepts across different digital gambling platforms that are exemplars of gamble-play, namely, slot machines, online poker and social casino apps as well as stock trading apps in the final chapter.

Chapter 4, "Gamble-play and popular culture: when slots meet Hollywood", deals with the relationship between gamblers and EGMs, as framed by the rhetorical devices of exotica and Hollywood branding. Building on the concept of the procedure-image, I argue that slot machines share aesthetic and procedural similarities with video games and that the gameplay's objective is not always merely to win money but to fulfil a desire to accomplish missions and embark on adventures, oftentimes influenced by Hollywood-style storytelling and characters. I contend that these 'missions' are communicated through procedure-images and are related to the chase, the overarching procedure that defines EGM consumption and gambler-pokie couplings. The chase consists of continuous play motivated by a desire to recoup losses. The aura of some of these procedure-images can be traced back to a postcolonial domination over foreign lands, peoples and cultures – faux Chinese and aboriginal lore, exotic deserts, untamed jungles and Arctic landscapes that need to be conquered. These tropes feed into class-related aspirations, postcolonial discourse and exotica, which are apparent in the imagery of many slot machines. I also analyse how Hollywood branding works as a strategy that frames the experience of play.

After this discussion about slot machines, I move on to an analysis of a particular digital poker platform: the online casino *PKR*. Chapter 5, "Gamble-play as *Second Life*: the case of *PKR*", conceptualises online poker sites as mediated spectacles – as envisioned by Guy Debord (1967). *PKR*, which went bankrupt in early 2017, is a historical exemplar of gamble-play that combines online poker with a virtual environment similar to *Second Life*, in which users are co-creators of the gaming experience. *PKR* encapsulates gamble-play, showing how the structural affordances of video games, such as avatar creation and the manipulation of a virtual camera, are incorporated into digital gambling platforms (King et al., 2010).

Chapter 6, "Mobile gamble-play apps: a casino in your pocket", revolves around the cultural innovation of mobile social gambling and its ramifications in gambling and gaming assemblages. I analyse the apps *Slots Journey*, *Slots by Zynga* and *Slotomania*, which are now popular on smartphones and tablets. These apps expand available spaces and opportunities for gamble-play, with considerable implications for questions of problem gambling, socialisation and human-machine interaction. Through the development of apps by companies such as Zynga (one of the leading developers of games for Facebook), mobile media platforms are being designed to open new markets and in preparation for the loosening of restrictions on multiple varieties of mobile gambling. I compare these apps with earlier EGMs in how they construct cultural spaces of gambling and argue that new forms of media subvert gambling practices and their accepted limits, pushing them further into the realm of everyday life. Slot or pokie apps recontextualise the rhetorical procedures of video gaming, particularly those of the quest and skill-based movement through levels, by writing them into the design of mobile digital slots.

Finally, Chapter 7, "Gambling with markets: stock trading apps and the logic of gamble-play", argues that the concept of gamble-play can be expanded into other digital media realms. I analyse the discourses surrounding the stock trading apps *Bux* and *Robinhood*, and how they bring the spheres of digital gambling and finance closer together.

References

Aarseth, E. (1997). *Cybertext: Perspectives on ergodic literature.* Baltimore, MD: The Johns Hopkins University Press.

Abt, V., & McGurrin, M. C. (1992). Commercial gambling and values in American society: The social construction of risk. *Journal of Gambling Studies, 8*(4), 413–420.

Albarrán-Torres, C. (2017) Where the stakes are higher: Transnational labor and digital gambling media. In G. Goggin & M. McLelland, (Eds.) *The Routledge companion to global internet histories* (pp. 425–435). London and New York, NY: Routledge.

Ardila, A. (2005). Spanglish: An anglicized Spanish dialect. *Hispanic Journal of Behavioral Sciences, 27*(1), 60–81.

Australian Associated Press (2014, February 4). Gambling: Australians bet more and lose more than anyone else. *The Guardian.* Retrieved from www.theguardian.com/society/2014/feb/04/gambling-australians-bet-more-lose-more

Barraclough, L. (2013, December 16). Endemol backs social casino gaming company Plumbee. *Variety.* Retrieved from http://variety.com/2013/digital/news/endemol-backs-social-casino-gaming-company-plumbee-1200962071/

Battersby, L. (2013, October 22). Australians of all ages are gamers now, survey finds. *The Sydney Morning Herald.* Retrieved from www.smh.com.au/digital-life/games/australians-of-all-ages-are-gamers-now-survey-finds-20131021-2vx72.html

Benjamin, W. (2008). *The work of art in the age of mechanical reproduction (Penguin Great Ideas).* London, UK: Penguin. (Original work published 1935)

Bitcoinist (2017, December 24). Blockchain gambling machine placed in land-based casino. *Bitcoinist.net.* Retrieved from http://bitcoinist.com/blockchain-gambling-machine-placed-land-based-casino/

Blodget, H. (2012, January 24). When online gambling is legalized, Facebook will be a $100 billion company. *Business Insider Australia.* Retrieved from www.businessinsider.com.au/facebook-gambling-2012-1

Bogost, I. (2007). *Persuasive games: The expressive power of video games.* Cambridge, MA: MIT Press.

Bowers, S. (2012, July 4). Alderney, the unlikely hub for a global, online gambling industry. *The Guardian.* Retrieved from www.theguardian.com/uk/2012/jul/04/alderney-hub-online-gambling

Caldwell, G. (1985). Some historical and sociological characteristics of Australian gambling. In G. Caldwell, B. Haig, M. Dickerson, & L. Sylan (Eds.), *Gambling in Australia* (pp. 18–27). Sydney, NSW: Croom Helm Australia.

Calhoun, C. (2006). The privatization of risk. *Public Culture, 18*(2), 257–263.

Cassidy, R., Pisac, A., & Loussouarn, C. (Eds.). (2013). *Qualitative research in gambling: Exploring the production and consumption of risk.* New York, NY, London, UK: Routledge.

Cervini, E. (2013, November 8). High stakes for gambling students. *The Age.* Retrieved from www.theage.com.au/national/education/high-stakes-for-gambling-students-20131108-2x5cl.html

Cook, I. (2009). The body without organs and Internet gaming addiction. In M. Poster & D. Savat (Eds.), *Deleuze and new technology* (pp. 185–205). Edinburgh, Scotland: Edinburgh University Press.

Cosgrave, J. F. (Ed.). (2006). *The sociology of risk and gambling reader.* London, UK, New York, NY: Routledge.

Cosgrave, J. (2010). Embedded addiction: The social production of gambling knowledge and the development of gambling markets. *Canadian Journal of Sociology, 35*(10), 113–133.

Cosgrave, J., & Klassen, T. R. (2001). Gambling against the State: The State and the Legitimation of gambling. *Current Sociology, 49*(1), 1–15.

Couldry, N. (2012). *Media, society, world: Social theory and digital media practice*. Cambridge, MA: Polity.

Cowie, T. (2013, January 11). Facebookie: social betting next big thing in gambling. *Crikey*. Retrieved from www.crikey.com.au/2013/01/11/facebookie-social-betting-next-big-thing-in-gambling/?wpmp_switcher=mobile

Cox, L. (2014, March 14). Strood woman Collette Smith's marriage in tatters by racking up £16k debt in husband's name after going on online betting binge. *Kent Online*. Retrieved from www.kentonline.co.uk/medway_messenger/news/gambling-obsession-14194/

Dayanim, B. (2014). Social casino gaming: An evolving legal landscape. *Gaming Law Review and Economics, 18*(1), 30–36.

Dean, J. (2010). *Blog theory: Feedback and capture in the circuits of drive*. Cambridge, MA: Polity.

Debord, G. (original 1967). Society of the spectacle. *Marxist*.org. Retrieved from www.marxists.org/reference/archive/debord/society.htm

DeGoede, M. (2005). *Virtue, fortune and faith: A genealogy of finance*. Minneapolis, MN: University of Minnesota Press.

DeLanda, M. (2006). *A new philosophy of society: Assemblage theory and social complexity*. London, UK, New York, NY: Continuum.

Deleuze, G. (1986). *Cinema 1. The movement-image*. London, UK: The Athlone Press.

Deleuze, G. (1992). Postscript on the societies of control. *October, 59*, 3–7.

Dreier, H. (2013, October 5). Online poker thriller 'Runner' quickly politicized. *Las Vegas Review Journal*. Retrieved from www.reviewjournal.com/business/casinos-gaming/online-poker-thriller-runner-quickly-politicized

Dunn, P. (2014, March 15). What will Internet gaming mean for gambling addicts? *Courier Post Online*. Retrieved from www.courierpostonline.com/article/20140316/NEWS01/303160045/Some-fear-easy-access-gambling-may-fuel-addiction?nclick_check=1

Duryee, T. (2013). Zynga bringing real money gaming to Facebook in the U.K. Retrieved from http://allthingsd.com/20130206/zynga-bringing-real-money-gaming-to-facebook-in-the-u-k/

Farnsworth, J., & Austrin, T. (2010). The ethnography of new media worlds? Following the case of global poker. *New Media Society, 12*(7), 1120–1136.

Fiedler, I., & Wilcke, A. (2011). *The market of online poker*. The University of Hamburg, Social Science Research Network. Retrieved from http://papers.ssrn.com/sol3/papers.cfm?abstract_id=1747646

Gainsbury, S. M., Russell, A. M., Hing, N., & Blaszczynski, A. (2017). Consumer engagement with and perceptions of offshore online gambling sites. *New Media & Society*, doi:10.1177/1461444817738783 (online first).

Gainsbury, S., & Wood, R. (2011). Internet gambling policy in critical comparative perspective: The effectiveness of existing regulatory frameworks. *International Gambling Studies, 11*(3), 309–323.

Gaming Intelligence (2016, October 18). Pariplay launches latest Atari-branded online slot. *Gaming Intelligence*. Retrieved from www.gamingintelligence.com/games/40300-pariplay-launches-latest-atari-branded-online-slot

Gibson, B., & Sanbonmatsu, D. M. (2004). Optimism, pessimism, and gambling: The downside of optimism. *Personality and Social Psychology Bulletin, 30*(2), 149–160.

Griffiths, M. (1993). Fruit machine gambling: The importance of structural characteristics. *Journal of Gambling Studies, 9*(2), 101–120.

Griffiths, M. D. (2013). Social gambling via Facebook: Further observations and concerns. *Gaming Law Review and Economics, 17*(2), 104–106.

Grubb, J. (2013). Social-casino developer Bee Cave Games moving into real-money gambling and slots. *Venture Beat.* Retrieved from http://venturebeat.com/2013/10/29/social-casino-developer-bee-cave-games-moving-into-real-money-gambling-and-slots/

Han, E. (2013). Poker machines rejected as pubs vote for food and fun. *Good Food.* Retrieved from www.goodfood.com.au/good-food/eat-out/poker-machines-rejected-as-pubs-vote-for-food-and-fun-20131122-2y1is.html

Hastings, E. (2013, October 13). Online gamblers more at risk of addiction. *Herald Sun.* Retrieved from www.heraldsun.com.au/news/online-gamblers-more-at-risk-of-addiction/story-fni0fiyv-1226739184629#!

Hayatbakhsh, M. R., Clavarino, A., Williams, G. M., Bor, W., & Najman, J. M. (2012). Young adults' gambling and its association with mental health and substance use problems. *Australian and New Zealand Journal of Public Health, 36*(2), 160–166.

Hing, N., & Breen, H. (2002). A profile of gaming machine players in clubs in Sydney, Australia. *Journal of Gambling Studies, 18*(2), 185–205.

Hjorth, L. (2011). *Games & gaming: An introduction to new media.* London, UK: Berg.

Hobbs, R. (1998). The seven great debates in the media literacy movement. *Journal of Communication, 48*(1), 16–32.

Holsworth, L., Tiyce, M., & Hing, N. (2011). Exploring the relationship between problem gambling and homelessness: Becoming and being homeless. *Gambling Research, Journal of the National Association for Gambling Studies Australia, 23*(2), 39–54.

Interactive Games & Entertainment Association and Bond University (2016). *Digital Australia 2016 report.* Retrieved from www.igea.net/wp-content/uploads/2015/07/Digital-Australia-2016-DA16-Final.pdf

ISGA (2014). ISGA (International Social Games Association). *i-sga-org.* Retrieved September 2014, from www.i-sga.org/

Jacques, O. (2013). Pokies high rollers spend big in northern mining towns. *Sunshine Coast Daily* Retrieved from www.sunshinecoastdaily.com.au/news/pokies-high-rollers-spend-big-northern-mining-town/2124528/

Jenkins, H. (2006). *Convergence culture: Where old and new media collide.* New York, NY: New York University Press.

Kelly, J. (2006). Poker: The very American career of the card game you can learn in 10 minutes and work on for the rest of your life. *American Heritage, 57*(6). Retrieved from www.americanheritage.com/content/poker

Kelly, R. (2013). Aristocrat Leisure hopes its bets pay off; Australian slot-machine maker's CEO Jamie Odell discusses the next growth phase and how the company is harnessing the popularity of social media. *The Wall Street Journal Online.* Retrieved from http://online.wsj.com/article/SB10001424127887323665504579028420024314700.html

Kemp, J. (2013, October 12). Oklahoma parents so engulfed in Second Life they allegedly starved their real 3-year-old daughter: cops. *NY Daily News*. Retrieved from www.nydailynews.com/news/national/oklahoma-parents-engulfed-online-fantasy-world-allegedly-starved-real-3-year-old-daughter-cops-article-1.1483479

King, D., Delfabbro, P., & Griffiths, M. (2010). Video game structural characteristics: A new psychological taxonomy. *International Journal of Mental Health and Addiction, 8*(1), 90–106.

Kruse, H. (2016). *Off-Track and Online: The networked spaces of horse racing*. Cambridge, MA: MIT Press.

Latour, B. (2005). *Reassembling the social: An introduction to actor-network theory*. Oxford, UK: Oxford University Press.

Lee, T. J. (2009). Distinctive features of the Australian gambling industry and problems faced by Australian women gamblers. *Tourism Analysis, 14*(6), 867–876.

Levy, B. (2014, July 28). Bitcoin looks for foothold in gambling industry. *Liberty Voice*. Retrieved from http://guardianlv.com/2014/07/bitcoin-looks-for-foothold-in-gambling-industry/

Lewis, H. (2013, August 23). 'Runner Runner': Gambling groups use Ben Affleck film to push for online supervision. *The Hollywood Reporter*. Retrieved from www.hollywoodreporter.com/news/runner-runner-gambling-groups-use-613663

Livingstone, C. (2017). *How electronic gambling machines work*. AGRC Discussion Paper 8. Melbourne: Australian Gambling Research Centre, Australian Institute of Family Studies.

Livingstone, C., Adams, P., Cassidy, R., Markham, F., Reith, G., Rintoul, A., ... Young, M. (2017). On gambling research, social science and the consequences of commercial gambling. *International Gambling Studies*, 1–14. www.tandfonline.com/doi/abs/10.1080/14459795.2017.1377748?journalCode=rigs20

Lott, M. (2014, February 18). Betting with bitcoin: Site lets Americans gamble on elections, sports with online-only currency. *Fox News*. Retrieved from www.foxnews.com/tech/2014/02/18/bitcoin-only-site-lets-americans-bet-on-elections-sports/

Lüders, M. (2008). Conceptualizing personal media. *New Media & Society, 10*(5), 683–702.

Lyall, I. (2013). Change in tax law will have significant impact on online gambling sector, says broker. *Proactive Investors United Kingdom*. Retrieved from www.proactiveinvestors.co.uk/companies/news/60196/change-in-tax-law-will-have-significant-impact-on-online-gambling-sector-says-broker-60196.html

Mahmoon, N. M. (2006). *The science of poker*. London, UK: High Stakes Publishing.

Malaby, T. (1999). Fateful misconceptions: Rethinking paradigms of chance among gamblers in Crete. *Social Analysis Issue, 43*(1), 141–165.

Malaby, T. M. (2003). *Gambling life: Dealing in contingency in a Greek city*. Urbana, IL: University of Illinois Press.

Malaby, T. (2006). Parlaying value capital in and beyond virtual worlds. *Games and Culture, 1*(2), 141–162.

Malaby, T. M. (2011). *Making virtual worlds: Linden lab and second life*. Ithaca, NY: Cornell University Press.

Mallard, A., Meádel, C., & Musiani, F. (2014). The paradoxes of distributed trust: Peer-to-peer architecture and user confidence in Bitcoin. *Journal of Peer Production, 4.* Retrieved from http://peerproduction.net/issues/issue-4-value-and-currency/peer-reviewed-articles/the-paradoxes-of-distributed-trust/

Manovich, L. (2000). Database as a genre of new media. *AI & Society, 14*(2), 176–183.

Mazur, J. (2009). *What's luck got to do with it: The history, mathematics, and psychology behind the gambler's illusion.* Princeton, NJ: Princeton University Press.

McDonald, G. (2005). *Deal me in: Online cardrooms, bigtime tournaments, and the new poker.* San Francisco, CA, London, UK: Sybex.

McGrath Goodman, L. (2014, August 14). How Washington opened the floodgates to online poker, dealing parents a bad hand. *Newsweek.* Retrieved from www.newsweek.com/2014/08/22/how-washington-opened-floodgates-online-poker-dealing-parents-bad-hand-264459.html

McMillen, J., & Donnelly, K. (2008). Gambling in Australian Indigenous communities: The state of play. *The Australian Journal of Social Issues, 43*(3), 397.

McMullan, J. L., & Kervin, M. (2012). Selling Internet gambling: Advertising, new media and the content of poker promotion. *International Journal of Mental Health and Addiction, 10*(5), 622–645.

Miller, Ed (2006). Bots, cheating and online poker. *Noted Poker Authority.* Retrieved from www.notedpokerauthority.com/articles/bots-cheating-and-online-poker.html

Millman, O. (2014). Euroa residents prepare to fight introduction of poker machines. *The Guardian.* Retrieved from www.theguardian.com/world/2014/mar/18/euroa-residents-prepare-to-fight-introduction-of-poker-machines

Molina, B. (2014). Atari resets with jump into social casino gaming. *USA Today.* Retrieved from www.usatoday.com/story/tech/gaming/2014/03/26/atari-social-casino/6915065/

Montfort, N., & Bogost, I. (2009). *Racing the beam: The Atari video computer system.* Cambridge, MA: MIT Press.

Morgan Stanley (2012). Social gambling: Click here to play. *Morgan Stanley Blue Paper.* Retrieved from http://linkback.morganstanley.com/web/sendlink/webapp/f/u4a8mcp4-3ohe-g001-b7cd-002655210101?store=0&d=UwBSZXNlYXJjaAA0NzE3NTY%3D&user=2t7a7p40q5buy-2365&__gda__=1479106416_6a55cefa848830ece67e9f0e40d5607a

Morganteen, J. (2014, February 12). Pataki: Online gambling will fuel terrorism, organized crime. *CNBC.* Retrieved from www.cnbc.com/id/101411401

Murfett, A. (2013). America, a land largely free of pokies – but that's changing. *Crikey.* Retrieved from www.crikey.com.au/2013/11/11/america-a-land-largely-free-of-pokies-but-thats-changing/

Mwiraria, T. (2017, December 14). Why is gambling so addictive? *Daily Nation.* Retrieved from www.nation.co.ke/lifestyle/gambling-addiction-illegal-gaming-Nairobi-Kenya/1190-4227814-11nfcp9z/

National Geographic (2017, July 6). Murka and National Geographic Launch Nat Geo WILD Slots. *National Geographic.* Retrieved from http://press.nationalgeographic.com/2017/07/06/murka-and-national-geographic-to-launch-nat-geo-wild-slots/

Nicoll, F. (2011). On blowing up the pokies: The Pokie Lounge as a cultural site of neoliberal governmentality in Australia. *Cultural Studies Review, 17*(2), 219–256.

Nicoll, F. (2013). Finopower: Governing intersections between gambling and finance. *Communication and Critical/Cultural Studies, 10*(4), 385–405.

Nitsche, M. (2008). *Video game spaces: Image, play and structure in 3D.* Cambridge, MA: MIT Press.

Nomura Equity Research (2013, January 30). Australia Gaming and Leisure. Research analysts: Nick Berry, Emma Goodsell, Darina Farahbakhsh.

Ohtsuka, K., & Ohtsuka, T. (2010). Vietnamese Australian gamblers' views on luck and winning: universal versus culture-specific schemas. *Asian Journal of Gambling Issues and Public Health, 1*(1), 34–46.

Owens Jr., M. D. (2008). The limits of coercion and the case for i-gaming self-regulation. *Gaming Law Review and Economics, 12*(2), 93–100.

Palmeri, C., Lepido, D., & C. Rahn (2014, July 16). Gtech Agrees to Acquire Slot-Machine Maker IGT for $4.7 Billion. *Bloomberg.* Retrieved from www.bloomberg.com/news/2014-07-16/gtech-agrees-to-buy-slot-machine-maker-igt-for-4-7-billion.html

Parlett, D. (1991). *A history of card games.* Oxford, UK: Oxford University Press.

Parry, W. (2013, October 22). Tropicana awarded online gambling permit. *Courier-Post.* Retrieved from www.courierpostonline.com/viewart/20131022/NEWS 01/310220018/Tropicana-awarded-online-gambling-permit

Pokerscout.com (2017) *PokerScout.* Retrieved December 2017 from www.pokerscout.com

Povoledo, E. (2013). Fears of social breakdown as gambling explodes in Italy. *The New York Times.* Retrieved from www.nytimes.com/2013/12/29/world/europe/fears-of-social-breakdown-as-gambling-explodes-in-italy.html?_r=0

Precious, T. (2013, October 15). Slot machine gives its life in Capitol Park. *The Buffalo News.* Retrieved from http://blogs.buffalonews.com/politics_now/2013/10/slot-machine-gives-its-life-in-capitol-park.html

PRNewswire (2014, January 2). Bitcoin gaming industry pioneer BetCoin launches new animated slot machine game… BetCoin Reels. *The Sacramento Bee.* Retrieved from www.sacbee.com/2014/01/02/6043483/bitcoin-gaming-industry-pioneer.html

Ramesh, R. (2014, January 9). David Cameron 'shares Ed Miliband's concerns about gambling machines'. *The Guardian.* Retrieved from www.theguardian.com/society/2014/jan/08/david-cameron-ed-miliband-gambling-machines?CMP=twt_gu

Reith, G. (1999). *The age of chance: Gambling in Western culture.* London, UK: Routledge.

Reuters (2014). Las Vegas casinos to accept Bitcoin virtual currency. *South China Morning Post.* Retrieved from www.scmp.com/business/banking-finance/article/1411035/las-vegas-casinos-accept-bitcoin-virtual-currency

Rodriguez, J. (2013). Are Bitcoins the next big online gambling frontier? *The Bitcoin Channel.* Retrieved from www.thebitcoinchannel.com/archives/22295

Rovell, D. (2011). Insider's breakdown of Poker's Black Friday. *CNBC.* Retrieved from www.cnbc.com/id/42649117/Insider_Breakdown_Of_Poker_s_Black_Friday

Russell, B. (2014, April 21). Most online betting services back to normal following Gibraltar blaze. *Express.* Retrieved from www.express.co.uk/news/uk/471487/Fuel-explosion-in-Gibraltar-causes-huge-fire-and-disrupts-online-betting-sites

Sapsted, T. (2013). Social Casino gaming: Opportunities for 2013 and beyond. *Design1Online.* Retrieved from http://design1online.com/downloads/white-papers/social_casino_games.pdf

Savat, D., & Poster, M. (2009). *Deleuze and new technology.* Edinburgh, Scotland: Edinburgh University Press.

Schüll, N. D. (2012). *Addiction by design: Machine gambling in Las Vegas.* Princeton, NJ: Princeton University Press.

Sieroty, C. (2013). Steve Wynn compares effort to outlaw online poker to Prohibition. *Las Vegas Review-Journal.* Retrieved from www.reviewjournal.com/business/steve-wynn-compares-effort-outlaw-online-poker-prohibition

Stutz, H. (2015, September 9). 'Big Bang Theory' slot machines are no 'Bazinga!'. *Las Vegas Review Journal.* Retrieved from www.reviewjournal.com/business/casinos-gaming/big-bang-theory-slot-machines-are-no-bazinga/

STV News (2014, March 24). Housekeeper 'stole £18,000 from retirees to fund gambling habit'. *STV News.* Retrieved from http://news.stv.tv/scotland/2692 92-kathleen-johnston-stole-18000-from-retirees-to-fund-gambling-habit/

Tanasornnarong, N., Jackson, A., & Thomas, S. (2004). Gambling among young Thai people in Melbourne, Australia: an exploratory study. *International Gambling Studies, 4*(2), 189–203.

Takahashi, D. (2017, December 4). How Aristocrat's $990 million Big Fish deal will shake up social casino games. *Venture Beat.* Retrieved from https://venturebeat.com/2017/12/04/how-aristocrats-990-million-big-fish-deal-will-shake-up-social-casino-games/

Taylor, T. L. (2009). The assemblage of play. *Games and Culture, 4*(4), 331–339.

The Irish Times (2014, February 4). Online poker addict cheated employer of €135,000. *The Irish Times.* Retrieved from www.irishtimes.com/news/crime-and-law/courts/online-poker-addict-cheated-employer-of-135-000-1.1678250

Vacchiano, M., & Mejía Reyes, C. (2017). Reflexiones sobre los juegos de azar en la sociedad contemporánea: hacia una biografía del riesgo. *Athenea Digital. Revista de pensamiento e investigación social, 17*(2). Retrieved from http://atheneadigital.net/article/view/v17-n2-vacchiano

Weber, K. (2013, December 12). Does God love online poker? Texas congressman has shocking answer. *The Christian Post.* Retrieved from http://global.christianpost.com/news/does-god-love-online-poker-texas-congressman-has-shocking-answer-110595/#Dr00t8U5VLvbwr8M.99

Willingham, R. (2013, January 13). Virtual pokie app a hit - but 'not gambling'. *The Sydney Morning Herald.* Retrieved from www.smh.com.au/digital-life/smartphone-apps/virtual-pokie-app-a-hit--but-not-gambling-20130112-2cmev.html#ixzz2QVlsCJs1

Worthington, A., Brown, K., Crawford, M., & Pickernell, D. (2007). Gambling participation in Australia: findings from the national household expenditure survey. *Review of Economics of the Household, 5*(2), 209–221.

Young, M., Barnes, T., Stevens, M., Paterson, M., & Morris, M. (2007). The changing landscape of Indigenous gambling in Northern Australia: Current knowledge and future directions. *International Gambling Studies, 7*(3), 327–343.

Ziolkowski, S. (2017). The World count of gaming machines 2016. *Gaming Technologies Association.* Retrieved from http://gamingta.com/wp-content/uploads/2017/05/World_Count_2016.pdf

Part I
Gamble-Play Theory

1 Towards a Theory of Gamble-Play

This chapter offers a description and theorisation of a new media and cultural form that I call 'gamble-play', a term central to this book, which helps explain changes in contemporary forms of digital gambling. This media and cultural form is the product of a shift that is taking place at the intersection of gambling, entertainment, social media and finance. Gamble-play is a set of media platforms and practices in which gambling situations are staged through digital means and chance events are produced through algorithms. Digital gamble-play privileges the 'fun' aspects of gambling over winning or losing, establishing new dynamics of seduction and control. Gamble-play consists of two related cultural tendencies. First, gambling practices become more gamelike. Second, gaming practices adopt the appearance of gambling.

In gamble-play, players acquire a gambling or gambling-like experience that may or may not involve the chance to win real money or tangible goods. In these transactions, players pay a mixture of money, labour, time and access to their digital social networks. Digital gamble-play is carried out in slot machines, desktop computers and mobile devices, such as smartphones and tablets. As a media practice, digital gamble-play has a ductile nature: its gameplay configurations flow across platforms, from the slot machine to the smartphone or tablet app to the desktop computer. Gamble-play dynamics influence other practices, such as stock trading through mobile apps, in which the procedures involved in financial transactions resemble games of chance.

I propose a conceptual framework that will help me explain digital gamble-play in the remainder of this book. This conceptual framework offers a "contingent system of interpretation" that allows me to make "certain empirical statements" and exclude "other forms of empirical statements" (Reckwitz, 2002, p. 257) related to digital gambling.

As a lead-up to this discussion, I will first exemplify the media shift embodied by digital gamble-play, as well as its deriving practices, with three vignettes. The subjects of these vignettes are hypothetical and do not resemble actual events or people. However, their situations are indicative of some of the digital gamble-play practices identified in this book:

1   New York, 9 am. Samantha is waiting for the bus, which has already been delayed for 20 minutes. She is getting anxious as she has an important business meeting in half an hour. She takes out her Android smartphone and texts her colleague to say she is running late. Then, to pass the time before the bus arrives, she accesses *Hit It Rich*. She likes playing slots on her mobile, even though she is not making or spending real money. Samantha finds the cartoonish characters appealing and enjoys the vibrant graphics, encouraging messages and vigorous sounds, particularly the ones in the level themed after her favourite childhood movie *The Wizard of Oz*. As a financial advisor, she deals with risk all day long, so she enjoys gambling for nothing. Before her bus finally arrives, she has a big win (10,000 credits!) and shares it with her Facebook friends (this will give her a few more extra credits).

2   2010. After a long day at his London office, Mike O'Reilly comes home and turns on his computer. He accesses *PKR*, the online casino in which he plays poker for real money. *PKR* is unlike other online casinos, however, as it is a sort of mix between the virtual environment *Second Life* and the professional poker tournaments he sometimes watches on ESPN. Before choosing a table, Mike buys virtual items for his avatar: a pair of flashy sunglasses and a gold chain. These items will help him bluff better – really disguise what he is up to. If he wins big, he plans to purchase a Sony PS4 digital game console in the *PKR Shop*, where he can directly exchange his in-game winnings for real-life items. (He can even donate to charities such as Ante Up for Africa using his *PKR* Points, which can also be changed for real money.)

3   Sydney, Australia. Kyle is out with friends in a pub. He has a couple of pints, and by 10 pm, he grows bored with the conversation (he is not really into sports and his 'mates' are involved in a never-ending argument about this or that rugby player). Kyle decides to play the pokies (slots). He walks into the VIP Lounge and inserts a $50 note into his favourite machine: *Gypsy Moon*, the slot machine or *pokie* on which he hit a small jackpot last month. He loses the $50 in the next 15 minutes, goes back to his mates and chats about the series finale of the TV show *Game of Thrones*.

Are these three individuals involved in the same sort of cultural and media practice? What are the similarities and differences in what they are doing? Are they playing or gambling? What place does real or simulated gambling have in their everyday media consumption habits? Moreover, are they all gambling? If so, what they are gambling with or for?

   This chapter is divided into three sections. First, I explain the method of Gilles Deleuze and Félix Guattari in creating new concepts "as a function of problems which are thought to be badly understood or badly posed" (Deleuze & Guattari, 1994, p. 16). Second, I further develop the concept of 'digital gamble-play', situating it historically in the trajectory of gambling media. Finally, I explain how the digitisation of gambling produces significant departures from the experiences offered in analogue platforms across three domains: tactile engagement, movement across space and time.

'Gamble-Play': The Relevance of Concepts

Coining a concept is an act of provocation. As an umbrella term, 'gamble-play' might be judged by some as problematic as it encapsulates a series of dissimilar platforms and practices in which different things are at stake: real money in slot machines and some forms of online poker, and virtual currencies in social casino apps. The fact that different things are at stake has vastly dissimilar consequences in terms of regulation and problem gambling – or "gambling problems", as psychologists Blaszczynski and Nower point out, arguing that individual circumstances should be analysed when treating gambling addiction (2002).

It is in this zone of indeterminacy, however, that my argument gathers strength and currency, and that my contribution to gambling and media studies is situated. Digital gamble-play refers to an emerging set of cultural practices that blur the distinction between digital games and gambling.

As a concept, 'digital gamble-play' alludes to the developing – but incomplete – consolidation of these markets. Other researchers have already identified the erosion of boundaries in different spheres of life. It is this 'wear and tear' that the term 'digital gamble-play' speaks to. Media theorist and gambling researcher Joyce Goggin, for instance, writes about "the destabilization of binaries that has, if only conceptually, blurred the perceived line that was once thought to divide work from play, and finance from fun" (2012, p. 442). A feature of digital gamble-play is the "destabilization of binaries" (Goggin, 2012, p. 442). Gamble-play reveals a negotiation between user agency driven by enjoyment (gaming) and industry calculation driven by profit (gambling). Gamble-play moves towards the exploitation of compulsive play *and* compulsive communication.

In *What is Philosophy?* (1994), Deleuze and Guattari write about the liberating power of concepts and their use in the consolidation of meanings and the creation of philosophical apparatuses. They contend that concepts are created "as a function of problems which are thought to be badly understood or badly posed" (Deleuze & Guattari, 1994, p. 16).

Deleuze and Guattari argue that a concept

> is a whole because it totalizes its components, but it is a fragmentary whole. Only on this condition can it escape the mental chaos constantly threatening it, stalking it, trying to reabsorb it.
>
> (Deleuze & Guattari, 1994, p. 16)

Concepts allow us to escape chaos, to identify and contain components, and to analyse them: in the case of contemporary gambling, these components are images, platforms, practices and the interrelation between different media forms (gambling media, digital games, film, television).

'Digital gamble-play' is a "fragmentary whole" (Deleuze & Guattari, 1994, p. 16) in the sense that it describes a set of media changes and cultural practices that are distinct. Yet these share a fundamental characteristic: they sprout from the staging of a chance event and involve an economy of danger, enjoyment and quantifiable success. Digital gamble-play is also fragmentary in that it contains an unfathomable number of elements: users, platforms, stakeholders and infrastructural components that are joined by volatile connections. Yet, as happens with other all-encompassing terms, such as, say, "ethnic media" (Deuze, 2006), 'digital gamble-play' is a point of departure for understanding a palpable reality and its cultural manifestations.

However, digital gamble-play is not so much a philosophical concept as a concept situated within a particular cultural history of media.

Moreover, Deleuze and Guattari recognise that concepts respond to particular histories and borrow from other concepts to make sense of reality:

> every concept always has a history, even though this history zigzags, though it passes, if need be, through other problems or onto different planes. In any concept there are usually bits or components that come from other concepts, which corresponded to other problems and presupposed other planes. This is inevitable because each concept carries out a new cutting-out, takes on new contours, and must be reactivated or recut.
>
> (Deleuze & Guattari, 1994, p. 18)

'Gamble-play' is gambling plus play: gambling that is increasingly more like play. This concept borrows from these two media forms and effectively "takes on new contours" (Deleuze & Guattari, 1994, p. 18). The following section deals with the zigzagging history of gambling and the ways in which the digitisation of processes and the subsequent cultural ramifications of gambling are taking place across different planes.

The Cultural Innovation of Gamble-Play

Regulated gambling, understood as the commercialisation of controlled and relatively safe experiences of risk, is a widespread cultural phenomenon around the world. Its manifold moral, legal, economic and even philosophical implications call for a variety of definitions. Common in these descriptions, however, is the constant negotiation between risk, skill and luck, and the reproduction of these as the defining elements of the gambling equation. As a cultural practice, gambling has inspired the creation of cities in previously deserted landscapes (such as Reno or Las Vegas in Nevada; see Dombrink & Thompson, 1990; Fox, 2007), the formation of satellite economies (for instance, card rooms across California, sites in Indian reservations in the United States and Canada or online casinos), numerous literary and audiovisual explorations (novels in the vein of Dostoyevsky's *The Gambler* (2010) or Paul Auster's *The Music of Chance* (1990); films including Hill's *The Sting* (1973) or Paul Thomas Anderson's *Hard Eight* (1996) and various scenes in the James Bond franchise; and TV's *Celebrity Poker Showdown* or *The National Heads-Up Poker Championship*) and technological artefacts (miniature cameras for the broadcasting of poker tournaments, logistics software, surveillance equipment, mobile apps).

Even though gamble-play practices move away from the dominant cultural notions of 'gambling', it is important to recognise that digital gamble-play does not supplant traditional forms of gambling. The gambling industry is a vast financial and informational network that produces gigantic profits that amount to more than USD $391 billion per year (Morgan Stanley, 2012). This is evidenced by the construction of important casino venues in cities including Sydney and the exponential growth of nascent gambling markets, such as Macau, which is bound to become the next gambling mecca. In this book, I do not argue that digital forms of game delivery will supplant analogue or land-based gambling but rather that gambling cultures are in a constant state of flux and that this has to do in part with technological change.

Gambling theorists have debated the definition of gambling. When trying to enunciate what exactly is being acquired in gambling, Bjerg goes as far as to say that the gambler "does not buy a thing, but nothingness itself" (2009, p. 54). This explanation counters the notion that the gambler is "buying a commodity in the form of entertainment and excitement" from the casino (Bjerg, 2009, p. 54). For Bjerg, gambling takes money out of circulation on the symbolic apparatus of capitalism as it leads it "astray into a universe of chance" (2009, pp. 47–48). Bjerg's notion of the "nothingness" of the gambler's purchase can be extrapolated to the consumption of gambling-like products (social gambling apps, such as *Hit It Rich*, as described in my opening vignette) in which money is 'fake', an in-game representation of wealth. Here, this "nothingness" acquires an even deeper dimension. His observation resonating with the notion of the immateriality of money in gaming, Harvie Ferguson points out that gambling is "simply the exchange of money itself; exchange liberated from the viscous medium of objects" and that in this process, "money gains the dignity of Being" (1999, p. xvii).

On the other hand, this cultural practice has received other, less abstract definitions from lawmakers. French gambling law, for instance, "stipulates that a game of chance is a game in return of a payment where chance prevails over skill and intelligence to obtain gain", and the *German State Treaty on Gambling* states that

> it is a game of chance when in the framework of a game played with a view to obtaining a chance to win financial consideration is required and the outcome (of the uncertain future events) hinges completely or predominantly on chance.
>
> (both cited in Lycka, 2011, p. 180)

Gamble-play does not always involve financial gain, and it is questionable if chance always "prevails over skill and intelligence" as the digitisation of gambling requires new sets of skills and literacies from players.

Gambling's ambiguous positioning in moral terms (Flavin, 2003; Quinn, 1892) has also led to the formation of illegal satellite activities that, nevertheless, have a considerable influence on how gaming cultures are configured and perceived. Currently, online gambling is a marginal practice in many territories, as are some of its recent variations, such as highly profitable Bitcoin casinos (Geuss, 2013). However, some digital gambling platforms that are at first considered to be illegal tend to be stabilised through legalisation, which implies the putting in place of legislative and fiscal normative frameworks (as happened recently in some US states, including New Jersey, Illinois and Nevada).

Even though games of chance have been present as either religious rituals or forms of entertainment since ancient times in both Western and non-Western societies (Binde, 2005a, 2005b; Lears, 2003), institutionalised commercial gambling gained notoriety only during the second half of the nineteenth century, particularly in itinerant gambling enclaves in the southern United States. It was then that some scientists, including Clausius and Boltzmann, aligned with the preoccupations of modernity, became fascinated with the mysteries of the unpredictable as "it became increasingly clear that at an elementary level the analogy of Nature with a game of chance was more precise than anyone had imagined; more precise than anyone had feared" (as cited in Ferguson, 1999, p. xvi). For Reith (1999), gambling is a ritual in which humankind continuously enters and exits the realm of chance, which is separate from the everyday.

Likewise, Jackson Lears points out that contemporary gambling games "recall ancient rituals, attempts to divine the decrees of fate, and conjure the wayward force of luck" (2003, p. 2). Some gamble-play platforms recall ancient cultures and rituals associated with chance. The social casino app *Babel Casino*, developed by Real Fun Games in Luxembourg, is described as follows:

> Be sure to keep the mighty ancient gods happy, for they just may decide to help you out from time to time! Play Blackjack, Roulette, and Slots. Complete challenging missions, satisfy your god's every

need to win even bigger prizes, and compete against your friends in the leaderboard! Place your bets in Ancient Babylon and may the gods be on your side!

(Real Fun Games, 2014)

In the following passage, Lears demonstrates the conflicts that can arise when the cultural practice of consuming chance events counters prevalent religious and moral values, but at the same time invokes timeless preoccupations concerning the inevitability of loss:

> In New Orleans and Harlem, among other places, Saint Anthony was the patron of gamblers – as well as the patron of lost objects. In a sense, the popularity of his images suggested the links between gambling and awareness of inevitable loss, between playing apparently pointless games with abandon and cultivating a certain kind of subversive Christianity.
>
> (Lears, 2003, p. 256)

However, Lears also indicates that gambling rituals implicitly express a view that conflicts with dominant Western values. He argues, "This outlook contrasted sharply with what became an American creed: the faith that we can master chance through force of will, and that rewards will match merits in this world as well as the next" (2003, p. 2).

Gambling has an ambivalent position. On the one hand, it presents itself as a shortcut to financial prosperity and social mobility. On the other hand, it is highly suspect as an inauthentic practice that can only lead to losses, undeserved wins and vice.

The current popularity of gambling in Western societies relates to a broader cultural trend identified by Beck in *Risk Society* (1992) and echoed by Young when he concludes that "social organization has moved from a concern with the distribution of wealth to a concern with the distribution and management of risk" (2010, p. 261). Young states that contemporary late capitalist societies produce a "demand for risk" (2010, p. 254) that is met with new gambling products. Gambling has survived, and even flourished, through times of financial crisis and scarcity (DeGoede, 2005).

Even though random outcomes have been electronically produced in slot machines since the 1960s and video was incorporated in the 1970s, what I refer to as 'gamble-play' became widespread in the 1990s with the proliferation of online casinos that offered games such as blackjack, poker and roulette. The recent expansion of gambling as a cultural force is motivated by the adoption of new screen-based ubiquitous technologies that aid in the reproduction of gaming situations. The translation of analogue gambling into ubiquitous screen environments holds implications for the nature of the games themselves, as defined by the domains of movement/stasis, changing experience of time and visual/tactile engagement. It also changes the ways in which stakeholders relate to each other and establish normative frameworks.

These transformations began about two decades ago and reached a highpoint in the 2010s with technical feasibility, cultural normalisation and regulatory stabilisation. In the late 1990s online gambling – initially roulette, sports betting and poker – was introduced as a new commercial enterprise aligned with the discourses and practices of the dotcom era, one of which was the promise of unforeseen financial gain through digital means. Some journalistic accounts reveal a sense of vexed expectancy regarding the new medium. Australian journalist Stuart Ridley, for instance, wrote in 1996,

> Professional gamblers have always found ways to put their money where their mouths/maths formulas/reputations are, but for the rest of us, gambling has normally occupied a special place – with millions of devotees placing small bets every week and the majority only observing the practice on a grand scale a few times a year. Mostly this kind of small-time betting involves visiting some kind of shrine to gambling, be it the local Casino [sic], club, news agency or racetrack. However, online gambling brings the bets right into the loungeroom.
>
> (Ridley, 1996, p. 41)

This quote reveals some of the most salient media-related changes derived from the move from local and analogue to digital and networked gambling spaces. First, it speaks to the notion that land-based gambling has to take place 'somewhere else'. The metaphor of the 'shrine' is evocative of a space where the rules and norms of the outside world are not fully applicable, where one goes to potentially have a transcendental experience outside of 'everyday life' – a notion that recalls Salen and Zimmerman's 2003 appropriation of the notion of a Magic Circle in Johan Huizinga's book on games and culture, *Homo ludens* (1955). Second, it mentions that gambling can be part of a person's routines, particularly in a country such as Australia where it is fully inscribed into the rhythms of the everyday (Caldwell, 1985a, 1985b; Lynch, 1990; McGowan, 2012). Third, this quote identifies (as early as 1996, before online poker became the first success story in the trajectory of digital gambling networks; see Albarrán-Torres, 2017) the potential infiltration of gambling activities into domestic spaces via digital technology. This has recently been a source of much concern among policymakers (Morgan Stanley, 2012) and governments who believe that the use of mobile devices for gambling and gambling-like activities will increase the risk of addiction and compulsive consumption.

The first online poker site to offer real-money wagering was the now defunct Planet Poker, established by Randy Blumer (see Smith, 2011). The inaugural hand was dealt on January 1, 1998. The site became commercially viable just a few months after its launch but suffered severe problems due to technical limitations of current technological networks, such as poor dial-up connections, faulty software and geographical limitations (Smith, 2011). Real-time co-presence proved difficult. In 1999, Paradise Poker challenged Planet Poker's monopoly and thus the relentless proliferation and ruthless competition of desktop-based online poker rooms began (see Smith, 2011). Currently, the URL www.planetpoker.com leads you to a site that is "a play for fun entertainment poker site designed to allow players to hone their poker skills in a safe environment without the pressure associated with financial risk" (Planet Poker, 2017).

Since then, digital gambling platforms have extended both beyond poker and beyond desktop platforms. The ways in which this expansion happens are significant to culture and reveal larger trends in digital media design, practices and consumption practices. The popularisation of online gambling reflected the zeitgeist of its era. Lears recalls that in the 1990s,

> money seemed magically to beget more money – or make it disappear – with no more apparent rhyme or reason than the arrangement of numbers on a screen…the hallowed distinction between gambling and investment became more difficult than ever to sustain.
>
> (Lears, 2003, p. 5)

Gambling is a growing part of media landscapes in the Global North. It is common to see poker tournaments in transnational outlets, such as ESPN and Fox Sports, and to see gambling referenced in movies and TV shows. Austrin and Farnsworth have also stressed that poker is "richly populated with its own celebrities and the celebration of success, both financial and reputational" (Austrin & Farnsworth, 2012, p. 337). Televised shows, such as the *World Series of Poker*, frame the game with high-octane narrative structures reminiscent of sports movies (Caesars Interactive Entertainment Ltd., 2017), which have been remediated in online poker platforms such as *PKR*. The *World Series of Poker* has its own mythology of champions, underdogs and come-from-behind victories (Grotenstein & Reback, 2006; McManus, 2004). As the credits roll, winners – mostly men – are given generous stacks of cash and are surrounded by attractive hostesses. The *World Series of Poker* is a deeply aspirational event, sometimes combining amateurs and professionals in its final showdown, which follows trends in entertainment media in which amateurs become professionals in front of the camera (Dreier, 2013a, 2013b).

The most advanced online gambling platforms are as technically and socially complex as virtual worlds like *Second Life*, which has been the subject of rigorous ethnographic studies (Boellstorff, 2008; Parmentier &

Rolland, 2009). In these studies, the authors explain the mechanisms of identity-creation in virtual worlds and analyse how offline personality traits are translated into virtual platforms. The difference between virtual worlds and digital gambling platforms is that the immersion into the latter can have much greater financial repercussions. However, both digital gamble-play platforms and virtual worlds reaffirm Julian Dibbell's provocation when he wrote that,

> in the strange new world of immateriality toward which the engines of production have long been driving us, we can now at last make out the contours of a more familiar realm of the insubstantial – the realm of games and make-believe.
>
> (Dibbell, 2006, p. 25)

There is a game aspect inherent in traditional gambling, but gamble-play emphasises it, making the insubstantial more prominent by focussing on the fun ride rather than the big win.

The Cultural Dynamics of Gamble-Play

The transformations associated with the emergence of digital gamble-play took place in new everyday practices based on changes in human-machine relations. The rise of digital gamble-play is associated with new forms of neo-liberal consumption and production. The gambler/player becomes the "entrepreneur of the self" (Foucault, 2008, p. 226; see also Dilts, 2011), an individual who is

> being for himself his own capital, being for himself his own producer, being for himself the source of [his] earnings.
>
> (Foucault, 2008, p. 226)

The new economic dynamic associated with gamble-play has various political implications as users allow digital gambling operators to infiltrate the rhythms of the everyday through informational networks. In some forms of digital gamble-play, such as social casino apps (*Zynga Poker, Big Fish Casino, Hit It Rich*) and online casinos (*PokerStars, PKR, 888*), users are often encouraged to socialise or even invest their social capital in the opportunity to engage in continuous play or heightened game experiences. For example, they might choose to share their accomplishments on Facebook if they wish to proceed to the next level on *Big Fish Casino* or practise their poker skills on one of *PokerStars'* Play Money tables, which have been promoted in the *PokerStars* website as follows:

> Whether you're new to poker, or just looking to improve your skills, Play Money chips are a great way to get in the game. There are ring

games and tournaments available across a wide range of Play Money buy-ins, and you can even boost your stack by purchasing chips.

(PokerStars, 2014)

The equation 'play + social clout = better game experience' has political implications and could be understood in terms of what Jodi Dean calls "communicative capitalism", an economic and political dynamic which relies "on the exploitation of communications" rather than on the exploitation of labour (Dean, 2010, p. 4; see also Dean, 2005). Gamble-play establishes new communicative configurations among gamblers or players and between users and companies. By doing so, it establishes connections with other media, such as film and digital games.

Communication is exploited in gamble-play… but also enjoyed. What users often look for is not a 'big win' but fun and controlled risk. What companies rely upon is not compulsive play but compulsive communication in the form of images, code and text that will, in turn, help them know their customers better and expand their networks and influence by following the conventions of networked socialisation. As the synthesis of a major media change, digital gamble-play disrupts the temporal, spatial and socialisation regimes generally associated with gambling.

As part of this new economic dynamic, money increasingly comes to be perceived as a game token, an admission price to the theme park of risk. This effect is present in casino gambling as well but is exacerbated

Figure 1.1 Screenshot of the social casino app *Slots Journey 2*, which encourages users to share personal data and connect to their Facebook profiles to enjoy a better game experience.

Image captured on February 16, 2017 from the author's Android device.

in gamble-play. Even if players do not risk money in all forms of digital gamble-play, they experience a sense of vertigo by being put in a situation of real or simulated danger of losing. For instance, many digital gamble-play platforms, such as online poker tables, allow the user to create an avatar, therefore producing a sort of disembodied experience. Disembodiment, or the capacity to expand our physicality through technology, alters the phenomenological mechanisms of gambling: for players, it might momentarily seem like someone else (the avatar) is losing money. In its website, *PKR* has described the use of its first-person camera as a sort of disembodiment:

> See the action from the point of view of your in-game character. Use the mouse to look around and even make eye contact with your opponents!
>
> (*PKR*, 2014)

As a practice that emphasises the play dimension of gambling, digital gamble-play sheds new light on previous work on gambling that deals with the joy of play and the dangers inherent in risk-taking. The philosopher and cultural theorist Walter Benjamin, for instance, wrote the short piece "Notes on a Theory of Gambling", in which he discusses the social and intimate experiences of play in modernity. He perceives gambling to be the ritualised exteriorisation of an interior negotiation between danger and pleasure, the two facets of gambling (Kusyszyn, 1984). Benjamin argues that the element of danger "is the most important factor in gambling, alongside pleasure" and that it "arises not so much from the threat of losing as from that of *not winning*" (2006, p. 212; emphasis in the original). Throughout this book, I will foreground the negotiation between pleasure and danger and how it features digital gambling platforms. Online gamble-play platforms, for instance, exacerbate the threat of *not winning* by being persistent environments that can be accessed at any time.

Unpublished in Benjamin's lifetime, "Notes on a Theory of Gambling" was written in the late 1920s, long before the inception of digital forms of gambling. Yet Benjamin is writing in the midst of the fast-paced changes brought about by technological innovation and an increasingly multifaceted urban landscape inhabited by the *flâneuse/flâneur*. The *flâneuse/flâneur* is "the viewer who takes pleasure in abandoning himself [herself] to the artificial world of high capitalist civilization" (Lauster, 2007, p. 140). It was during Benjamin's life that diverse mediated experiences, such as cinema and panoramas, were establishing new sets of relationships between humans, technology and the world as well as new regimes of vision, cultural consumption and spectatorship (Friedberg, 2006) that are now interlinked with gamble-play.

Benjamin writes in relation to gambling,

gambling generates by way of experiment the lightning-quick process of stimulation at the moment of danger, the marginal case in which presence of mind becomes divination – that is to say, one of the highest, rarest moments in life.

(Benjamin, 2006, p. 212)

Benjamin identified, then, the specific dynamics of gambling by observing players in the early-twentieth-century European arcades, a site of rapid technological change not unlike ours. Even though Benjamin mainly referred to the roulette, a mechanical device that converts the movement of the ball into discrete variables, his understanding of how technology can generate a transcendental experience is still current. Gamble-play devices can lead a person to believe that in winning they are "being rewarded by fate" or that they have "seized control of destiny" (Benjamin, 2006, p. 212).

As happens with other types of digital networked media, digital gamble-play platforms "capture their users in intensive and extensive networks of enjoyment, production, and surveillance" (Dean, 2010, p. 4). Players wish to experience one of those "rarest moments in life" evoked by Benjamin (2006, p. 212). These moments are what Deleuze and Guattari would call an "incorporeal transformation" (2004, p. 89), which is "the change of status in of a body or the change in its relations to other bodies which occurs when it is subject to a new description" (Patton, 1991).

Users enjoy being placed in a network that provides situations of controlled risk and allows the production of content, such as avatars and commentary. By entering these networks, however, users are subsequently categorised as consumers and digital marketing subjects, what Cheney-Lippold calls "algorithmic identities" (2011). This conversion opens the door to new types of control and risk concerning issues, such as privacy and cyberfraud, particularly in unregulated markets, such as Bitcoin casinos. It also opens up new possibilities for control through a better understanding of customers for, as Young states, contemporary gambling industries evidence the desire "to manipulate the outcomes of chance, to predetermine the outcomes in order to maximize revenues" (Young, 2010, p. 258).

Cheney-Lippold argues,

As the capacity of computers to aggregate user data increases and algorithms are improved upon to make disparate data more intelligible and useful, the ability for real-time cybernetic modelling to monitor, compute, and act becomes more efficient. So as more data is received about a certain user's behavior online, new coded computations can be done to change who the user is believed to be and what content that user might desire.

(Cheney-Lippold, 2011, p. 168)

By encouraging the generation of "algorithmic identities" through "coded computations" (Cheney-Lippold, 2011, p. 168) informed by the user's cultural preferences in terms of taste and consumption patterns, gamble-play becomes one of the many materialisations of Deleuze's notion of the "societies of control" (1992). Deleuze explores these ideas in the essay "Postscript on the Societies of Control", an influential critique of contemporary technosocial structures. In this essay, Deleuze argues that human groupings have moved on from the Foucauldian spaces of enclosure present in modernity to spaces of flow where people, text, images, procedures and discourses converge. In a society of control, information access and management produces individuals who are not a "discontinuous producer of energy" but "undulatory, in orbit, in a continuous network" (Deleuze, 1992, pp. 5–6). Gamble-play media establish continuous engagement with users, offering an experience that is perpetual and not the one-off, discontinuous experience of casino gambling.

Deleuze also describes technosocial structures and the ways in which they allow a more fluid form of government and corporate control over individuals. This form of control is the one subtly exercised by gamble-play operators. Deleuze claims that we have moved historically from the disciplinary societies envisioned by Foucault and organised around "spaces of enclosure" (the school, the factory, the prison, et cetera) created and maintained by institutions, to "ultrarapid forms of free-floating control" (Deleuze, 1992, p. 4). Deleuze argues that individuals do not enter and exit spaces of enclosure in a sort of ordered life progression but are always unfinished projects, perpetually seeking betterment while never truly achieving it. This formulation is an illustrative description of compulsive gambling in which the project of becoming a millionaire is seldom achieved. For their part, gamble-play platforms foster competition, such as at online poker tables and on social casino apps that rank players according to their winnings, involving the player in a never-ending becoming.

In escaping the spaces of enclosure of casinos and card rooms – for the most part exceptions in the flows of the everyday – digital gamble-play allows operators to infiltrate networks that the gamer/gambler can enter and exit continuously as they are persistent, always-on spaces or even other environments, such as *Second Life* (Boellstorff, 2008). Some social casino apps including *Zynga Poker* and *Big Fish Casino* send constant 'push notifications' if the user goes through extended periods of time without playing. Consumers of digital gambling do not enter the casino but carry the casino around in their pockets, access it from their computer desktop or find it in almost every corner, as happens in Electronic Game Machine markets that present ubiquitous opportunities to gamble.

In digital gamble-play actions and images are waiting to be invoked. This is made possible through computers, "metamedia", which according to Manovich, "can represent most other media while augmenting them with many new properties" (2013, p. 101). Manovich argues that computers are used to generate "a number of new types of media that are not simulations of prior physical media" (Manovich, 2013, p. 329; see also Giddings, 2007). Accordingly, gambling platforms generated and accessed via computers are not copycats of older gambling media but media in their own right as they are "a combination of particular techniques for generating, editing and accessing content" (Manovich, 2013, p. 335). Gamble-play media generate new types of content, such as a user's game history, avatars, player rankings and so on, that converge in newfound mechanisms of seduction and control.

Either for real or virtual stakes, in gamble-play the focus tends to be on the gameplay and the narratives associated with the gambling experience rather than the stake. This is exemplified, for instance, with the branding of slot machines and social casino apps using Hollywood franchises and icons that are culturally resonant. The platform designs, business models and marketing campaigns that I refer to throughout this book show how digital gamble-play products are sold as an experience in which what matters most is not necessarily how much money (real or virtual) you win or lose but how much fun you have while trying to succeed. Gamble-play events produce an "incorporeal transformation" into either a winner or a loser (Deleuze & Guattari, 2004, p. 89). An incorporeal transformation is "the change of status in of a body or the change in its relations to other bodies which occurs when it is subject to a new description" (Patton, 1991).

In gamble-play, what is promoted is not always the monetary prize but the ludic and social practices involved in attempting to win as well as the state-of-the-art technology used to stage gambling "spectacles" (Debord, 1967). The ludic rather than the agonistic or competitive components are exacerbated. This type of dynamic has been noticed by video game theorists, such as Alexander Galloway, who states that "labor itself is now play, just as play becomes more and more laborious" (2013, p. 29).

Gamble-play is not about outcome but about gameplay.

The Dynamics of Digital Poker and Slots

I study online poker and slot machines in both their real-money and play currency variants, a significant departure from previous gambling studies, which only consider gambling to be those games of chance that involve real money and are demarcated from everyday life (Reith, 1999). Poker is generally considered a game that involves both chance (in the dealing of the cards) and skill (in reading one's opponents and making calculations on the cards at play). Traditional slots are considered to be purely defined by chance, although some players have the illusion of mastery over the machine.

It is now necessary to describe these two forms of play: digital poker and slots. Online poker tables can be defined as a simulation or virtual representation of real-life or RL (Boellstorff, 2008) poker tables. The goal in digital poker is to win money by capturing the pot, which contains the bets made by players during the round. Players place the bets hoping that they have the best hand (two cards) or that they can convince other players that they do (bluff). Players can fold (relinquish their cards and their bet), call (equal the bet), or raise the bet on each hand (McDonald, 2005). Digital poker involves both skill (in anticipating the actions of the other players and preventing other players from reading you) and chance (the cards are dealt randomly). Online poker tables and mobile poker apps replicate the basic procedures of traditional poker and institute new codes proper to interactive and networked entertainment, such as the generation of avatars that perform bluffing and telling, or the sharing of social media status updates related to the game. A digital poker game needs two main types of agent, "a dealer together with multiple players that represent either human players or computer players" (Billings, Davidson, Schaeffer, & Szafron, 2002, p. 209).

Programmers and designers face various technical challenges when trying to simulate poker electronically. Poker is

> a game of imperfect information, where multiple competing agents must deal with probabilistic knowledge, risk assessment, and possible deception, not unlike decisions made in the real world.
>
> (Billings et al., 2002, p. 202)

The modelling of a digital opponent is a significant challenge for artificial intelligence designers (Moravčík et al., 2017) as various factors come into play: hand strength (how strong a hand is in relation to other hands), hand potential ("the probability that a hand will improve to win, or that a leading hand will lose, after future community cards appear"), bluffing (the probability that a weak hand could win) and opponent modelling ("a likely probability distribution of the opponent's hand") (Billings et al., 2002, p. 209). These factors are significant as values such as trust and reputation come, literally, into play. In digital poker, players face the random distribution of cards, the unpredictability of what other players will do next and the black-boxed operations defined by codes and algorithms.

The question that has fascinated gambling researchers, mathematicians and philosophers, from Cardano to Pascal (Mazur, 2009), resurfaces and acquires currency in digital poker. Is poker a game of chance or a game of skill? Recent studies have indicated that in fact digital poker is something that can be learnt and is defined by skill. DeDonno and Detterman (2008), for example, conducted an experiment in which participants played *Turbo Texas Hold'em* for Windows. In two tests, they compared the results of participants who had received a set of instructions on how to play better, and those who did not. Those who were instructed outperformed those who were not. They concluded that

> Luck (random factors) disguises the fact that poker is a game of skill... skill is the determining factor in long-term outcome.
>
> (DeDonno & Detterman, 2008, p. 36)

The skills required in gamble-play platforms involve not only strategies in the game itself but also other platform-specific abilities, such as creating an effective avatar or understanding how the procedures in each platform work.

On the other hand, slots or pokies are gaming machines that traditionally require that "a minimum of three reels be put in motion with the result being determined by the combination of objects displayed when the reels come to a stop" (Ziolkowski, 2014, p. 5). The winning amount depends on the ranking of a particular image/object compared to the other images/objects in the reel. Digital slots follow the same principle as their mechanical predecessor, but a Random Number Generator, or RNG, produces the outcomes. Digital slots are played in physical venues, such as VIP Lounges and casinos, in real-money online casinos – most of them unregulated – and through social casino smartphone and tablet apps, where winnings are in the form of virtual currency and where pure randomness is not enforced by law as they are considered gaming, not gambling.

The digitisation of play in both poker and slots poses significant challenges to the theorisation of digital gamble-play in terms of the phenomenology of play. In general, major media shifts that emanate from the digitisation of play happen along three domains:

1   tactile/visual engagement with the machine;
2   movement/stasis in relation to the player's position in real and virtual space; and
3   changing experience of time. Users can get lost in their own perception of time, as in traditional slot machines, or they may share the same time as others, as in an online poker game.

It is useful to locate the experience offered by each type of digital gambling platform in these domains as this analysis offers insight into how people relate to gambling media experientially.

Tactile/visual engagement refers to how users engage physically with the gambling platform: how they use their bodies to play. This is particularly relevant when talking about online poker as traditional poker implies a heavily tactile engagement with objects (chips, cards) and other people (mainly with the dealer). In digital poker, this engagement is reframed with visual cues that require a more limited tactile engagement from the user, mostly clicks either with a mouse or digitally on touch-screens, and a more pronounced dexterity to interpret and manipulate visual and aural cues and signs.

Online poker platform designers strive to replicate the tactile dimension of the game. Mobile apps based on gameplay through touchscreens also bring back the tactility of traditional poker. Standard desktop on-line poker platforms, however, are a primarily visual medium, although they also involve some tactility. What matters most in online poker is not only the codification of sensation – such as what one 'feels' while watching one's opponent bluff – but the codification of information – how to interpret the actions of human and non-human actors as represented in digital images.

In the case of slots, some contemporary machines played in venues such as casinos, pubs and clubs increase the sensorial stimulation of the gambling experience, both tactilely and visually, by having larger and more complex hardware that includes various screen formats, sophisticated speakers and even vibrations when the user hits the jackpot. For example, the *Michael Jackson: King of Pop* slot machine, developed by Bally Technologies (the biggest US manufacturer of gaming machines), "showcases a custom surround-sound chair for an unprecedented audio experience" (Bally Technologies, 2014). Bally Technologies manufactures slot machines themed after other cultural icons, such as the film *Titanic*, providing a multisensory experience with images, sounds and vibrations that are familiar to the gambler. International Game Technology (IGT) has gone further into providing gamblers with an intense bodily experience. In 2017, the slot machine manufacturer released its 4D Sphinx slot model, in which users "can actually move, and sometimes feel, the jewels, rings and butterflies hovering in front of them"; additionally, "the game is able to track the location and movement of a player's hands in front of the screen, and those gestures are integrated into the game" (Moore, 2017).

In some digital gambling platforms, users can move across real or virtual space. These forms of movement are particularly apparent when comparing static slot machines with mobile social casino apps. While traditional slot machines require the gambler to sit in front of the device, slot apps allow movement between different places and contexts. Play escapes *enclosures* and enters *flows*. Digital gamble-play bleeds into everyday spaces in quite significant ways (Albarrán-Torres & Goggin, 2014).

In other forms of digital gamble-play, such as online poker, users can navigate across different poker tables on their screen. Online, poker escapes the confines of the felt table and allows movement through simultaneous games. Many online poker players play on various windows at a time (LaPlante, Kleschinsky, LaBrie, Nelson, & Shaffer, 2009) and some platforms including *PKR* have featured multi-table capacities built into their platforms. Some digital poker tables offer a schematic representation of the game where avatars are static. Others, such as *PKR*, have allowed the avatar to move inside the virtual room, following the conventions of digital games and virtual worlds.

Gambling has typically been characterised by specific temporal regimes. Benjamin argues that

> The phantasmagorias of space to which the *flâneur* devotes himself find a counterpart in the phantasmagorias of time to which the gambler is addicted. Gambling converts time into a narcotic.
>
> (Benjamin, 1999, p. 12)

Most land-based gambling venues, the casino and the VIP Lounge among them, are designed to make gamblers enter a state of euphoria in which time becomes independent, and the overall gambling experience a "narcotic" (Ritzer & Stillman, 2001). In traditional gambling, each player experiences time differently depending on the intensity of play. In gambling, "each round is a self-contained island in time, existing independently of what came before or what will come after" (Reith, 1999, p. 136). Time becomes a gooey substance under the casino lights.

In digital gamble-play platforms, by contrast, there are visual cues designed to inscribe a sense of urgency in the gameplay, such as clocks or, as is the case in most online poker platforms, indicators that opponents are waiting. Time becomes homogenous as most digital gamble-play platforms rely on a shared communicative experience, on the co-presence necessary to sustain play.

Through these three domains – sensorial engagement, spatiality and temporality – we can grasp the media changes and technocultural innovations of digital gamble-play. The sensorial and temporal dynamics of gambling and play change when translated into digital environments and are also transformed depending on whether play is mediated through a static or a mobile device.

Digital gamble-play platforms also oscillate between being media that are evidently present – such as 3D online casinos or the most pyrotechnic online slots – and media that lend themselves to be experienced in subtle ways to let users concentrate on the game – such as some online poker tables. This can be understood through the two logics identified by new media theorists Jay David Bolter and Richard Grusin when they discuss variants of media in terms of regimes of representation: immediacy and hypermediacy. The logic of immediacy "dictates that the medium itself should disappear and leave us in the presence of the thing represented" (Bolter & Grusin, 1999, p. 6). Contrarily, the logic of hypermediacy leads us "to become aware of the new medium as a medium" (Bolter & Grusin, 1999, p. 6). In this book, I am interested in the ways in which these two logics "not only coexist" in digital gambling platforms but also are "mutually dependent" (Bolter & Grusin, 1999, p. 6).

Conclusion

Gamble-play is a new cultural form in which the fun aspects of gambling are privileged over winning and losing. This dynamic generates new negotiations between seduction and control in gambling markets. It also generates new forms of play that are gambling-like but do not offer the possibility of winning real money. The practices of gamble-play are establishing new types of relationship between players and the 'house' as products adopt the affordances and conventions of digital networked media.

In this chapter, I situated gamble-play historically in the trajectory of contemporary gambling cultures. Then, I explained how gamble-play media operate across three domains: tactile/visual engagement with the machine, movement/stasis of the player in real or virtual space and changing experiences of time. Defining where gamble-play media are situated in these domains allows us to grasp the phenomenological dimension of play. The chapter also explains how gamble-play media, digital poker and digital slots, in particular, depart from the experiences offered by traditional gambling, a cultural shift explored in the remaining sections of this book.

References

Albarrán-Torres, C. (2017) Where the stakes are higher: transnational labor and digital gambling media. In G. Goggin & M. McLelland (Eds.). *The Routledge companion to global internet histories* (pp. 425–435). London, UK, New York, NY: Routledge.

Albarrán Torres, C., & Goggin, G. (2014). Mobile social gambling: Poker's next frontier. *Mobile Media & Communication*, 2(1), 94–109.

Auster, P. (1990). *The music of chance*. New York, NY: Viking.

Austrin, T., & Farnsworth, J. (2012). Celebrity, infamy, poker. *Celebrity Studies*, 3(3), 337–339.

Bally Technologies, Inc. (2014). Bally Technologies – Your partner in innovation. *ballytech.com*. Retrieved September 2014, from www.ballytech.com/

Beck, U. (1992). *The risk society: Towards a new modernity*. London, UK: Sage.

Benjamin, W. (1999). *The arcades project*. Cambridge, London: Harvard University Press.

Benjamin, W. (2006). Notes on a theory of gambling. In J. F. Cosgrave (Ed.), *The sociology of risk and gambling reader* (pp. 211–213). London, UK: Routledge.

Billings, D., Davidson, A., Schaeffer, J., & Szafron, D. (2002). The challenge of poker. *Artificial Intelligence*, 134(1), 201–240.

Binde, P. (2005a). Gambling, exchange systems and moralities. *Journal of Gambling Studies*, 21(4), 445–479.

Binde, P. (2005b). Gambling across cultures: Mapping worldwide occurrence and learning from ethnographic comparison. *International Gambling Studies*, 5(1), 1–27.

Bjerg, O. (2009). Too close to the money: A theory of compulsive gambling. *Theory, Culture & Society, 26*(4), 47–66.

Blaszczynski, A., & Nower, L. (2002). A pathways model of problem and pathological gambling. *Addiction, 97*(5), 487–499.

Boellstorff, T. (2008). *Coming of age in Second Life: An anthropologist explores the virtually human*. Princeton, NJ: Princeton University Press.

Bolter, J. D., & Grusin, R. (1999). *Remediation: Understanding new media*. Cambridge, MA: MIT Press.

Caldwell, G. (1985a). Some historical and sociological characteristics of Australian gambling. In G. Caldwell, B. Haig, M. Dickerson, & L. Sylan (Eds.), *Gambling in Australia* (pp. 18–27). Sydney, NSW: Croom Helm Australia.

Caldwell, G. (1985b). Poker machine gambling in NSW and ACT clubs. In G. Caldwell, B. Haig, M. Dickerson, & L. Sylan (Eds.), *Gambling in Australia* (pp. 261–268). Sydney, NSW: Croom Helm Australia.

Cheney-Lippold, J. (2011). A new algorithmic identity: Soft biopolitics and the modulation of control. *Theory, Culture & Society, 28*(6), 164–181.

Dean, J. (2005). Communicative capitalism: Circulation and the foreclosure of politics. *Cultural Politics, 1*(1), 51–74.

Dean, J. (2010). *Blog theory: Feedback and capture in the circuits of drive*. Cambridge, MA: Polity.

Debord, G. (1967). *Society of the Spectacle*. Marxist.org. Retrieved from www.marxists.org/reference/archive/debord/society.htm

DeDonno, M., & Detterman, D. K. (2008). Poker is a skill. *Gaming Law Review, 12*(1), 31–36.

DeGoede, M. (2005). *Virtue, fortune and faith: A genealogy of finance*. Minneapolis, MN: University of Minnesota Press.

Deleuze, G. (1992). Postscript on the Societies of Control. *October, 59*, 3–7.

Deleuze, G., & Guattari, F. (1994). *What is philosophy?* New York, NY: Columbia University Press.

Deleuze, G., & Guattari, F. (2004). *Capitalism and schizophrenia: A thousand plateaus*. London, UK: Continuum.

Deuze, M. (2006). Ethnic media, community media and participatory culture. *Journalism, 7*(3), 262–280.

Dibbell, J. (2006). *Play money: Or, how I quit my day job and made millions trading virtual loot*. New York, NY: Basic Books.

Dilts, A. (2011). From 'entrepreneur of the self' to 'care of the self': Neo-liberal governmentality and Foucault's ethics. *Foucault Studies*, (12), 130–146. Retrieved from https://rauli.cbs.dk/index.php/foucault-studies/article/view/3338

Dombrink, J., & Thompson, W. N. (1990). *The last resort: Success and failures in campaigns for casinos*. Reno, NV: University of Nevada Press.

Dostoyevsky, F. (2010). *The Gambler and other stories*. New York, NY: Penguin Classics.

Dreier, H. (2013a). Online poker thriller 'Runner' quickly politicized. *Las Vegas Review Journal*. Retrieved from www.reviewjournal.com/business/casinos-gaming/online-poker-thriller-runner-quickly-politicized

Dreier, H. (2013b). 8 pros, 1 amateur compete for $8.4m WSOP prize. *Herald Online*. Retrieved from www.heraldonline.com/2013/11/03/5366475/8-pros-1-amateur-compete-for-84m.html#storylink=cpy

Ferguson, H. (1999). Preface: Gambling, chance and the suspension of reality. In G. Reith (Ed.), *The age of chance: Gambling in western culture* (pp. xiv–xix). London, UK: Routledge.

Flavin, M. (2003). *Gambling in the nineteenth-century English Novel: "a leprosy is o'er the land"*. Brighton, UK: Sussex Academic Press.

Foucault, M. (2008). *The birth of biopolitics: Lectures at the Collège de France, 1978–1979* (trans. Graham Burchell). New York, NY: Palgrave McMillan.

Fox, W. L. (2007). *In the desert of desire: Las Vegas and the culture of spectacle*. Reno, NV: University of Nevada Press.

Friedberg, A. (2006). *The virtual world: From Alberti to Microsoft*. Cambridge, MA: MIT Press.

Galloway, A. (2013). *The interface effect*. New York, NY: Polity.

Geuss, M. (2013). Firm says online gambling accounts for almost half of all Bitcoin transactions. *Ars Technica*. Retrieved from http://arstechnica.com/business/2013/08/firm-says-online-gambling-accounts-for-almost-half-of-all-bitcoin-transactions/

Giddings, S. (2007). Dionysiac machines, video games and the triumph of the simulacra. *Convergence: The International Journal of Research into New Media Technologies, 13*(4), 417–431.

Goggin, J. (2012). Regulating (virtual) subjects: Finance, entertainment and games. *Journal of Cultural Economy, 5*(4), 441–456.

Grotenstein, J., & Reback, S. (2006). *All in: The (almost) entirely true story of the World Series of Poker*. New York, NY: St. Martin's Press.

Huizinga, J. (1955). *Homo ludens: A study of the play-element in culture*. Boston, MA: Beacon Press.

Kusyszyn, I. (1984). The psychology of gambling. *The Annals of the American Academy of Political and Social Science, 474*, 133–145.

LaPlante, D. A., Kleschinsky, J. H., LaBrie, R. A., Nelson, S. E., & Shaffer, H. J. (2009). Sitting at the virtual poker table: a prospective epidemiological study of actual Internet poker gambling behavior. *Computers in Human Behavior, 25*(3), 711–717.

Lauster, M. (2007). Walter Benjamin's myth of the "flâneur". *The Modern Language Review, 102*(1), 139–156.

Lears, J. (2003). *Something for nothing: Luck in America*. New York, NY: Viking.

Lycka, M. (2011). Online gambling: Towards a transnational regulation? *Gaming Law Review and Economics, 15*(4), 179–195.

Lynch, R. (1990). Working-class luck and vocabularies of hope among regular poker-machine players. In D. Rowe & G. Lawrence (Eds.), *Sport and leisure: Trends in Australian popular culture* (pp. 189–208). Sydney, NSW: Harcourt Brace Jovanovich.

Manovich, L. (2013). *Software takes command*. New York, NY, London, UK: Bloomsbury.

Mazur, J. (2009). *What's luck got to do with it: The history, mathematics, and psychology behind the gambler's illusion*. Princeton, NJ: Princeton University Press.

McDonald, G. (2005). *Deal me in: Online cardrooms, bigtime tournaments, and the new poker*. San Francisco, CA, London, UK: Sybex.

McGowan, R. (2012). Australian gambling culture and economic development. *Gaming Law Review and Economics, 16*(12), 729–734.

McManus, J. (2004). *Positively fifth street: Murderers, cheetahs, and Binion's World Series of Poker*. New York, NY: Picador.

Moore, T. (2017, December 8). IGT adds stimulating dimension to slot machine. *Las Vegas Sun*. Retrieved from https://m.lasvegassun.com/news/2017/dec/08/igt-adds-stimulating-dimension-to-slot-machine/

Moravčík, M., Schmid, M., Burch, N., Lisý, V., Morrill, D., Bard, N., ... Bowling, M. (2017). DeepStack: Expert-level artificial intelligence in heads-up no-limit poker. *Science, 356*(6337), 508–513.

Morgan Stanley (2012). Social gambling: Click here to play. *Morgan Stanley Blue Paper*. Retrieved from www.morganstanley.com/

Parmentier, G., & Rolland, S. (2009). Les consommateurs des mondes virtuels: Construction identitaire et expérience de consommation dans Second Life. *Recherche et applications en marketing, 24*(3), 43–56.

Patton, P. (1991). The world seen from within: Deleuze and the philosophy of events. *Theory & Event, 1*(1), Johns Hopkins University Press. Retrieved February 12, 2018, from Project MUSE database.

Quinn, J. P. (1892). *Fools of fortune or Gambling and gamblers*. Chicago, IL: The Anti-Gambling Association.

Reckwitz, A. (2002). Toward a theory of social practices: a development in culturalist theorizing. *European Journal of Social Theory, 5*(2), 243–263.

Reith, G. (1999). *The age of chance: Gambling in Western culture*. London, UK: Routledge.

Ridley, S. (1996). You can bet on it. *Internet.au, 13*, 41–45.

Ritzer, G., & Stillman, T. (2001). The modern Las Vegas casino-hotel: The paradigmatic new means of consumption. *M@n@gement, 4*(3), 83–99.

Salen, K., & Zimmerman, E. (2003). *Rules of play*. Cambridge, MA: MIT Press.

Smith, E. (2011). Planet Poker Era. *Poker History*. Retrieved from www.pokerhistory.eu/history/planet-poker-first-online-poker-room

Young, M. (2010). Gambling, capitalism and the State: Towards a new dialectic of the Risk Society? *Journal of Consumer Culture, 10*(2), 254–273.

Ziolkowski, S. (2014). The World Count of Gaming Machines 2013. *Gaming Technologies Association*. Retrieved from www.gamingta.com/pdf/World_Count_2014.pdf

Films and television shows cited

Anderson, P. T. (Director). (1996) *Hard Eight* [Motion picture]. United States: Samuel Goldwyn Company.

Hill, G. R. (Director). (1973) *The Sting* [Motion picture]. United States: Universal Pictures

Mulé, M., Scott, B., Malina, J., & Newman, A. (Producers). (2003–2006) *Celebrity Poker Showdown* [Television series]. United States: Bravo Network.

Digital games cited

Big Fish Games (2012) Big Fish Casino. *www.bigfishgames.com*. Retrieved from www.bigfishgames.com/online-games/19475/big-fish-casino/index.html

Caesars Interactive Entertainment Ltd. (2017) *World Series of Poker*. Retrieved from www.wsop.com

Cassava Enterprises. (n.d). *888poker* (Android version). Retrieved from http://au.888.com/

PKR Limited (2014). PKR Let's Play. *pkr.com*. Retrieved September 2014, from www.pkr.com/en/ [Note: PKR declared bankruptcy in 2017].

Planet Poker (2017). Planet Poker Internet Cardroom – Real Poker, Real People. *planetpoker.com*. Retrieved from www.planetpoker.com

Rational Entertainment Enterprises Limited (2014). PokerStars.com. *pokerstars.com*. Retrieved, from www.pokerstars.com/

Real Fun Games (2014). *Babel Casino* (Version 1.2.1). Retrieved from https://itunes.apple.com/us/app/babel-casino/id691350993

Rosedale, P. (Designer). (2003) *Second Life*. United States: Linden Lab

Zynga (2007) Zynga Poker. *zynga.com*. Retrieved from http://zynga.com/game/poker

Zynga (2014). Hit it Rich Slots Play Online Slots. *zynga.com*. Retrieved from http://zynga.com/game/slots

2 Smoke and Mirrors
Procedural Rhetoric in Gamble-Play

This chapter explains how gamble-play assemblages are formed and sustained through procedures, interactive images and constant communication among players and between players and the house. Interactive images are a fundamental part of the media innovations brought about by the digitisation of gambling platforms. Interactive images are the entry point for practices of digital gamble-play, such as connecting with other gamblers and engaging in continuous play. Such connections are achieved through the articulation of procedures – particular ways of doing things (Bogost, 2007) – that promise gamblers the often-misleading possibility of their becoming a constant winner.

Images in gamble-play are exteriorisations of "procedural rhetoric" (Bogost, 2007). Procedural rhetoric is "a new type of persuasive and expressive practice" that is primarily present in various forms of interactive media in which computing processes are used "persuasively" (Bogost, 2007, p. 3). This conceptualisation of gamble-play resembles Thomas Malaby's theorisation of games as "grounded in human practice and as fundamentally processual" (2007, p. 210). Gamble-play operators design platforms that lead players to do things in particular ways and engage in practices that are foreign to traditional forms of gambling, such as the selection and creation of avatars and the sharing of results on digital networks. These procedures define the media specificity of gamble-play platforms.

Interactive images are particularly significant in their move from predominantly tactile media – such as chips and cards in traditional poker – to principally visual platforms in online casinos. Interactive images are also essential in comprehending how digital gamble-play bridges online and offline 'universes of reference' (Guattari, 1995), which configure knowledge, habits and values associated with particular techno-social paradigms (Chesher, 2012), in this case, following the paradigm of digital gamble-play. Images also generate new kinds of relationships between human and computer agents by being placed in audiovisual interactive platforms that work as rhetorical tools that motivate consumption and engagement.

The role of interactive images in recent media innovations in gambling is particularly evident in poker. Analogue poker involves a co-present, tactile engagement, both with objects such as chips and cards and with other people, including the dealer, other players and spectators. In digital poker platforms, including *PokerStars* or the now-bankrupt *PKR*, engagement is reframed with visual and acoustic cues that support interaction and move players to engage with the platform and the gambling operator through procedures that lead towards constant play, communication, brand loyalty and affiliation.

Gamble-play operates through *procedure-images*, which are programmed events manifest in a complex flow of audiovisual cues. As well as drawing from Bogost, the term procedure-image adapts Gilles Deleuze's concept of the movement-image, which interrogates our engagement with the early-twentieth-century technology of cinema (Deleuze, 1986). The movement-image "ultimately concerns self-perception, self-understanding, and belief" (Crockett, 2005, p. 181). Procedure-images in gamble-play platforms reshape players' "self-perception" and "self-understanding" as subjects that are prone to particular "incorporeal transformations" (Deleuze & Guattari, 2004, p. 89) through play – transformations into winners, losers and members of gambling communities based on emotional attachments to other players.

I will now discuss the cultural significance of Deleuze's 'movement-image' and place it vis-à-vis the 'procedure-image'. In his treatise on cinema, *Cinema 1 The movement-image*, Deleuze argues that cinema generates images that contain movement, not images to which movement is added. Procedure-images in interactive media, such as digital gambling platforms, are neither images that simulate procedures nor images to which procedures are added. They are procedures in and of themselves. This assertion, which will be fleshed out later in this chapter, implies a new regime of engagement with the image that will help us to better understand procedural rhetoric in digital gamble-play. The procedure-image establishes new paradigms, just as the time-image and the movement-image derived from cinema established new phenomenological and discursive regimes related to, respectively, action and memory (Deleuze, 1986, 2005). Images in gamble-play platforms are also movement-images, but they imply the presence of a new subject, a player who can alter the actions displayed on the screen by following pre-established procedures.

Procedure-images aid in the construction of a particular rhetoric, or persuasive discourse, related to gambling and its consumption as they are fundamental in the formation of "intensive and extensive networks of enjoyment, production, and surveillance" (Dean, 2010, p. 4). In this chapter, I focus mainly on online poker sites, both desktop and mobile, although I also refer to slot machines when discussing particular procedure-images related to kitsch and exotica. The concepts of procedure-images and procedural rhetoric can also be used in the analysis of slot machines and social casino apps, the other two varieties of gamble-play that I explore in this book.

Procedural rhetoric in gamble-play typically establishes negotiations between user agency and operator control. On the one hand, it allows users to interact and feel a sense of control over the outcome. On the other hand, it affords communication that strengthens engagement, consumption and brand affiliation. Procedural rhetoric in gamble-play also reveals how the dynamics of other types of media, such as social networking sites, influence the configuration of digital gambling platforms. This takes form particularly in persistent environments that support player co-presence. Online casinos are always on and at the player's disposal, much like virtual worlds in the vein of *Second Life* or *World of Warcraft* (Bainbridge, 2010; Boellstorff, 2008).

This chapter is structured as follows. First, I use Deleuze's image categories (1986, 2005) as a departure point for identifying the key distinctive features of the imagery in digital gambling assemblages. I propose a modification, or rather an addition, to Deleuze's movement-image, which was originally based on cinema. The movement-image calls for a new regime for understanding image systems. Contrary to the Platonic precept of images as representations/illusions, Deleuze contests that images should be approached with distinct ontological categories. For instance, regarding the movement-image, Deleuze states in *Cinema 2* that "The movement-image is the object; the thing itself caught in movement as continuous function. The movement-image is the modulation of the object itself" (2005, p. 27). I then explore how procedure-images are exteriorisations of procedural rhetoric. In the case of digital poker, the house tries to persuade gamblers to keep betting and partaking in other communicative acts, thus expanding the reaches of the operator's player pool and guaranteeing profit derived from real or simulated bets. Finally, I explain how procedure-images in gamble-play constitute a set of discourses that are categorised in five instances of procedural rhetoric:

1 Gambling is an adventure!
2 Learn through experience, you will get better;
3 Do not feel alone, your friends and foes are here;
4 Remain loyal, the 'house' loves you; and
5 Do not miss out! There is always something to be won!

In order to identify how procedural rhetoric and procedure-images work in digital poker, I provide examples of the interface design, in both lobbies and tables, of some of the world's most popular online casinos, according to www.pokerscout.com, the website on which Fiedler and Wilcke (2011) based the first large-scale snapshot of the online poker market. Some of the interfaces analysed for this book are as follows: the ill-fated *PKR, Cake Poker, Mansion Poker, EuroPoker, Ladbrokes, Paddy Power Poker, BetFred Poker, 24thPoker, Poker Heaven, Unibet, Bwin, 888, PokerStars, PartyPoker, William Hill, Poker 770* and *Everest Poker.*

From the Movement-Image to the Procedure-Image

Video game theory provides insights into how images articulate procedures in gamble-play platforms. Nitsche identifies five analytical planes for the scrutiny of video games (2008, p. 15). This categorisation is useful when discussing other screen-based technologies: in this case, digital gamble-play interfaces. As discussed in the Introduction to this book, these five spaces are as follows: *rule-based space, mediated space, fictional space, play space* and *social space.*

The mediated space, through procedure-images, defines the interplay between the other four planes. The dynamics of the mediated space actualise the rule-based space and bring it from the realm of the virtual to the realm of the sensorial.

Digital images related to digital gambling forms such as poker can be seen in a multitude of offline and online "mediated spaces" (Nitsche, 2008, p. 15). The vast technocultural network of overlapping digital gamble-play assemblages is visible through the multitude of digitally produced and distributed procedure-images. This imagery (cards, player avatars, logos, promising six-figure prizes) is, so to speak, the surface layer of digital gamble-play assemblages. Zooming in on these images is fundamental for unveiling the workings of these complex networks.

Gamble-play design constantly *remediates* gambling practices. Remediation is the unstable refashioning and appropriation of existing media by new, developing media (Bolter & Grusin, 1999). The materiality of the game (cards in predigital poker, screens in digital iterations) not only defines its rules but also user experience.

In a traditional poker game, gamblers exchange money through the intermittent showing and concealing of information in the form of images printed on cards and bodily expressions (Hayano, 1982). This procedural exchange of information is mediated by a set of cards distributed randomly, whose combinations determine who wins the hand. In traditional commercial poker (organised, for example, in casinos and card rooms), the performance of the other players, their mastery of 'poker faces' and the ambience created by the house are inputs that must be taken into account by the gambler and by anyone who studies their actions, reactions and decision-making processes. Poker is as much about reading other players as it is about having the skill to play your cards right.

In digital poker, by contrast, player performance and ambience manifest as interactive images. These images include avatars and virtual environments. These virtual environments vary in complexity, from the schematic representation of the poker table in *Virgin Poker* (Gamesys, 2013) to the complex 3D rendition of a casino in *PKR*, where the user could choose virtual camera modes when the casino was in operation (Figure 2.1).

Figure 2.1 Promotional image of the orbit view of the 3D casino *PKR* (image captured on May 6, 2014 from www.pkr.com/en/game-info/viewing-options/; this web page has since been removed).

Procedure-images place digital poker closer to the visual end in the visual/tactile engagement spectrum. The ways in which digital poker players show (raise, show) and conceal (bluff) information is mediated by computer code and performed through audiovisual interactions that both replicate and transform the exchanges present in brick-and-mortar poker games, where information is conveyed in a multi-sensorial fashion. In digital poker, users and software agents exchange information primarily through images and sounds arranged in a variety of screen-based interfaces (among hundreds, *888*, *PartyCasino* and *Zynga Poker*). Touchscreens bring tactility back to digital poker.

The staging of a digital poker game requires the player to 'fill in the blanks' and experience movement and action (not an *illusion* of movement but movement per se). Scott McCloud (1993) illustrates how mental processes articulate closure when we read and interpret sequential images. McCloud's illustration of the inner workings of comic books can be useful when analysing other sequential arts, such as film, and interactive platforms, such as digital poker. McCloud points out that the mind's eye creates the action that takes place in between the panels of a comic book. He calls this phenomenon "closure" and describes it as the "phenomenon of observing the parts but perceiving the whole" (McCloud, 1993, p. 63). This action can be sequential or disjointed and can represent split-second time-lapses, minutes, hours or years. In digital gamble-play, players are required to anticipate their actions and those of their adversaries. They accomplish this by analysing past experiences, as platforms usually provide a digital archive of each player's gaming history, and by studying the conditions of the current game, exteriorised through procedure-images. The gambler inhabits various temporal frames in any given instant. They follow a sequence of actions and reactions through exercises in deduction, logic and anticipation until achieving temporary states of closure.

To exemplify the process of closure in a gamble-play platform, consider the pioneering app *Zynga Poker*, which was made available on Android, Apple and Facebook in 2012. An aerial shot shows the following elements: the table, the hand that was just revealed by one of the players, the stakes and the state of each player in relation to their expected actions (call, raise and so on). Although the platform is almost still, there are *things happening*. There are various indicators of time, such as the glowing contours of the player profiles, which appear to be bathed in neon light. Additionally, by placing chips in two different positions, the system simulates their physical displacement: the mind *fills in the blanks* and creates movement. Each card, in turn, is an image that represents shifting values over time as the game progresses and winning hands change. In gamble-play, movements signify game states as much as actions (Figure 2.2).

The phenomenological logic of these processes can be understood through Deleuze's image categories: mainly the movement-image (and to a lesser extent, the time-image), through which he offers a theory of film. Deleuze challenges the notion that cinematic images are mere representations of reality or translations of discourses and argues that they are a new expressive force in their own right, related to the ways in which the technical production of action and memory alter our perception and

Figure 2.2 A screenshot of the mobile app *Zynga Poker* (captured on February 17, 2017 from the author's Android device). Transparency in the player's avatars indicates the passage of time.

understandings of the world (Deleuze, 1986, 2005; Crockett, 2005). Deleuze contends that filmmakers generate discourse through images in the same way that philosophers construct theoretical frameworks through language (1986, 2005).

In his first book on the film image, *Cinema 1 The Movement-Image* (1986), Deleuze constructs an ontological approach to the cinematic image, focussing on its inherent movement. Deleuze bases his interpretation of images on Henri Bergson's phenomenology. He claims that cinema and other cultural manifestations based on moving images conform image-universes in themselves. Images do not form a *representation* of reality but a reality that is set apart.

In the Deleuzian image ontology, an image exists in the present and thus implies a past and a future that merge through movement. Images are the antithesis of *stasis* or stillness. This approach represents a fundamental shift in how we conceive images in a world increasingly populated by audiovisual constructs as

> cinema does not give us an image to which movement is added, it immediately gives us a movement-image. It does give us a section, but a section which is mobile, not an immobile section + abstract movement.
>
> (Deleuze, 1986, p. 2)

Images are not an illusion. They are not the shadows, such as in Plato's famous allegory of the cave. Images are not dependent on whatever goes on in the tangible world, behind the prisoner's back. Images equal reality... another reality. Movement-images inhabit a system defined by mobility and by the fluid relationship between its components. Movement and time, argues Deleuze, are not abstract notions in the image-universe but a manifestation of its own unique reality, of an image-universe or image-world.

Technological development has altered the ways in which we engage with screen images. At the end of the nineteenth century, movement-images established a regime of vision and experience that is still prevalent in myriad screen-based technologies. Even still images (advertisements, for instance) have cinematic qualities and give us "a section which is mobile" (Deleuze, 1986, p. 2). The brain becomes the screen. There is a vital force inside images, a force that rejects *stasis* or stillness. A technical innovation, cinema, creates "a new image of movement, a new form of motion, the movement of film and the way it alters perception and self-perception, as well as understanding" (Crockett, 2005, p. 178).

In light of the ethos of informational networks defined by mobility, ubiquity and potentiality, we can extrapolate Deleuze's theoretical framework further and flesh out our new category: the *procedure-image*. If action and movement characterised the relationship of modern cultural production with the image (as put into motion by Georges Méliès, Eadweard Muybridge and the Lumière brothers), then inter-action and computer code dictate the pace of the currents and under-currents of networked cultures (associated with Bill Gates, Steve Jobs, Mark Zuckerberg and many other programmers, designers and digital entrepreneurs).

Procedure-images are an extension of the semiology of cinematic signs elaborated by Deleuze based on Peirce's semiotics. Deleuze identifies three types of signs: chronosigns that are related to "the distinction set up by Bergson between peaks of present and sheets of time" (Crockett, 2005, p. 180), lectosigns that refer to the capacity for storytelling and the speech-act, and noosigns that reveal "the capacity of the film to gen-erate insight" (Crockett, 2005, p. 180). Procedure-images convey time, storytelling and insight in the form of rhetoric through procedures. The capacity of procedure-images to convey narrative and discourse is one of the most salient features of the media innovation synthesised in the concept of 'gamble-play'. However, unlike moving images in cin-ema, procedure-images require the direct physical engagement of the user. Procedure-images exist to be actualised, activated by the user. The narrative in gamble-play media and other interactive platforms, such as video games, is not fully predetermined but co-generated by the user's interaction with procedure-images. This provides users with a sense of mastery over what happens on the screen, a sense of control that is the cornerstone of how gamble-play interfaces generate and sustain user engagement.

Images in interactive digital environments hold the potential for in-teraction. They do not create an illusion of interaction: they exist to interact. They were programmed to facilitate communication between human and computer agents by carrying out procedures. How procedure-images work in games can be explained through the dynamics of digital chess pieces, which are images that exist to invite interaction and move play forward. The ways in which the player can move the pieces – the potential procedures – are what mediate engagement and competition, either with a human adversary or with the computer. What makes a pawn be a pawn is the associated procedure of only moving forward one square at the time, or capturing diagonally in the same ratio. A rook can only move in a straight line: displacement, action and interaction are embedded within it. In Peircean terms, chess pieces as images perform time, narrative and discourse (Crockett, 2005, p. 180). This breaks with the reality/representation dichotomy and institutes a reality/reality equa-tion, as Deleuze argues.

The digital art project *Thinking Machine* (2003), created by Martin Wattenberg and Marek Walczak, provides a useful visualisation of how the procedure-image works. *Thinking Machine* is an internet-based ap-plication that shows the possibilities considered by the computer (black) in a game of chess with a human user (white). The work's creator describes its function as follows:

> *Thinking Machine* explores the invisible, elusive nature of thought...
> A map is created from the traces of literally thousands of possible
> futures as the program tries to decide its best move. Those traces
> become a key to the invisible lines of force in the game as well as a
> window into the spirit of the thinking machine.
>
> (Wattenberg & Walczak, 2003)

When the machine is processing data a network of curves is overlaid on the board. The orange curves represent the possible future moves (procedures) of the machine (often many turns in the future), while the green ones indicate possibilities for the player. These possibilities will only become *actual* when either the machine or the human player moves the chessmen. Until this happens, interaction is virtual but nonetheless *real*.

What would the results rendered by a *Thinking Machine* programmed to visually represent the possible moves in a game of online poker look like? We would witness the formation of a tangled web of divergent thought and algorithmic processes; that web would extend and connect with other webs/assemblages that would form a fractal-like network in perpetual motion and transformation. We can also imagine what sort of diagram would result from the visualisation of the set of relationships that led to a financial transaction conducted in an online casino (Figure 2.3).

In view of this example, we can paraphrase, then, the Deleuzian proposition (Deleuze, 1986, p. 2): "... *digital poker* does not give us an image to which *interaction* is added, it immediately gives us a *procedure-image*. It does give us a section but a section which is interactive, not a *non-interactive* section + abstract *interaction*". Images are not slaves to interaction but rather constitute the interaction itself, an interaction that is not abstract but virtual, a potentiality. Most digital screens are an arrangement of procedure-images. The word processor in which this book is being typed, for instance, shows the image of a 3.5-inch floppy disk on the upper-left corner of the window. Like poker cards and chips, the image of the floppy disk – by now a nearly obsolete storage device – is a standard representation for specific procedures (saving) and capacities (mobility, portability). Floppy disk equals SAVE just as the image on the reverse of a card equals concealment. When the card is revealed through another procedure, the values are calculated, and the player wins or loses the hand.

The procedure-image carries procedural interaction from the virtual to the actual, from the algorithm to the interface. In digital poker, an unturned card promises the potential of changing the course of a game. For the player, the image *is* the interaction. This implies that the procedure-image acquires meaning through its placement in an

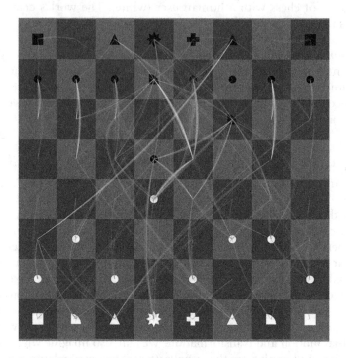

Figure 2.3 The Thinking Machine 6, an internet-based application that visua-
lises the possibilities explored by the machine during a game of chess.
This is a visual representation of what I call the procedure-image.

image-universe. In the case of mediated poker, the image-universe is a
gamble-play assemblage, populated by numbers, currency symbols and
agonistic imagery.

In discussing the interactive nature of images, Schwab adds when in-
terpreting the Deleuzian image ontology:

> On the one hand, an image is effectuated by factors originating from
> what is, will be, or counts in this respect as its environment; the
> image receives or is those effects – a reaction. On the other hand,
> the image is itself the origin or originator of effects; in this respect
> the image effectuates toward its environment, perhaps in *statu
> nascendi*-an action. To be an image is thus to be a form of exchange
> or interaction – action and reaction – between something and its
> environment, and to have or to constitute being and determinacy as
> such a form.
>
> (Schwab, 2000, p. 111)

For Schwab, then, an image holds the potential to change the image-world
that contains it. Schwab also concludes that the movement-image "exists as a relation, as relating to or in a given milieu; indeed, it seems to

exist *only* by virtue of relating", and that to be an image "is to organize being in a specific relational way" (Schwab, 2000, p. 111). Similarly, the procedure-image exists by virtue of establishing relations between actors. In digital poker, the frame of reference of each card, chip, monetary amount and avatar is indistinguishable from the actions, reactions and interactions that trigger its very existence and which are triggered by it.

Programmers and game designers construct a thought-system through interactions and communicate through procedure-images. Online casino designers actualise the connections between the infrastructures involved in gamble-play assemblages and perpetuate the ethos of capitalistic modes of production and consumption of risk.

In digital poker interfaces, numbers that represent money or other values become procedure-images. They present movement, the passage of time and, above all, the potential for interaction and transformation. Numbers that represent real or virtual currency are transferred from the abstract financial-universe to the concrete image-universe and thus acquire new values and meanings, where their financial quality does not reign over other qualities. Money acts as information and is then reframed as procedure-images. The monetary value of currency seems to be diluted as it gains ludic values. If you enter your personal bank account through the internet and notice that $1,000 dollars are missing, the link between the number-images and the monetary value they represent is tight, inseparable. However, in digital poker interfaces this link weakens. Numbers are then associated with other values, including the hope for the big win or a deficit that needs to be surmounted in order to recuperate losses.

As currency enters the image-universe, a dissonance is established: digital gamble-play interfaces are image-systems that seem to deal with intangible goods, when in fact outside the interface the wealth that changes hands has a monetary value. Numbers in digital gamble-play platforms, such as online poker tables, are as abstract as the chips on a traditional poker table.

Procedural Rhetoric in Digital Poker

Video game theorist Ian Bogost (2007) believes that audiovisual interactive products such as video games convey discourses that persuade the player to act in particular ways and establish systems of thought, similarly to the way that Deleuze believed cinema could convey discourse. In the case of digital gamble-play, game designers try to persuade the user to consume compulsively, as is the case in slot machine markets, or to communicate compulsively, as happens in social casino apps.

Bogost argues that video games invite players to enact procedures or particular ways of doing things and that, in turn, these procedures can be used persuasively and rhetorically. Bogost calls this process procedural rhetoric, defining rhetoric as "persuasive expression" (2007, p. viii). He states that one authors code that enforces rules to generate some kind of representation, rather than authoring the representation itself... the ability to execute a series of rules fundamentally separates computers from other media.

(Bogost, 2007, p. 4)

For Bogost, procedural authors – platform and video game designers, among others – make arguments through the authorship of rules of behaviour and the construction of what he calls "dynamic models" (Bogost, 2007, p. 29).

I propose an approach that marries the Deleuzian ontology of the image and Bogost's awareness of the expressive and persuasive capabilities of audiovisual interactive interfaces. In screen-based technologies such as gamble-play platforms, procedure-images are the building blocks of the "dynamic models" identified by Bogost.

Images in gamble-play come into being procedurally. Schwab notes, "To be an image is thus to be a form of exchange or interaction – action and reaction" (2000, p. 111); for images in digital gamble-play, I would add procedural expression as actions and reactions convey procedures or particular ways of doing things. This is the new formulation: to be a procedure-image is to be a form of procedural expression as the nature of their interaction is procedural.

In that sense, digital poker reframes the ways in which certain procedures are enacted in poker. Media innovation implies a shift from material cards, chips and tables to virtual cards, tables, chips, adversaries and dealers. This change generates new practices and actors.

Traditional poker involves a series of procedures that depend on human decisions based on interpretations of signs, rules, gestures and environmental cues. The dealer and the players, as well as the casino managers, carry out these interpretative processes (Kingma, 2010). Bogost states in relation to this dynamic,

> Nondigital board and card games offer further examples of human enacted processes; the people playing the game execute the rules.
> (Bogost, 2007, p. 10)

Gamblers execute the rules through the repetitive codification of objects including cards and chips as well as of other player's expressions. They also have to deal with distractions:

> clanging slot machines, noisy acts in the front lounge, gawking tourists walking between the casino and the elevators, and the general hubbub produced by hundreds of other casino gamblers on the move.
> (Hayano, 1982, p. 31)

In digital poker, many of these "human enacted processes" (Bogost, 2007, p. 10) are taken over by the computer and exteriorised by procedure-images. The digitisation of poker triggers a media change as

> procedurality is intrinsic and fundamental to computers, and because computers are much more flexible as an inscription medium than human agents, they are particularly suited to procedural expression.
>
> (Bogost, 2007, p.10)

For Bogost, computers are "inflexible systems that cannot empathize, that attempt to treat everyone the same" (2007, p. 6). The digitisation of poker transforms the social and game dynamics of traditional gambling as computers take over roles previously held by humans. As Morse and Goss (2007) explain,

> Internet operations… do not require extensive employee staffing to serve the needs of customers. Employees who run the games, such as dealers and croupiers, are instead replaced by computerized versions of online patrons. The pit boss and the supervisory personnel who are otherwise employed to watch over these employees are also unnecessary, as computer algorithms are designed to ensure against human foibles that might otherwise cheat the house in their advantage.
>
> (Morse & Goss, 2007, p. 182)

To clarify the notion of procedural rhetoric Bogost provides, among others, the example of *The McDonald's Video game*, developed by the Italian collective Molleindustria. In this video game, the player has to perform a set of procedures that imply the "questionable business practices that developers want to critique" (2007, p. 30). Instead of showing pictures of how McDonald's cows are slaughtered or a document detailing the low wage scheme in their business model, Molleindustria created a game that not only "entails persuasion – to change opinion or action" but also "entails expression – to convey ideas effectively" (Bogost, 2007, p. 29). Through procedural rhetoric, users are made aware of industry malpractices.

Similarly, designers of gamble-play platforms engage in persuasive and expressive practices. First, they establish a series of rules that regulate the dynamics of the casino and the possible behaviours of the player. These rules follow the basic dynamics of traditional gambling but also introduce other dynamics that make each interface alluring and immersive for the player. Then, they create interfaces composed of procedure-images that establish procedural links with the gamblers and stimulate the growth of groups of players by introducing social networking functions.

Procedural Rhetoric in Gamble-Play Platforms

Gambling Is an Adventure!

Digital gamble-play is not just about losing, winning or chasing money: it is about confronting adventures and challenges. Procedure-images that exteriorise these adventures and challenges are present in both slot machines and online poker tables.

When the surroundings in which play happens are familiar, gamble-play images can promise adventure in exotic settings. In gamble-play interfaces located in demarcated physical spaces, such as 'VIP Lounges' in Australian pubs, we find imagery such as pyramids, jungles, Wild West landscapes and other untamed territories. The aesthetic currents that intersect in the image-worlds of digital slots contain images that pin the player against indomitable or foreign image-worlds (Chinese ancient lore, ancient Egypt, Arctic landscapes). The connection to the aura of traditional gambling resides in the physical space, while in the slot machine the user encounters a sense of adventure.

In the case of online poker, virtual environments recall the audiovisual arrangements of familiar gambling scenarios, such as casinos, domestic spaces and underground poker circuits. The mediated space in digital poker translates the basic tropes of the social space in traditional poker. As such, avatars in virtual poker tables are positioned similarly to the way adversaries would position themselves in a physical casino, and even though the machine deals the cards, this procedure is carried out by the procedure-image of a dealer.

The gambler, therefore, does not have to tame an exotic place but to acquire a particular digital literacy. The player has to learn how to use the interface and read the machine and other players, represented by procedure-images. The sense of adventure in the *Bwin* online poker platform, for example, is exacerbated by the sense of urgency communicated by markers, such as the swift movement of the chips and cards as well as background music (Figure 2.4).

Learn through Experience, You Will Get Better

Even though they carry out similar processes, procedure-images in each online casino require a different set of skills. In order to secure consumer loyalty, online casinos encourage players to learn how to play their particular platforms and become better players. This learning process involves constant play and communication.

Each gamble-play platform requires the player to internalise a specific set of codes and procedures. In online digital poker, for example, these codes involve the basic procedures of traditional poker (call, bet, fold,

Figure 2.4 Table at the *Bwin* casino. Procedure-images make reference to the basic elements of real-life poker tables and establish a sense of urgency with the swift movements of cards and chips. Image captured from an online interactive tutorial (accessed on November 14, 2017 at https://poker.bwin.com/en/poker/howtoplay/home/tutorial).

check and, in the more complex platforms, bluff). They can also support other possibilities exclusive to digital interfaces, such as playing in multiple tables, creating avatars, communicating with players or identifying pokerbots (Wood & Griffiths, 2008). These possibilities can be either provided by the operators or spontaneously created by the users.

Procedures particular to each platform can be learnt. Throughout the learning process, strategies can be developed to maximise winnings and economise efforts. Online casinos promote this learning process through free play schemes and low-stakes games. For instance, in its lobby *Bwin* shows a procedure-image that connects the player to "Trial Games: Play Money" tables. Other interfaces like *Cake Poker* have a very clear distinction between "Play Money" and "Real Money"; *888* offers something similar.

As they build a player pool and promote a culture of professionalisation, casinos constantly offer help in the assimilation of their platforms. Learning how procedure-images interact in each platform is fundamental for all gamblers. Hayano identified this in his pioneering study of traditional professional poker circles:

An early childhood experience with card-playing, though not an invariable prerequisite to later professional playing, nonetheless prepares the individual as a kind of informal, antecedent socialization...

professional poker-playing requires that the player at least acquire minimal playing skills and spend time learning and losing as an amateur.

(Hayano, 1982, p. 19)

Online casinos provide inexperienced users with the equivalent of that "early childhood experience" (Hayano, 1982, p. 19). More so than in traditional poker, digital poker requires a significant level of skill to decipher procedure-images – a master chess player would be able to imagine the visual patterns produced by *Thinking Machine*. By decoding procedure-images through continuous play, gamblers can master the platform and gain advantage over other players. Winning does not only imply getting lucky when receiving cards but also involves the ability to read other players, learn patterns and repeat actions. The claim that poker is a game defined by skill (Dedonno & Detterman, 2008) is supported in digital poker, where digital literacy is needed and continuous play encouraged partly by the reward of learning.

There is a culture of poker training on the internet. Alongside online forums and message boards where tips are shared casually, there are online poker academies that service those who wish to perfect their game or build a long-term career in online poker. Through procedure-images, online casinos train players to maintain a fair balance between chance and skill. A recent survey of the online casino market (Fiedler & Wilcke, 2011) indicates that for most players chance prevails, while skill is the territory of just a few professional gamblers. We can identify, then, two online gambling cultures defined by the level of professionalism. For amateur players, procedure-images that support learning and practice are a constant reminder that gamble-play is a learning process. Professionals have achieved a level of mastery of the interface and the game.

Do Not Feel Alone, Your Friends and Foes Are Here

In digital poker, procedure-images take the place of croupiers, security personnel, pit bosses, opponents and dealers (Morse & Goss, 2007, p. 182). Through digitisation, the social dynamics of casino poker change through procedure-images. These are mainly avatars – in-game characters designed or chosen by players as stand-ins in virtual environments.

If you sit at a poker table in a traditional casino, chances are you will play among strangers. You will be certain of the number of players you are competing against and, if you trust the 'house', you will be confident that the dealing of cards will be fully fair and random. The fairness of the game is not that certain in digital poker. Behind any given avatar in an online poker game, there could be an indeterminate number of human players collaborating in a practice known as 'team play and colluding' in online poker forums. Alternatively, there could be pokerbots decoding information and making decisions.

When playing online poker, procedure-images constantly remind players that poker is a social endeavour and that they are not gambling alone. They reveal that other players are co-present in the virtual environment. *Unibet*'s lobby, for instance, displays a button to contact your 'Buddies' or get real time assistance through the "Help" button. Procedure-images invite the gambler to seek help if encountering problems when playing or navigating through the system. The relationship to the house is transformed. Through the presence of avatars at the poker table, the player is also fully aware of the online identity of the other players, whom she may have encountered in the past.

Participatory practices in online gambling are familiar from wider trends in online culture, where users usually play multiple roles. Chats are available in many of the lobbies in the online casinos I surveyed. Gamblers can also have 'Friends' in each platform and interfaces constantly show buttons through which they can be contacted.

Gamblers develop loyalty to online casinos not only because of the credit they acquire but also because of the sense of community and competition that gamble-play platforms try to nourish through procedure-images. By configuring procedure-images in particular ways, casinos constantly remind players of tournaments where they can pit their skills against those of their buddies (Figure 2.5).

Figure 2.5 In its poker tables, *Unibet* offers the opportunity to interact with avatars called 'Buddies'.

Procedure-images in other forms of gamble-play provide an opportunity for gambling companies to intensify the interaction between casinos and gamblers, and to facilitate communication between gamblers. This enhances the inherent social aspects of some gambling practices. Competition is one of these social dynamics. For example, the app *SlotsCrown*, developed by Pixalim Studios and launched in 2013 for Apple's iOS,

> features Facebook login to connect and play slots with friends via a fun Leaderboard that shows your top friends and the current King of SlotsCrown in the throne. The Leaderboard uses players' Facebook profile photos to truly personalize the slots gameplay experience.
>
> (Pixalim Studios, 2013)

The leader board, a ranking system which reminds us of other mobile gaming platforms that stimulate competition among friends, such as Apple's Game Center, adds an element of socialisation to an activity that is otherwise an isolated affair. The allure of these type of features has been recognised by academics such as Stephen Andrade, computer graphics professor at Johnson and Wales University, who is reported as saying, "Digital natives want to know where they stand compared to others – and they want others to know their status as well" (as quoted in Schwartz, 2014) (Figure 2.6).

Figure 2.6 Promotional screenshot advertising the Leaderboard feature in the *SlotsCrown* social casino app in Apple's App Store.

Remain Loyal, the 'House' Loves You

Digital gamble-play platforms want you to remain loyal. In the case of real-money online poker, there are literally thousands of options for poker enthusiasts on the internet. Most poker players, however, stick to one choice after scouting for the interface that suits them best. Some of these choices have to do with nationality as some online casinos cater to specific territories, such as *Bwin* in the UK, for instance. Other choices have to do with how different interfaces suit different gamblers.

Choosing an online casino is a matter of taste and trust. According to Wood and Griffiths (2008), trust relies on

> size and reputation of the operator, the speed with which winnings were paid out, the clarity of the Web site design, the technical reliability of the service, and the accessibility and effectiveness of the customer service.
>
> (Wood & Griffiths, 2008, p. 80)

When a player first encounters an online casino, trust is courted by the display of procedure-images that link to certifications that promise to guarantee the fairness of the gameplay and the ethical approach by the casino concerning responsible gambling. In online casinos, logos establish spaces for brand affiliation. Just as with any entertainment consumption good, branding (both inside and outside the casino space) helps shape the identity of the player as well.

Online gambling sites establish nuanced procedural-image patterns that players learn through repetition. The particularities of each platform make it hard to jump seamlessly from one casino to the next one. Gamblers have invested time and money in deciphering particular configurations of procedure-images. Players become versed not only in how to play poker but also in how to adapt their play to specific interfaces, with specific audiovisual arrangements (colours, shapes, particular information) that generate particular affects.

Like traditional gambling companies, online casinos offer loyalty programs. In their lobbies and in social networking sites (primarily Twitter and Facebook), they offer bonuses, giveaways, free cash, 24/7 help and entries to exclusive tournaments (Figure 2.7).

Do Not Miss Out! There Is Always Something to Be Won!

Gamble-play platforms allow users to play at any given moment and, if accessed through mobile devices, almost anywhere. Digital gamble-play platforms are persistent: they can always be accessed, retaining an

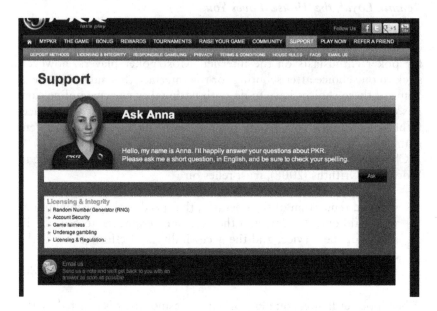

Figure 2.7 Automated support system of the now inactive 3D casino *PKR*. Image captured on May 19, 2014 from www.pkr.com/en/support/

ongoing state of play. Digital gamble-play platforms epitomise the danger recognised by Walter Benjamin when he wrote that,

> The particular danger that threatens the gambler lies in the fateful category of arriving 'too late,' of having 'missed the opportunity'.
>
> (Benjamin, 2006, p. 212)

Being persistent environments, gamble-play platforms seduce players by always being at their disposal. The always-on servers of digital poker always hold the potential to be actualised by the player. Much like in Las Vegas's "cathedrals of consumption" (Ritzer, 1999), neo-baroque theatrical settings (Ndalianis, 2017), online casinos and digital poker interfaces in physical environments always have their lights on and welcome new customers. In their lobbies, online casinos show all that is going on in their virtual networks, and the games that the gambler can enter.

Gamblers in physical casinos rarely (if ever) have a comprehensive overview of all the games that are taking place around them. Experienced and professional gamblers play at specific tables, but the majority of visitors choose tables at random. Procedure-images in online casinos, however, provide information on all that is happening in their spaces, much like information boards at airports or train stations.

In its virtual lobby, for example, *Poker770* shows a comprehensive overview of the operations that are taking place in its servers (the number of online players, the number of tables and the information on all the games). This schematic conception of the gambling space, configured by images, allows gamblers to interact as they wish. Procedure-images function as a navigational tool even in the most schematic casino environments. Procedure-images direct the player through a sequence of actions.

Conclusion

In this chapter, I stressed the importance of procedure-images in digital gamble-play. Images seduce gamblers, promising an "incorporeal transformation" through play (Deleuze & Guattari, 2004, p. 89). Although other interactive media, such as video games, also communicate through procedure-images, the dynamics of procedure-images are more evident in gambling. Gambling has more measurable repercussions in a player's everyday life. Operators make profit from continuous play, which is why procedure-images mobilise particular rhetorical tools to foster constant engagement in individual sessions as well as over time.

In particular, this chapter shows how concepts derived from game studies, such as procedural rhetoric, are appropriate tools for the analysis of gamble-play interfaces. First, I explored Deleuze's movement-image and developed the term procedure-image, establishing the ways in which it configures procedural rhetoric in gamble-play. Then, I related the procedure-image to Bogost's notion of procedural rhetoric and concluded by exemplifying five instances of rhetorical practice in gamble-play platforms.

Considering recent developments in mobile technologies, such as tablets and smartphones, the gambler's experience will continue to change, as will the complexity and nature of procedure-images and the morphology of gambling networks. As touchscreen technologies establish new regimes of vision and interaction, the ways in which users relate to procedure-images in digital gamble-play interfaces are increasingly relevant in the shaping of gambling and play cultures as well as the generation of new affects and mechanisms of seduction and control.

Just as Deleuze's (1986) movement-image and the action-image established a vocabulary of the cinematic regime of vision, procedure-images construct new regimes of computer-mediated communication and human-machine interaction. This ontology can be used in further research to analyse other social-visual spaces, such as video games, mobile apps or GPS systems. This framework will be referenced in the remainder of this book when dealing with interfaces and audiovisual arrangements in digital gamble-play products.

References

Benjamin, W. (2006). Notes on a theory of gambling. In J. F. Cosgrave (Ed.), *The sociology of risk and gambling reader* (pp. 211–213). London: Routledge.

Boellstorff, T. (2008). *Coming of age in Second Life: An anthropologist explores the virtually human*. Princeton, NJ: Princeton University Press.

Bogost, I. (2007). *Persuasive games: The expressive power of video games*. Cambridge, MA: MIT Press.

Bolter, J. D., & Grusin, R. (1999). *Remediation: Understanding new media*. Cambridge, MA: MIT Press.

Bainbridge, W. S. (2010). *The Warcraft civilization: Social science in a virtual world*. Cambridge, MA: MIT Press.

Chesher, C. (2012). Between image and information: The iPhone camera in the history of photography. In L. Hjorth, J. Burgess, & I. Richardson, (Eds.), *Studying mobile media: Cultural technologies, mobile communication and the iPhone* (pp. 98–117). London and New York, NY: Routledge.

Crockett, C. (2005). Technology and the time-image: Deleuze and postmodern subjectivity. *South African Journal of Philosophy, 24*(3), 176–188.

Dean, J. (2010). *Blog theory: Feedback and capture in the circuits of drive*. Cambridge: Polity.

Dedonno, M., & Detterman, D. K. (2008). Poker is a skill. *Gaming Law Review, 12*(1), 31–36.

Deleuze, G. (1986). *Cinema 1. The movement-image*. London: The Athlone Press.

Deleuze, G. (2005). *Cinema 2. The time-image*. London and New York, NY: Continuum.

Deleuze, G., & Guattari, F. (2004). *Capitalism and schizophrenia: A thousand plateaus*. London: Continuum.

Fiedler, I., & Wilcke, A. (2011). The market of online poker. The University of Hamburg, Social Science Research Network. Retrieved from http://papers.ssrn.com/sol3/papers.cfm?abstract_id=1747646

Guattari, F. (1995). *Chaosmosis: an ethico-aesthetic paradigm*. Sydney: Power.

Hayano, D. M. (1982). *Poker faces: The life and work of professional card players*. Berkeley: University of California Press.

Kingma, S. F. (2010). Dutch casino space: The spatial construction of gambling pleasure. In S. F. Kingma (Ed.), *Global gambling: Cultural perspectives on gambling organizations* (pp. 144–170). London and New York, NY: Routledge.

McCloud, S. (1993). *Understanding comics*. New York, NY: Kitchen Sink.

Malaby, T. (2007). Beyond play: A new approach to games. *Games & Culture, 2*(2), 95–113.

Morse, E., & Goss, E. P. (2007). *Governing fortune: Casino gambling in America*. Ann Arbor: The University of Michigan Press.

Ndalianis, A. (2017). Baroque theatricality and scripted spaces: From Movie Palace to Las Vegas Casinos. *Postmodern Studies, 55*, 283.

Nitsche, M. (2008). *Video game spaces: Image, play and structure in 3D*. Cambridge, MA: MIT Press.

Pixalim Studios. (2013). Pixalim Studios Releases SlotsCrown – Social Slots Machine App for iOS. *Digital Journal*. Retrieved from www.digitaljournal.com/pr/1616174#ixzz2mT280GNx

Pokerscout.com. (2017). *PokerScout*. Retrieved from www.pokerscout.com

Ritzer, G. (1999). *Enchanting a disenchanted world: Revolutionising the means of consumption*. Thousand Oaks, CA: Pine Forge Press.

Schwab, M. (2000). Escape from the image: Deleuze's image-ontology. In G. Flaxman (Ed.), *The brain is the screen: Deleuze and the philosphy of cinema* (pp. 109–139). Minneapolis: University of Minnesota Press.

Schwartz, D. (2014). The coming social (gaming) revolution. *Vegas Seven*. Retrieved from http://vegasseven.com/2014/04/22/coming-social-gaming-revolution/

Unibet/Betchoice Corporation. (2017). *Unibet*. Retrieved from www.unibet. com.au

Watterberg, M., & Walczak, M. (2003). *Thinking Machine*. www.bewitched. com. Retrieved from www.bewitched.com/chess

Wood, R. T., & Griffiths, M. D. (2008). Why Swedish people play online poker and factors that can increase or decrease trust in poker web sites: A qualitative investigation. *Journal of Gambling Issues, 21*, 80–97.

Digital games cited

Blizzard Entertainment. (2004). *World of Warcraft*. Blizzard Entertainment.

Cake Network. (2004). *Cake Poker*. CakePoker.com [Note: site no longer operating]

Cassava Enterprises. (n.d.). *888poker* (Android version). Retrieved from http://au.888.com/

Electraworks Limited. (2014). Party Poker Get your game on. *partypoker.com*. Retrieved from www.partypoker.com/

Electraworks Limited. (2017a). *PartyCasino*. Retrieved from https://casino. partycasino.com/en/casino

Electraworks Limited. (2017b). *Bwin*. Retrieved from www.bwin.com

Gamesys. (2013). Virgin Poker (Facebook version) [Mobile application software]. Retrieved from https://apps.facebook.com/virginpoker/

Ladbrokes Digital Australia Ltd. (2017). *Ladbrokes*. Retrieved from www. ladbrokes.com.au

Mansion Poker. (2015). *Mansion Poker*. Retrieved from www.mansionpoker.com

Paddy Power Services Limited. (2017). Paddy Power Poker. Retrieved from https://poker.paddypower.com

Pixalim Studios. (2013). *Slotscrown*. Apple Store.

Petfre (Gibralta) Limited. (2011). *BetFred Poker*. Retrieved from www.betfred.com

PKR Limited. (n.d.). PKR Let's Play. *pkr.com*. Retrieved September 2014, from www.pkr.com/en/ [Note: PKR declared bankruptcy in 2017, web page inactive].

PokerNews. (2015). *Poker Heaven*. Retrieved from www.pokernews.com/poker-heaven-com/ [Note: game no longer operating].

Poker.Org. (2017). *Poker770*. Retrieved from www.poker.org/poker770/download/

Rational Entertainment Enterprises Limited. (2014). PokerStars.com. *pokerstars.com*. Retrieved from www.pokerstars.com

Rosedale, P. (Designer). (2003). *Second Life*. United States: Linden Lab.

Unibet/Betchoice Corporation. (2017). *Unibet*. Retrieved from www.unibet. com.au

Zynga. (2007). Zynga Poker. *zynga.com*. Retrieved from http://zynga.com/game/poker

3   Gamble-Play Media and Practices of Consumption

> the casino system provides a near-perfect analogy for the consumer society.
> —David B. Clarke (2003, p. 12)

Twenty-first-century gamble-play operates through processes of cultural normalisation that make gambling an acceptable form of digital entertainment. In this chapter, I offer a description and theorisation of consumption in digital gamble-play, bringing to light the strategies used by gambling operators and social casino app developers to generate and sustain user engagement. Operators adapt to media convergence, the paradigms of participatory media and the prevalence of social networking as an essential mode of online interaction.

Consumption of gamble-play media may or may not involve the chance to win real currency. In such transactions, users pay with a mix of money, labour, time and access to their digital social networks. Even if some gamble-play products are 'free', playing has other costs, often in the form of time and social influence, such as recommending the application to users' contacts, publicising results and so on. These terms are accepted to the detriment of social media etiquette as some online contacts perceive this type of information as spamming (Finin et al., 2008).

This new framework has significant political and economic implications for how digital gambling assemblages are formed, sustained and expanded. Not all gamble-play products allow the gambler to actually make money. In traditional understandings of gambling, the opportunity to make a profit through winning is the main good being purchased.

Gamble-play reflects new dynamics based on the promise of new forms of socialisation. For example, in applications such as *Fresh Deck Poker* – developed by Brainwave K and available on Facebook, iOS and Android platforms – or *Betting Billionaire* – created by Invendium Ltd – users engage in gambling-like processes that do not render winners in this traditional sense. The prize comes in the form of reputation rather than financial gain.

To understand how consumption is framed in digital gamble-play, we need to explore the varieties of digital media practices (Couldry, 2012) that consumers engage in. By practices, I mean *what people can do* with gamble-play platforms and how these actions relate to engagement with other media forms, such as social games and social networking sites. Practices are understood as a "the regular, skilful 'performance' of (human) bodies", which holds true for "modes of handling certain objects as well as for 'intellectual' activities such as talking, reading or writing" (Reckwitz, 2002, p. 251). Practice implies regularity of action (Reckwitz, 2002), and in gamble-play, this regularity is core for the maintenance of gamble-play assemblages:

> [Practices] imply certain routinised ways of understanding the world, of desiring something, of knowing how to do something.
> (Reckwitz, 2002, p. 251)

This chapter is structured as follows. First, I provide an account of how consumption is a gateway into understanding the identities and practices generated by new media forms and why its conceptualisation is important in the study of gambling, an approach I have explored in previous academic publications (Albarrán-Torres, 2016). Second, I discuss the ways in which gamble-play is part of more general trends of "media convergence" (Jenkins, 2006), which leads to the cultural normalisation of gambling, both through product design and through platform affordances. Third, I discuss the notion of "practice" as a "routinised type of behaviour" (Reckwitz, 2002, p. 249) and discuss how this explains consumption of digital gamble-play, resulting in new configurations of seduction, enjoyment and control. I then deliberate on the paradigms of participatory cultures – much discussed in academic literature on digital cultures, often on a celebratory, quasi-utopian note – and their applicability to the practices of consumption in digital gamble-play. Finally, I enumerate a set of digital media practices that define how gambling is consumed in online and mobile gambling platforms in a way that promotes regularity and repetitiveness of action. These practices include searching, search-enabling, showing and being shown, archiving and sustaining a public presence (Couldry, 2012).

Gamblers as Active Consumers

Theorising consumption practices in digital gambling allows us to understand subjects that are quite different from the passive consumers generally conceptualised by gambling studies. Theories of gambling consumption are often limited because they are guided by the frame of problem gambling (Ricketts & Macaskill, 2004; Volberg, 2001). Contemporary gambling technologies, however, are designed to cater to digital media consumers, some of whom have not experienced predigital betting. Theories of consumption in cultural studies have also advanced the understanding of gambling practices (Bjerg, 2009; Cosgrave & Klassen, 2001; Reith, 2007), as we will see.

The consumption of particular forms of low-stakes gambling in the Global North, such as slot machines and now online platforms and apps, is regulated by policies that treat these products as a sort of 'gateway drug' into gambling addiction. This is particularly the case when dealing with populations deemed to be vulnerable by researchers and policymakers, such as low-income families, pensioners, housewives or children. In Australia, for instance, problem gambling awareness leaflets and stickers are placed next to gambling machines, and the popularity of slot apps has prompted anti-gambling advocacy groups to speak out, particularly in the state of South Australia (Willingham, 2013). Studies have also shown that gambling addiction carries a public stigma that "has deleterious effects by undermining the mental health of stigmatised individuals and posing a major barrier to problem acknowledgement, disclosure, treatment-seeking and recovery" (Hing et al., 2016, p. 860).

Gambling studies have largely overlooked the agency of gamblers as active consumers, focussing instead on extreme forms of consumption related to compulsive gambling and addiction, particularly in games where chance prevails over skill. These games include roulette, slot machines, lottery, lotto or bingo as opposed to poker, whist, backgammon or even chess.

Gambling studies researchers have generally grouped gamblers in specific demographic groups according to age, socio-economic status or geographical location. Among others, these groups include pensioners (Hing & Breen, 2002), migrants (Ohtsuka & Ohtsuka, 2010; Scull & Woolcock, 2005; Tanasornnarong et al., 2004), young adults (Hayatbakhsh et al., 2012) and older players (Hope & Havir, 2002). These studies focus on the dangers that those in each category face in terms of potential problems with gambling. These studies do not consider consumption to be a meaning-making process in which the consumer is an active participant. Gambling is seen as something that is being *done to* people, not something that people *do*.

Reith points out that the notion of problem gambling is a cultural and policy construct "articulated in terms that are oppositional to the ideology of a 'consumption ethic' based on the values of self-control, self-actualization, responsibility, and reason" (Reith, 2007, p. 33). Reith points to an inherent contradiction in contemporary notions of the consumption of gambling. On the one hand, commentators conceptualise consumers as potential addicts and threats to the neo-liberal state and its virtue, with little room for the consideration of 'normal' subjects. On the other hand, the state is constantly deregulating gambling activities and obtaining considerable tax revenue derived from these. This has resulted in "a massive proliferation of commercial gambling as a global enterprise, with a central place in Western economies" (Reith, 2007, p. 35).

This contradiction has resulted in particular cultural notions around problem gambling. In countries such as Australia, as recent research reveals (Jean, 2013), attitudes towards people who are arguably addicted to gambling are different than those towards individuals afflicted by alcohol or drug abuse. While "Australians tend to be sympathetic towards people with alcohol and other drug addictions who seek help", problem gambling is seen as a "moral failing" (Jean, 2013).

Opposed to notions of gambling as a force that disrupts the social and moral order by triggering addiction, others claim that there is an emancipatory power inherent in wagering. For Clarke, the casino is "ruthlessly egalitarian, shamelessly democratic" (2003, p. 12) in that the distribution of wealth is random. In regard to women's consumption of poker, for example, Abarbanel and Bernhard problematically state that the "glass-ceiling concept that typically applies to most feminist microstructural theory does not quite fit in the poker world" (Abarbanel & Bernhard, 2012, pp. 368–369):

> women are not explicitly oppressed in poker with lower pay or lack of promotion, nor does the game overtly discriminate along any lines. Given that, in the long run, luck is even across opponents, poker seems to constitute a rare meritocracy.
>
> (Abarbanel & Bernhard, 2012, p. 369)

By drawing from cultural studies, we can conceptualise gamble-play in a way that recognises consumer agency more comprehensively. In the past 40 years, our academic understanding of consumers has developed to recognise the ways in which consumption is a meaning-creating process, a notion that is appropriate to understanding digital gambling. Consumption is now well established in the agenda of the social sciences. In the 1970s, cultural studies developed the notion that consumers "are not 'passive dupes' of mass culture, but that they act, resist and exercise creativity in their consumer practices" (Arvidsson, 2006, p. 17). Consumers generate and transform meanings while actively putting these meanings into circulation.

The product mix that delineates consumers' personal or collective taste is certainly a meaning-creating activity that defines how consumers present themselves. Consumption implies practice. Individuals express their identities by choosing what goods to buy or which services to hire. Even alternative practices such as purchasing old clothes in thrift shops are associated with broader cultural patterns, such as the hipster movement (Cowen, 2006).

Cultural studies have tackled the formation of identities through the study of clothes, taste and consumer behaviours and habits. Campbell

(2005), for instance, states that "individuals consume principally out of a desire to engage in creative acts of self-expression" and that they "already have a stable sense of identity" (2005, p. 24). He argues against the idea of the average consumer being "the helpless puppet of external forces" (Campbell, 2005, p. 24). This counters past notions of the overwhelming power that mass culture holds over individuals (Adorno & Horkheimer, 1944/2000) and provides subjects with a much stronger sense of autonomy and self-dependency.

Understood as a meaning-making process, consumption helps us understand the mechanisms of gambling markets, in which various state and corporate interests are put into motion. The profitability of gambling, moreover, is dependent on a constant engagement between consumers and producers. Gambling industries rely on wagering being deeply rooted in people's everyday consumption habits and meaning-creating practices. That is why understanding the practices involved in the consumption of gamble-play sheds light on how operators sustain and expand their market reach.

Although research on creative consumption has been more common with the popularisation of the internet and other forms of digitally mediated communication since the 1990s, it predates the expansion of web cultures. For two decades, researchers of consumer cultures, amalgamated under the rubric of consumer culture theory or CCT, have explored

> the heterogeneous distribution of meanings and the multiplicity of overlapping cultural groupings that exist within the broader socio-historic frame of globalization and market capitalism.
> (Arnould & Thompson, 2005, p. 869)

Lay and casual gamblers, and the dynamics of their consumption, are rarely addressed in academic or journalistic publications. Gamble-play involves "the heterogeneous distribution of meanings" (Arnould & Thompson, 2005, p. 869), not only the passive consumption of gambling products.

Jean Baudrillard's more critical conceptualisation of consumption is useful for understanding the cultural shift represented by gamble-play. He (1998) offers a critique of contemporary consumption, seeing a premeditated order in the way in which products are offered in capitalist societies. He considers consumption to be a scheme in which consumers are "mutually implicated, despite themselves, in a general system of exchange and in the production of coded values" (Baudrillard, 1998, p. 46).

For Baudrillard, contemporary consumers consider "the experience of pleasure an obligation" (Baudrillard, 1998, p. 48), a notion that certainly resonates with the ways in which online casinos and social gambling apps are designed and promoted, as we will see later in this chapter. Gambling particularly brings to mind Baudrillard's thinking when he writes about the maximization of existence by the multiplication of contacts and relations, by the intensive use of signs and objects, and by the systematic exploitation of all the possibilities of pleasure.

(Baudrillard, 1998, p. 48)

Consumption practices in digital gambling platforms promise this "maximization of existence" (Baudrillard, 1998, p. 48) through the multiplication of relations *and* the possibilities of winning. Procedure-images in digital gambling platforms illustrate this maximisation by showcasing images that show financial and even sexual freedom as well as ultimate plenitude.

Baudrillard argues that the consumer society is also defined by networks of objects that can "*mimic* disorder to better seduce" but are "always arranged to trace out directive paths" (Baudrillard, 1998, p. 31). He argues that the consumer does not strive in chaos but rather proceeds logically "from one object to the next", getting caught up in a "*calculus* of objects" as opposed to frenzied purchasing (Baudrillard, 1998, p. 31).

Although Baudrillard's argument preceded current informational networks, his conceptualisation of consumption as a system explains the ways in which diverse industries, markets and discourses come together in online and mobile media environments. This is particularly evident in the entertainment sector (cinema, television, digital games, gambling), which offers consumers unique, tailored product mixes. For example, advertising on social networking sites such as Facebook depends on the user's online activity, connections and preferences. Streaming services such as Netflix offer particular recommendations based on the viewer's assumed taste. Digital media users are co-creators of the "directive paths" (Baudrillard, 1998, p. 31) that delineate their consumption and are limited by the affordances of each platform.

Gambling industries rely on encouraging continuous and repetitive behaviours from consumers. Since the mass popularisation of gambling in the first half of the twentieth century (Reith, 1999), these industries have negotiated entry into consumers' everyday lives through "directive paths" (Baudrillard, 1998, p. 31). They have done so not only with the varieties of play analysed in this book (slots and poker) but also through state and privately sponsored lotteries, games including roulette and bingo, sweepstakes and sports betting. Gambling industries have increasingly conducted consumer research and product development to foster consumption:

The development of the commercial strategies of market research, advertising, and branding has been used to develop a variety of products and opportunities to gamble… games of chance have been commoditized as heterogeneous products, offering a diverse range of choices for ever-increasing numbers of consumers.

(Reith, 2007, p. 35)

As gambling companies have put diverse promotional and recruiting mechanisms in place, consumer networks have experienced exponential growth in digital environments. Digital gambling platform design takes into account the nature of digital content, which can be easily archived, reproduced and distributed (boyd, 2011). For example, if you play in a social casino such as *DoubleDown Casino* or *Jackpot Party Casino Slots* using your Facebook profile, your contacts could receive information on your wins or get recommendations – promotional material known as Suggested Pages – based on the games you play and the pages you like.

The following section explains how gambling has become a part of the range of options from which active consumers can choose. By framing this argument around media convergence, I will explain how gamble-play is incorporated into everyday digital media consumption.

Gambling at the Altar of Convergence

The design and revenue models of digital gambling products have experienced recent changes that bring gambling closer to other media forms, such as computer and casual games. For example, the landing pages of online casinos are dramatically different from when they were first launched in the mid-1990s. They have evolved from simple websites with a few hyperlinks to portals with various subpages that encourage particular practices, such as the formation of communities, as well as links to social networking sites, such as Twitter, Facebook and YouTube. Some of these sites are geographically and linguistically specific, emphasising locality. *PokerStars*, for example, has sites in most Western European languages.

These changes are a calculated approach to engage and maintain customers through new practices that were previously foreign to gambling but are part of more widespread digital media cultures. For example, *PokerStars* has made efforts to be branded as a property that goes beyond gambling and is incorporated into the user's hypermediated lifestyle. In early 2014, the company hired the public relations firm 'W' with the purpose of

> repositioning [*PokerStars*] as a lifestyle brand, and broadening the appeal beyond its traditional market... This would take it into areas like music, the arts and a wider lifestyle space... and things more interesting to a wider audience than the traditional poker player.
>
> (Owens, 2014)

This strategic move shows how online gambling companies try to enter everyday consumption practices and to be a part of the acceptable range of options for leisure and entertainment for the middle class (Reith, 2007). Thomas Raymen and Oliver Smith argue that gambling is an "integral feature of the wider masculine weekend leisure experience" (2017, p. 1). Among other strategies, this is accomplished by hiring celebrity sponsors who work as brand ambassadors for online gambling sites. That is the case with former *Playboy* Playmate Pamela Anderson, of *Baywatch* fame, who has been the spokesperson of the Facebook app *BamPoker*. This is clearly directed to the male heterosexual gaze. In cross-platform branding efforts, online casinos also sponsor televised competitions and their teams of professional players regularly participate in both online and face-to-face tournaments. These professional players are often portrayed as successful in their move between land-based and online gambling.

Besides established online casinos like *PokerStars*, newer social gaming companies have identified the opportunities in marrying gambling with the affordances of online and mobile media. For instance, Laurence Escalante, CEO of Virtual Gaming Worlds, which operates the hugely popular Facebook app *Chumba Casino* – a business modelled on sweepstakes – has stated in relation to the transference of the social dynamics of land-based informal gambling into social media:

> We found it crazy [Escalante and his friends, *World of Warcraft* aficionados] we could go into a virtual world and kill a dragon together... but we couldn't replicate that Friday night poker night.
>
> (quoted in Gardner, 2013)

The sweepstakes model of some social casino apps profits from a loophole in Facebook's policies: some jurisdictions, including the United States, don't consider sweepstakes to be gambling. *Chumba Casino* experienced a steady expansion after offering sweepstakes (Gardner, 2013). These desires for hybrid platforms are behind the recent development of gamble-play media. Historically, gambling has often been judged as the epitome of highly intensive and indulgent capitalist consumption (Bjerg, 2009) as it implies a blatantly ludic and, for some, senseless circulation of money. However, consumption needs to be reframed for digital gamble-play, which is an increasingly networked and social experience. Online gambling escapes previous temporal and spatial constrictions, such as the limited availability of venues or the restrictive and highly regulated spaces of casinos (Kingma, 2010).

Gambling industries have followed wider tendencies towards media convergence. Convergence describes cultural shifts in which "consumers are encouraged to seek out new information and make connections among dispersed media content" (Jenkins, 2006, p. 3). These patterns are apparent in cultural industries such as music, film, comic books, manga, anime, digital games and television, which offer multiplatform products that support new types of consumer practices. For example, television networks produce apps, comic books, merchandise and even digital games to accompany their shows, as has been the case in titles such as *Better Call Saul* (AMC) and *Stranger Things* (Netflix).

Media convergence is increasingly found in the gambling sector. Chon et al. identify the main industry changes associated with convergence:

> (a) the consolidation through industry alliances and mergers, (b) the combination of technology and network platforms, and (c) the integration between services and markets.
>
> (Chon et al., 2003, p. 143)

Technological development and the digitisation of content allow for the flow of concepts and brands between platforms. Operators produce parallel avenues for corporate communication and branding. These include Facebook fan pages, Twitter accounts, apps and televised tournaments as well as merchandise that ranges from T-shirts to branded poker chips and digital games, such as the *World Series of Poker*, developed by Activision and upon its release available for the Xbox, PlayStation and Wii consoles.

Convergence repositions gambling as an acceptable entertainment option. Inscribed in the dynamics of content, audience and platform convergence in the entertainment industry, and developing in parallel to other forms of interactive media, such as computer and mobile games, gambling has widened its market to include segments previously foreign to wagering activities. Reith argues that by borrowing marketing and branding strategies from other industries, transnational gambling operators have broken into the middle class, thus establishing modes of consumption previously foreign to wagering.

> Participation [in gambling activities] has not only increased but also widened to include, for the first time, the middle class – the group traditionally most hostile to all forms of gambling – in a move that has finally 'normalized' the activity'.
>
> (Reith, 2007, p. 35)

Digital gambling has been introduced to the array of entertainment options (cable television, comic books, cinema, digital games) from which the tech-savvy, middle-class consumer of the Global North can choose. Following this move towards the cultural normalisation of gambling as an acceptable form of consumption, online gambling companies actively pursue the transnational legalisation of real-money online gambling. A representative of the online casino *888* in Singapore, for example, is reported as saying that the company is committed to "fostering, so far as possible, the trend towards liberalization and regulation of online gaming throughout the world" (quoted in Watts, 2013).

This cultural normalisation is also the product of a more amicable consumer perception of gambling products derived from branding strategies. Research by Humphreys and Latour (2013) suggests that the ways in which an industry frames its products help shape consumers' attitudes. By labelling gambling products as "gaming", digital gambling operators move "nonusers to judge online betting as more legitimate" (McGandy, 2013). Humphreys and Latour's research reveals that the coming together of the cultural connotations associated with the gambling and gaming industries has the potential to open new markets and lessen public scrutiny.

As evidenced by the recent acquisition of social gaming start-ups and companies by major players in the gambling industry, such as Australian slot machine manufacturer Aristocrat, there is an industry-wide effort to shift the perception of gambling from a vice-inducing practice to a fun, harmless and even inspiring activity. As Kacapyr-Cornell states in reference to Humphreys and Latour's study, "'rags-to-riches' narratives prompted favourable associations while 'get-rich-quick' narratives prompted unfavourable associations" as merit and hard work are perceived as more honourable than trying your luck (Kacapyr-Cornell, 2013). These rags-to-riches myths are perpetuated in digital gamble-play environments, such as online casinos, which showcase their most successful poker players and their stories of personal achievement; see, for example, PokerStars' Team PokerStars (www.pokerstars.com/team-pokerstars/).

The digitisation of gambling also helps operators to blur the divide between 'gambling', 'gaming' and 'play'. In fact, the analogue gambling industry has attempted to blur this conceptual divide for decades, mainly in relation to devices that allow for everyday consumption of risk with low stakes. These devices include slot and video poker machines strategically located in places that are sites of the user's daily activities, such as shopping malls and gas stations in Las Vegas and, to much controversy, public ferries in Vancouver, Canada (Austin & Smyth, 2013). As Schüll points out when discussing slot machine gambling in Nevada during the 1980s and 1990s,

> The low-stakes devices fit comfortably with the redefinition of gambling as 'gaming' by industry spokespeople and state officials who hoped to sway public endorsement of the activity as a form of mainstream consumer entertainment rather than a form of moral failing or predatory entrapment.
>
> (Schüll, 2012, p. 5)

This redefinition of gambling into an activity more closely related to gaming is particularly evident in poker. The rebranding efforts of the gambling industry and their impending success are evidenced by strategies such as the transmission of the *World Series of Poker* on ESPN or the formation of poker leagues aligned to sports federations around the world. This has allowed for poker to enter everyday media consumption in ways that are perceived as less damaging or predatory. Televised poker tournaments, for instance, are rooted in a narrative of success and self-realisation, much in tone with the values of hard work and rational thinking that dominate Western neo-liberal world views.

On the other hand, consumer familiarity with screen technologies such as personal computers and digital games "further facilitated the cultural normalization of screen gambling" (Schüll, 2012, p. 5). Professionals in the gambling industry are aware that digital gambling cohabits with other forms of screen-based entertainment. Take, for example, the notions expressed by veteran slot machine designer Joe Kaminkow. Over the span of three decades, Kamikow has worked for Aristocrat and designed over a 1,000 slot machines, some based on pop culture and entertainment, with models derived from *Sex and the City*, *Ghostbusters*, *Flashdance* and the Rolling Stones, among other cultural icons. Kamikow told a reporter, when questioned about industry trends at the intersection between game design and digital media:

> I think people are always looking for more entertainment. Think about how people today watch television at home, sitting on the sofa with a laptop or tablet, checking Facebook, playing games, shopping, checking Yahoo or Twitter and messaging. People just want to be connected.
>
> (quoted in Stutz, 2013)

The multiscreen, multiplatform media delivery options offered by online casinos and social gambling apps are strikingly different from traditional gambling experiences. Some digital gamble-play platforms go in tandem with the most current trends in screen and entertainment technology. We can think, for example, of online casinos, such as *888*, which since 2012 offers a 3D viewing experience in its poker tables in which the user needs to wear 3D glasses to access a more immersive game experience.

On a similar note, consumers' familiarity with screen-based socialisation – mainly through social networking sites – facilitates the insertion of social networking features and conventions in digital gambling platforms. Contemporary forms of digital gambling have appropriated the affordances of social networking, digital games and social gaming, a trio of growing new media assemblages. For example, online casinos provide a platform for gamblers to converse, create and sustain an identity, and group around common interests or characteristics, such as gender or language, which aligns with the affordances and conventions of social networking sites or SNSs.

Various sociotechnical assemblages of digital games, social media and gambling converge in digital gamble-play. These assemblages include online casinos and other providers of gambling experiences either for real or play money as well as digital media marketplaces, such as Apple's App Store, Google Play and the Facebook App Centre, through which social casino apps are distributed. As convergent media, digital gamble-play assemblages undergo processes of constant expansion and transformation. These assemblages are what Bogost (2006), based on Deleuze and Guattari, defined as "complex networks", systems that "self-organize through adaptation and emergence" (Bogost, 2006, p. 139). Designers of gambling platforms adapt to new media environments and generate novel products. Digital gamble-players seek, comment, archive and generate information across platforms that include Facebook pages, YouTube videos, Twitter accounts, apps, online casinos, television shows, and even dozens of poker strategy books, such as *Winning Poker: 200 Rules, Techniques and Strategies* (Matthewson & Diamond, 2004) and *The Poker Blueprint* (Nguyen & Davis, 2011).

In a different type of convergence, unregulated real-money online slot machines make direct reference to other cultural spaces and consumer demographics. For example, the unregulated digital slot machine *Girls and the City*, operated by Bingo Cabin and promoted through Facebook via Suggested Posts, contains images of women that resemble erotic dancers in adult clubs, sites of sexual-economic exchange with their own codes and set relationships of power (Frank, 2007). *Girls and the City* brings together two offline cultural spaces – the pokie room and the strip club – that are generally associated with desire, titillation, crime, abuse, vice and problematic forms of consumption. *Girls and the City* is advertised as "Fun Australia Games for Men", clearly alluding to a heterosexual male ideal consumer, a well-defined subject – as opposed to the similarly titled *Sex and the City* land-based slot machine, themed after the popular HBO series and probably targeted to a predominantly female demographic. Gambling colonises the space of the strip club and vice versa.

The meanings that circulate in online casinos and social casino apps are also jacked into the intertextual web of meanings diffused by media including television, film, magazines and the internet as well as such cultural forms as sport (Figure 3.1). *888*, for example, has sponsored sporting events, such as boxing matches. Likewise, sports figures including tennis player Boris Becker, cross-country skier Marcus Hellner, soccer player Gianluigi Buffon and field hockey player Fatima Moreira de Melo are part of *Team PokerStars*. Similarly, after online gambling was legalised in the US state of New Jersey in late 2013, two major sports teams in North America, the New Jersey Devils (National Hockey League) and the Philadelphia 76ers (National Basketball Association), struck promotional deals with the online casino *PartyPoker* (Associated Press, 2014).

Figure 3.1 Facebook app *Hit It Rich,* featuring popular culture icons, such as *Willy Wonka, Ted* and B-movie icon Elvira.
Captured on November 14, 2017 from the author's Facebook account.

The National Basketball Association (NBA) and the National Hockey League (NHL) are two cornerstones of US and transnational popular culture, and their link to digital gambling is a telling sign of the cultural normalisation of online gambling as a mass consumer product and its insertion into other cultural assemblages related to sports spectatorship and leisure.

The relationship between gambling and sport goes far beyond sponsorships. In Australia, for instance, Australian Football League (AFL) and NRL (National Rugby League) clubs profit financially from the thousands of slot machines located in their venues. Some critics have pointed out that they are contradictory as they foster addiction while championing community values (Grant, 2013).

Convergence also happens on an operational level. As two of the largest companies that run poker tables online, *PokerStars* (founded in 2001) and *888* (operated by 888 Holdings and established in 1997) are exemplars of the newfound capacities of digital platforms and the networked practices of contemporary media assemblages. These capacities – among them ubiquity, interaction and networked socialisation – bridge the divide that separates gambling and social networking as fully distinct digital cultural practices.

This convergence of media assemblages triggers deep-rooted transformations in gambling towards popular culture. As Griffiths points out when discussing the coming together of gambling and online interaction, social networking sites "have the potential to normalize gambling behaviour as part of the consumption patterns of a non-gambling leisure activity" (2013, p. 105). This normalisation happens on three fronts:

1   in social casino gaming, primarily through mobile devices (wagering-like activities for play money);
2   through the marketing efforts of established gambling providers in social networking platforms; and
3   in the social networking capabilities built into online gambling platforms (*PokerStars* and *888* among them).

The notion of user participation is key in the cultural normalisation of gamble-play. The next section situates digital gambling affordances in the discourse of participatory culture and the notion that online users become producers of their online experience.

Gamble-Play Practices and the Paradigm of Participatory Cultures

As an act that implies the "production of coded values" (Baudrillard, 1998, p. 46), consumption is determined by practice: what people *are able to do* with media. To identify the distinct ways in which users interact in digital gambling platforms I first explore the concept of practice, which will lead to the understanding of participatory culture.

Andreas Reckwitz's definition of practice (2002) can frame gambling practices in which people and things interlink through particular activities. It is also useful in understanding how social media practices, norms and affordances generate new practices associated with gambling. Reckwitz (2002) argues that a practice

> *is a routinised* type of behaviour which consists of several elements, interconnected to one another: forms of bodily activities, forms of mental activities, 'things' and their use, a background knowledge in the form of understanding, know-how, states of emotion and motivational knowledge.
>
> (Reckwitz, 2002, p. 249)

Digital gambling involves bodily activities (clicking, excreting hormones while anxiously waiting for outcomes), mental activities (calculating the next move in a hand of online poker or the odds in an online slot machine), 'things' such as platforms and devices, a 'background knowledge' on the rules of the game and the nuances of each specific platform, and a spectrum of states of emotion that ranges from hope to expectation to perhaps disappointment.

There are also physiological explanations of how bodies respond to the affects triggered by gambling. Meyer et al. (2004) measured the neuroendocrine response to gambling among both problem and non-problem gamblers. In their sample group, both heart rate and the levels of the stress hormone norepinephrine increased during a blackjack session. Dopamine levels were significantly higher in problem gamblers. Cortisol levels increased in both groups. The researchers concluded that casino gambling induces the activation of the HPA-axis and the sympathoadrenergic system (Meyer et al., 2004). Similarly, Wulfert et al. conducted a study to measure the physical response of gamblers, and concluded that "the experiment yielded evidence that the participants became significantly more physiologically aroused during a horse race when they expected to win money than when they simply predicted the outcome of the race without wagering" (2005, p. 314).

Although gamblers are autonomous agents who can and do engage in creative forms of play, their routinised behaviours are also ultimately limited by what the digital environment allows them to do. Virtual environments such as Massive Multiplayer Online Role-Playing Games or MMORPGs, and arguably online casinos, are

> collectively produced realities, but this collective production process is in turn guided, restrained and empowered, in short, governed, by the restrictions and possibilities offered by the environment.
>
> (Arvidsson, 2006, p. 108)

In online casinos and gambling-like platforms there is a monetary stake, either real or fake, so there is a strict set of rules and restrictions imposed by the house. Prevalent practices in digital game cultures that alter the mechanics of play, such as *modding* or game modification (Kücklich, 2005) are heavily limited in gambling platforms. The new role that gamblers play within these networked markets has the potential to be disruptive of institutional structures, but that potential is rarely fulfilled.

Gamble-play media are multiplatform, convergent media where gamblers bet, converse and sustain a public presence. These activities become *practice*, routinised behaviours. In online casinos, shiny lights and alluring characters invite gamblers to partake in a game and take a shortcut to financial plenitude but also to engage in continuous, possibly lifelong consumption. In short, digital interfaces allow for the expansion of consumption beyond the bet. Online casinos manage a gambler's consumption through Consumer Lifetime Management (CLM), a strategy which "aims at maximizing the overall life-time revenue of customers through a diversified range of services" (Arvidsson, 2006, p. 116). These services both "tie the consumer closer to the company" and make the company's services "penetrate deeper into his or her life" (Arvidsson, 2006, p. 116). Gambling has also learned from other big industries. As Livingstone et al. argue, "the gambling industry has learned many lessons from 'big tobacco' and 'big alcohol' and uses very similar tactics to maximise its profits" (2017, p. 5). Likewise, research has indicated that Unhealthy Commodity Industries (UCI), such as tobacco, alcohol, food, beverage and gambling, use very similar rhetoric in their advertising (Petticrew et al., 2017).

CLM helps the gambler to establish and maintain routinised gambling behaviours. CLM is intensified with the use of mobile technology, which according to forecasts will be the main delivery platform for digital gambling and social casino gaming (Nomura Equity Research, 2013). In mobile apps, for example, gambling companies maintain constant communication with the consumer through mechanisms such as 'push notifications', which are reminders about special promotions, a friend's activity in the game or lack of play. An example of these messages is a personalised email sent by the app *myVegas* when a player hasn't accessed the platform for an extended period of time, and which simply reads, "We miss you!".

Online casinos heavily promote brand affinity among their clients. The bet is the focal experience, the central practice, but certainly not the only one. Operators encourage user participation in forums, tournaments, chats and social media platforms. These experiences turn into routinised behaviours, some of which partake in what is known in academic literature as 'participatory cultures'.

As Deuze recognises when citing Jenkins, participation is "both a topdown corporate-driven process and a bottom-up consumer-driven process" (Deuze, 2006, p. 268). The idea of consuming gambling and gambling-like products on a participatory fashion counters popular imaginations of gamblers as irrational and isolated consumers. Participation in digital gambling, however, can also be seen as an orchestrated effort by gambling service providers to align to a user's current media practices as a way to make gambling and gaming part of their daily consumption of entertainment.

> [Participation] enables companies to foster consumer loyalty and generate low-cost content aimed at an audience that seems to be increasingly willing to put their voluntary engagement in the service of commercial corporations.
>
> (Deuze, 2006, p. 268)

Participation also establishes a kind of consumer sovereignty and aids in the shaping of practices of consumption in digital gambling platforms, and in their cultural normalisation. Initially, participatory cultures around online poker were generated extemporaneously. Mid-1990s gamblers created forums and discussion groups to assess the quality and reliability of early online casinos – especially due to the fact that many of these operated on the periphery of legality – to share gambling tips and to identify industry malpractices, such as the operation of pokerbot software that imitates a gambler's behaviour and participates in poker hands by inserting electronic adversaries.

Some online and offline casinos, as well as app developers, have identified and capitalised on the dynamics of these participatory cultures. They have constructed their corporate communications around the notion that online gamblers communicate with each other, that they cooperate, serve as consumer rights advocates, act as sporadic mentors and pupils in online poker schools (including the *PokerStars* sponsored www.pokerschoolonline.com) and generate knowledge around the vast and multifarious world of online poker (Laquintano, 2010). Loyalty and bonus programs are also constructed around the notion of a new sort of gambler/consumer who accesses gambling and gambling-like products from static and mobile devices. Gambling service providers are highly reliant on users' recommendations and in the expansion of product and brand reach through the user's online social networks. Casinos invest significant amounts of money to gain loyal customers who will be involved in constant play (Lucas & Spilde, 2017).

Online casinos are making strategic efforts to capture the participatory culture that has so far been generated in their periphery but outside their control. Chat rooms, forums and blogs have been incorporated into the home pages and standalone software of casinos such as *888* and *PokerStars*. Casinos and social casino apps providers strive to redefine how and where consumption is carried out. They do so by offering gamblers platforms in which they can participate, mingle and merge their gambling networks with other spheres, such as their Facebook and Twitter communities, all of which are easily accessible through desktop and mobile devices.

Digital gamblers use online casinos in a variety of ways that intermittently reframe and reconstitute common practices of traditional gambling (Kinnunen et al., 2012). They access real-currency gambling sites to win money, of course, but they also extend the socialisation inherent in land-based gambling, to brag about their wins and to share tips, experiences and opinions on different casinos. Gambling is no longer the consumption of bets for consumption's sake, where socialisation is an extra. The consumption of bets in online realms invokes certain codes and practices that are inherently related to patterns of socialisation in digital media, such as the logics of sharing and adding 'friends'.

Gamblers have come to make social connections with other participants in online casinos. They are no longer nameless adversaries sharing a poker table in a physical casino. They become 'friends' with whom the gambling experience is shared, much as in informal poker nights among acquaintances. This trend aligns with social media conventions (boyd & Ellison, 2007; Webster, 2010).

Not all commentators have been optimistic about the presumed emancipatory capabilities of participatory culture, in which current gambling platforms were incubated. A look back at Beer's 2009 assessment of participatory web cultures is specifically relevant when studying the trajectory of gamble-play. Beer reveals certain scepticism towards claims that Web 2.0 platforms could be catalysts of collective action and empowering forms of consumption:

> It is perhaps not surprising that Web 2.0 – which has been defined as the shift toward user-generated content and the move from desktop storage to webtop access (Beer and Burrows, 2007) – has become associated in popular depictions with empowerment and liberation as 'the people' apparently reclaim the internet and exercise their 'collective intelligence'.
>
> (Beer, 2009, p. 986)

Beer goes on to affirm that there exist "increasingly powerful and active technological environments that operate without the knowledge of those upon whom they are taking an effect" (Beer, 2009, p. 990). This is certainly the case in the constricted environments of contemporary digital gamble-play, where various mechanisms are put into place to extract information out of users and categorise them as a market research subjects. As we will see, online casinos are still such environments, where

> users are generating metadata 'tags' that organize and categorize the user-generated content, where social networking site profiles often provide detailed impressions of people's lives, where these profiles are clearly integrated as mundane and ordinary parts of how people live, and where the emphasis is on the 'invention' of new content, new 'social relations' and even new ways of presenting content in the form of creative visualizations of ordinary things.
>
> (Beer, 2009, p. 996)

Beer argues that consumers are increasingly producers in online spaces:

> Whether we give any credibility to this progressional model of versions of the web or not, what we can see is that there is a wide-scale shift towards a model in which user generated content is increasingly important.\
>
> (Beer, 2008, p. 621)

Although gambling is generally seen as a solitary practice, online casinos and other gamble-play operators build platforms that allow users to create content around poker games and even slot machine apps. *PKR*, for example, allowed users to create avatars in an act of self-commodification. The gambler's avatar was an important actor in this particular gambling assemblage as it can be tailored to achieve the desired self-presentation and convey different emotions at the poker table. Similarly, both *PokerStars* and *888* push for the creation of detailed profiles. Through these profiles gamblers showcase their abilities and present themselves within the gambling community. They also provide valuable data to the operator, information that is, in turn, used to extend participation.

Current forms of online interaction related to gamble-play foster a more active kind of consumption, one in which the user invests time, effort and labour to engage in gamble-play. Terranova has judged this type of dynamic as "free labor", where "knowledgeable consumption of culture is translated into productive activities that are pleasurably embraced and at the same time shamelessly exploited" (Terranova, 2000, p. 37; see also Hesmondhalgh, 2010). Beyond the stakes, digital gamble-play often involves free labour.

The Use of Perks in the Consumption of Gamble-Play

Traditional gambling operators have long used bonuses and perks to sustain consumption. Clarke (2003) uses casinos to exemplify contemporary forms of capitalist consumption, in which perks accompany the acquisition of a good or service:

> Evidently, the customers perceive benefits from the nominally free drinks their gambling subsidizes: they get both 'free' drinks *and* the chance to win fabulous amounts of money... What is most significant about this system, however, is the way in which it seems capable of conjuring up an increased 'total amount of benefit' – for both consumers and casino operators – simply by diverting the system of supplying drinks through the supplementary detour of games of chance.
>
> (Clarke, 2003, p. 11)

Online gamble-play has adapted strategies appropriate to the medium. In online casinos, for instance, perks include loyalty and new membership bonuses as well as exclusive content and entry into sweepstakes and members-only tournaments. In 2014, online casino *Royal Panda* even offered the opportunity to win a trip to space by playing its online slot *Starburst* (Reuters, 2014). In most desktop and mobile apps, users can earn bonuses and other perks by sharing information or inviting their contacts to download the app.

Recent efforts from the gambling industry indicate a move towards including real-life benefits derived from wins and bonuses in virtual gambling, which pushes the limits of gaming even further into the realm of gambling. The MGM casino, one of the biggest in the Las Vegas Strip, originally launched the app *MyVegas*, developed by PlayStudios, in June 2012. Initially, users could play with virtual money to win virtual prizes.

Since November 2013, however, it allows players to cash in their winnings in selected establishments in Las Vegas for prizes that range from free meals to tickets for shows or swimming with dolphins (Chapman, 2013). Partners include Wolfgang Puck and House of Blues as well as The Mirage, Mandalay Bay and the Excalibur casinos, among other venues. The gameplay itself is simple and repetitive, but the allure may lie in the fact that "[in] theory, the game is free to play forever, and players could fund an entire holiday in Las Vegas just from pressing that green button" (Street, 2013).

Some of the slots available in *MyVegas* are extensions of the casino and its partners' branding strategies, with titles such as *New York New York, Excalibur* and *Mirage*, all adorned with cartoonish designs that make reference to popular social gaming titles, such as *Farmville* or *Angry Birds*. The app constantly invites the user to add Facebook friends to the player roster, offering bonus credits (Figure 3.2).

These corporate strategies are an effort by the traditional gambling industry to prolong the punter's relationship with the casino institution and to bring the casino into the online social life of gamblers. They are efforts to perpetuate gambling practices as a "routinised type of behaviour" (Reckwitz, 2002).

As Stutz reported before the initial launch of *MyVegas* in 2012, one year before the cash-in capabilities were activated,

> MGM Resorts Senior Vice President of Business Development Tom Mikulich said the company envisions myVegas as a way reach the about 30 million members of MLife, the casino operator's player

Figure 3.2 With the app *MyVegas*, players can play slots through Facebook and win credits that they can then exchange for goods and services in participating physical venues, such as the MGM Grand, the Bellagio or The Mirage in Las Vegas.
Image captured November 6, 2017 from the author's Facebook account.

loyalty program, when they're away from the Strip. MLife customers playing online will be able to win nongaming incentives, such as show tickets and dinners at company restaurants- "Through myVegas, we can tighten our emotional connection between our brands and our customers", Mikulich said. "That's what we mean by convergence."

(Stutz, 2012)

This perpetual "emotional connection" is associated with values such as commitment and belonging and allows the casino to be a ubiquitous presence in the gambler's life. This strategy further extends the reach of its loyalty programs, facilitating perks on a continuous, perhaps everyday basis. The conversion of in-play credits to real-life benefits significantly challenges preconceptions of what social casino apps entitles the consumer to. Other online casinos are following suit. CaesarsCasino.com is one of the first casinos launched after the US state of New Jersey legalised online gambling in 2013. As users play roulette, video poker, blackjack or slots online, they accumulate rewards that can be used in land-based venues: "Play the games you love and reap the rewards at nearly 40 resorts and casinos around the world" (the casino is available at CaesarsCasino.com).

Current forms of gamble-play consumption could be interpreted as part of the trend towards consumers taking active role in production. Ritzer and Jurgenson (2010) and others (Beer & Burrows, 2007; Zwick et al., 2008) have referred to this as 'prosumption', a new stage in capitalism in which the consumer is given the role of co-producer. Ritzer and Jurgenson (2010) point out,

> Prosumer capitalism is based in a system where content is abundant and created by those not on the payroll.
>
> (Ritzer & Jurgenson, 2010, p. 30)

They list business models in which the end user finished the production process, such as in the IKEA model, where consumers assemble furniture at home, or reality TV, where lay audience members become protagonists.

Early accounts of prosumerism praised its liberating qualities (Toffler, 1980). However, others argue that prosumerism is translated into free or cheap labour (Terranova, 2000) as value is generated at the expense of users and the benefit of industry. In the case of digital gamblers, the labour invested in playing, creating an online gambling persona and commenting in outlets such as social media and chats generates capital and expands gambling networks. In his analysis of MMORPGs, Arvidsson argues that commercial success "hinges on the ability to monopolize the valorisation of user productivity" (2006, p. 108). In the case of digital gambling, all this points towards a form of consumption in which users pay for perks by being involved in constrained forms of production.

Gamble-play involves different forms of prosumption that most often generate value for the operator. Successful players become celebrities, acquiring a status to which other novice gamblers aspire. Platforms including the now defunct *PKR* have made gamblers active participants of the experience by providing avatar generation tools and control over the audiovisual dynamics of the environment. Through recommendations, constant play and repetitive usage, the gambler becomes a market research subject. By nature, earlier gambling is a repetitive task and the more gamblers play and socialise online, the more valuable a gambling platform becomes. Gamblers are actively involved in the process of shaping the experience of betting in both institutionalised (official platforms) and non-institutionalised ways (chats, YouTube videos or discussion forums, among others).

In the final section of this chapter I analyse how some digital gambling platforms, including two of the biggest online casinos in the world (*888* and *PokerStars*), afford particular digital media practices that reframe gambling consumption.

Couldry identifies different practices that online users perform when engaging with contemporary media forms. These practices are searching and search-enabling, showing and being shown, presencing, archiving and commentary (Couldry, 2012). This taxonomy works as an analytical framework for identifying the strategies employed by gambling operators to invite particular kinds of consumption.

Searching and Search-Enabling

At the beginning of any gambling session, the player must search for an online casino and, once in the casino, for a poker table. Finding a gambling platform is among the practices that set online gamble-play apart from traditional gambling. Some players are better informed than others, a fact that establishes relationships of power among them. These kinds of knowledge might include being proficient in a particular language or having a level of insight into who plays online poker when and from which locations. One of the online paradigms of online poker is that there are marked differences in skill levels between, for example, American and European players.

Couldry states that the vaster the online realm becomes,

> the more salient will be the differences between people's search strategies and skills: here socio-economic status and education provide big advantages even if over time they can be overcome by experience.
> (Couldry, 2012, p. 45)

This dynamic gives an obvious advantage to casinos that have larger marketing budgets and a larger pool of players who can recommend the casino. At the same time, the more popular the casino is, the higher search engines will rank it. Casinos employ Search Engine Optimisation (SEO) methods to guarantee a high ranking. If you search for "online poker" in Google, *PokerStars* and *888* are likely to be the top two results.

There is an enormous array of gambling platforms online. Abundance in digital environments makes it important for users to gather the skills or digital literacy necessary to search and discern among various options. The number of sites is so vast and ever-changing that it is almost impossible to assess the exact number of gambling platforms that exist in the internet and mobile networks (Farnsworth & Austrin, 2010).

Finding online casinos can also be a serendipitous activity as digital gambling operators make the opportunity to gamble readily available by promoting their products among myriad already-established publics that could share some demographic characteristics with potential players. Some online casinos are advertised in platforms that some could deem immoral (pornographic sites) or illegal (torrent downloading sites; sports streaming sites). Pop-up windows advertising online gambling appear in sites such as Torrentz.com and The Pirate Bay, or YouPorn, where users and companies upload their pornographic videos, in a model similar to YouTube. Likewise, banners and over-the-screen advertising for sports wagering (companies such the UK-based *Bet 365*) are shown during unlicensed video streaming of sporting events (McMullan & Kervin, 2012).

New technological and cultural trends constantly trigger the generation of novel gambling platforms, which complicates searching practices. We can think, for example, of Bitcoin-only casinos, such as bitzino.com, casinobitco.in, satoshibet.com and bc-casino.com, which exist in the periphery of legality and raise governmental and user concerns about the use of digital currencies for wagering as bitcoins are far from being a stable currency (Adams, 2013).

Online casinos constantly disappear or are moved to mirror sites when legislative or taxation regimes change in the territories where the servers are located. As many jurisdictions prohibit online gambling for real money, servers are located in countries with laxer legislation. When there is a crackdown on gambling sites, some operators keep online casinos afloat by getting new domain names or moving servers, which shows the adaptability of digital gambling assemblages. As a user known as "Renee" wrote in the blog *Tight Poker* after 13 US online casinos were shut down in 2011, gambling operators find ways to endure:

> there is still hope for internet poker since poker giants, and internet gambling firms are still trying to find ways to survive. For example, as soon as the online poker sites were indicted, Bodog.com became Bodog.eu, and they would have definitely won over several thousands of players from the poker giants who were indicted.
>
> (Renee, 2011)

In online gambling, searching also involves finding the platforms that best suit individual players and correspond to regular online practices, such as adding friends, liking content or tailoring avatars. These affordances are built into the design of online casinos, such as *888* and *PokerStars*. Couldry further explains that "searching is a key practice through which people shape their distinctive conditions of action" (Couldry, 2012, p. 45). Online casinos also offer practice games so the user can test out the platform. This contrasts with land-based gambling, where immediate options are more limited in places that are not gambling hubs on the scale of Las Vegas, Monaco, Gold Coast, Reno or Macau, and where practice games are not an option. The opportunity to play with no real stakes might explain the vast popularity of predigital kitchen table or friendly poker games (Cotte & Latour, 2009; Zurcher, 1970).

There are a variety of sites that provide user-generated reviews to aid other gamblers in their search for online casinos. OnlineCasino.com.au, for instance, ranks casinos according to categories such as bonuses, security, jackpots, deposit methods, software, customer support and audited payout percentages. Although digital gamblers generate most of the content in these sites, the sites also work as a legitimising tool for online gambling providers.

Couldry takes a critical stance similar to Terranova's (2000) when discussing the labour dynamics of internet publics. He argues that the internet "is already inhabited by institutional predators who know very well the potential of peer-to-peer recommendation to enhance their marketing goals" (Couldry, 2012, p. 46).

Following this logic, *888*'s online community platform, My 888poker, invites users to partake as follows:

> Whether you're interested in reading poker blogs or just making friends who love to play poker like you, My 888poker is the place for you.

The accumulation of value through the users' connections is further evidenced by promotions such as the ones offered by *DoubleDown Casino Slots & Poker* in Facebook. In its "Facebook Like Challenge day" (which was organised on November 26, 2013) it promised free credits if users engaged in actions such as liking and sharing.

Self-Commodification in Gamble-Play: Presencing, Showing and Being Shown

Digital platforms allow gambling to be a more public activity, largely due to its cultural normalisation as an accepted middle-class leisure activity (Reith, 2007). As such, gamblers construct an online identity delimited by the affordances of each platform. The practice of showing is a useful concept to describe this media innovation. Couldry states that the term 'showing' "helps us grasp the mass of media-related acts that make something publicly available: many of those acts were unknown in a pre-digital age" (2012, p. 47).

Showing is a common practice in most online casinos and social casino apps as it allows users to state their ranking among a group of players, which adds another performative dimension to gambling. This practice is present in other gaming platforms, such as the Apple Game Center, where players can compete against their connections. In online casinos such as *PokerStars* or *888*, showing and being shown translates not only to showcasing each player's wins and eventually becoming an online poker star but also to demonstrating knowledge and gambling know-how.

It is important to state, however, that although some online gamblers like to be shown, others relish anonymity and avoid establishing connections with other gamblers beyond the game (Cotte & Latour, 2009).

However, recent developments in platform design, such as the joining of the user's gambling and social networks (mainly Facebook), lead to a partial and perhaps forced eradication of this anonymity. Users become co-creators of their gambling experience by engaging in acts of voluntary and involuntary self-promotion. Some major players in the social casino industry, including Zynga, have launched versions for Tencent, the immensely popular Chinese-language social network.

Showing gameplay and sharing strategies at the poker table through YouTube, for example, is a common practice through which gamblers acquire social standing and recognition. Players record and distribute a game to share poker tips and get other players' feedback (Figure 3.3).

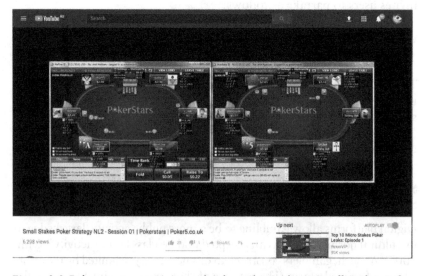

Figure 3.3 Poker strategy training video by poker5videos, *Small Stakes Poker Strategy NL2-Session 01*, uploaded on April 21, 2013, accessed on November 4, 2017 at www.youtube.com/watch?v=qeUGEHTIv8k.

Amateur players have access to a vast pool of poker knowledge in the form of user-generated videos. This is exemplified by YouTube videos, such as *Small Stakes Poker Strategy NL2-Session 01*, uploaded in April 2013, in which the user poker5videos provides spoken commentary on one of his games in PokerStars (poker5videos, 2013). poker5videos explains his strategy throughout the hour-long game. Other players respond to the video through text comments, offering their own insights and opinions on the strategy ("You play very risky but considering that you're in a stake table that has new players your strategy pays off :D looking forward to the rest," says user TheGeorgewday; "your breathing is really annoying", complains tsanko ivanov). The author also asks other users to point out the mistakes he made during the game, later admitting that

> at 08:35 I checked back because i wanted to try and get value from my opponents bluffing range, when the turn came i thought the best line would be to check/call. Then when the river came is should have raised or folded, i thinking calling there was the worst option. (sic)
>
> (poker5videos, 2013)

Couldry argues that the practice of showing in large social groupings

> regularizes mediated co-veillance in everyday life, transforming everyday action and performance into spectacle and audiencing.
>
> (Couldry, 2012, p. 49)

Through leagues, social media accounts (mainly on YouTube, Twitter and Facebook) and official teams, online casinos such as *PokerStars* and *888* promote practices of spectacle and audiencing. Other gambling-themed apps perpetuate narratives of personal achievement as performance. *Betting Billionaire*, for example, promises a "chance to live the millionaire lifestyle you always dreamed of and try to become a Billionaire". The user achieves this by using "your knowledge of sporting events to bet big on Football, Tennis, Horse Racing, Basketball and more" and competing "against your friends to see who knows their stuff". In the gameplay, you can "Spend your winnings on the latest bling from cool cars to luxury homes. Your friends will be so jealous when you buy your own private island" (*Betting Billionaire* page in Facebook's App Centre, 2013). The cultural dynamics of *Betting Billionaire* resonate with Baudrillard's notion that "to be the vehicle of the *egalitarian* myth, happiness needs to be *measured*" (Baudrillard, 1998, p. 50). Although this is not gambling per se as the user does not receive a payout, it presents an interesting dynamic in which real-life events influence simulated wagering (Figure 3.4).

Figure 3.4 Betting Billionaire Facebook app.
Image captured on February 16, 2017 from the author's Facebook account.

Practices of showing have produced some interesting intersections between poker and sport. These intersections are evidence of media and
branding convergence. Take, for example, the *PokerStars* 2012 promotion involving champion tennis player, but poker novice, Rafael Nadal:

> But while he may have already achieved everything in the tennis
> world, Rafa is yet to win a poker tournament, and is looking for-
> ward to taking on the challenge of building his skills as he competes
> online at PokerStars. You can follow Rafa as he takes his first steps
> on the journey towards becoming a winning poker player, and we'll
> be keeping this page updated with his progress every step of the way.
> (PokerStars, 2012)

Nadal's learning process was showcased in the *PokerStars* website and
users could upload videos to give him advice and tips. Similarly, *888* has
its own group of Ambassadors, one of whom is renowned Australian
cricketer Shane Warne. Warne "is usually scheduled to play in a number

of poker tournaments each and every year and can be seen playing at 888. com's poker tables" (888, 2013; Warne's full profile: www.888poker. com/ambassadors/shane-warne.htm).

Likewise, members of the elite Team PokerStars Pro (which includes the most successful gamblers) have personal blogs, Twitter feeds and Facebook pages. They are also grouped by country, which adds a sense of nationalism similar to that of sports such as tennis and soccer. The gambler becomes a commodity. Some of these players have evocative names, such as the legendary Chris Moneymaker (@CMONEYMAKER), who has the type of gambling rags-to-riches story that is perceived as positive and a result of hard work (Humphreys & Latour, 2013). His gambling journey is promoted by *PokerStars* as one of the foundational myths of online poker:

> Inspired by the tale of how an amateur managed to beat hundreds of world-class players and earn a huge cash prize, millions of people began playing online and in card rooms across the globe.

We can also think, for example, of Liv Boeree, an English member of Team PokerStars. She has a Twitter account with more than 73,000 followers (@Liv_Boeree) and is presented with a captivating life story: "She previously studied at the University of Manchester, achieving a first-class degree in Astrophysics, before going on to find fame as a model and TV presenter on a range of different shows". Then, the story continues, she found her true calling in online poker.

There are other digital media practices associated with showing and being shown. *Presencing* is

> a whole set of media-enhanced ways in which individuals, groups and institutions put into circulation information about, and representations of, themselves for the wider purpose of *sustaining a public presence.*
>
> (Couldry, 2012, p. 50)

Online casinos provide platforms that allow for players to sustain a public presence that can span anywhere from a one-off poker game to months or years. The maintenance of a public presence builds brand loyalty as the user invests money, time and creativity in generating it. For example, when users set up *PokerStars* on their computers, they have to enter a User ID or nickname, which will be the name "that people will see when you are playing". The user is then asked to confirm that they are over 18 years of age and to state how they learnt about PokerStars – options include "Cinema Advertising", "Friend Referral", "Search Engine", "Latin America Poker Tour (LAPT)", "European Poker Tour (EPT)", "Online Forum", "Newspaper", "Web Site", "Billboard", "Radio",

"TV", "Magazine" and "Asia Pacific Poker Tour (APPT)". This section is not optional, and evidences an effort from the casino to get information on how its player pools are created and better understand the expansion of its own networks.

Who you are allowed to be in an online casino is determined by code and design. Even though digital platforms allow gamblers to do more things as consumers, code still establishes limits and hierarchies. The creation of clear-cut categories also aids in the categorisation of gamblers and their conceptualisation as market research subjects. *PokerStars* created the website *PokerStars Women* (www.pokerstars.com/poker/women), dedicated to female players, who can share their tips and knowledge as well as access "promotions and events open exclusively to women". There are gender-specific features, such as the Women's Poker League and the Women's Sunday tournament, which subjectify female players as distinct from males.

The subjectification of gamblers according to gender has also been the subject of academic studies. Abarbanel and Bernhard (2012), for example, have stated that female gamblers exhibit a combination of what they call "feminine and masculine traits" while playing, establishing a sort of negotiation between natural risk aversion and aggressive play. The authors also highlight how women's poker leagues are on the rise in countries such as the United States, which is exemplified by *PokerStars Women*. They stress the fact that "while many women have experienced difficulty in finding acceptance in the male-dominated poker world, the avenue of women-only tournaments has allowed them to experience a sense of *communitas*" (Abarbanel & Bernhard, 2012).

Archiving in Gamble-Play

Traditional gambling is defined by the moment: the instant, ephemeral nature of the experience (Reith, 1999). However, digital gambling platforms allow for the bet to be a moment that is on record. Digital gambling platforms require the user to have a profile, and this profile is then associated with the player's gambling history. In slot apps, for example, gameplay is based on the accumulation of credits or the completion of levels. The insertion of levels into the gameplay of an activity as ephemeral as slot machine playing significantly changes the temporal and narrative dynamics of the experience. As Chesher explains in relation to digital games, "There is a form of object permanency by which players' actions have ongoing effects" (2007).

One archives online gambling experiences to form a coherent story of success and defeat, just as one builds an existential archive on social media sites such as Facebook (Good, 2013). Similarly, users can broadcast their poker games via online video platforms, such as YouTube, commenting on them and offering tips for free. This practice is similar to the broadcasting and archiving of video game playing through genres such as the walkthrough, or even machinima – short films made with digital game footage – which grow out "of the creative energies of popular culture enthusiasts, fuelled by increasingly accessible digital media production tools and online video distribution" (Ito, 2011, p. 51).

Casino platforms encourage this idea of gambling as an archivable practice. *PokerStars*, for example, frames the acquisition of poker skills as a learning experience that can be recorded and archived. In its website *Poker School Online* it has a PokerSchool League where gamblers can enter tournaments to learn and play for fake money. The casino seeks an eventual conversion to real-money wagering.

Once the gambler commences to play for real money, the online casino keeps a detailed record of deposits and cashouts. In *PokerStars*, for example, this is done through a stand-alone program, Desktop Cashier. This feature is not part of the land-based gambler's experience unless they are part of a casino's loyalty program and every transaction is recorded.

The Infrastructure of Commentary

User commentaries and reviews are fundamental in the expansion and sustenance of gambling assemblages. Couldry identifies the emergence of an *infrastructure of commentary*, whereby commentaries are archived and made visible online (Couldry, 2012, p. 55). Many online organisations are heavily reliant on commentary as positive opinions draw new consumers and negative ones steer them away. Digital gambling, particularly poker, is an activity with a heavy reliance on trust. Positive commentaries can increase the number of players in a digital poker site; negative commentaries will repel potential converts and draw negative attention to the casino as a potential site that exposes users to deviant practices and scams. Official and unofficial pages on platforms such as Facebook provide avenues for commentary and casinos are obliged to provide quick-response customer service.

Gambling online is a leap of faith as even the more credible casinos are prone to financial collapse or malpractice, as the infamous Black Tuesday showed. Gamblers rely heavily on what other gamblers offer as a perceived legitimate, non-biased commentary. Casino promoters posing as lay gamblers often infiltrate this infrastructure of commentary, however.

As Cooper (2012) states in an article published in *The New York Times*,

> placing bets on illegal Web sites requires a leap of faith – that the electronic cards are shuffled fairly, that other players cannot see your hand and that the Web site will pay you if you win.
>
> (Cooper, 2012)

It would be pertinent to add that the presence of pokerbots (fully digital players generated by the machine who camouflage as real players) is one of the foremost and most insidious worries that players have to face. As McMullan states in regard to Wood and Griffiths's 2008 study analysing the main concerns of Swedish online poker players, "players believed that poker bots operated by gambling sites, as well as computer viruses operated by other players, were depriving them of winnings" (McMullan, 2012, p. 101). Ed Miller, a self-proclaimed "poker authority", wrote on his website, www.notedpokerauthority.com, that "two excellent players who have mastered colluding will be damn near unbeatable" (Miller, 2006). He also stated that "the most direct threat to online poker is colluding bots. By themselves, bots are a major threat to online poker. Bot software is now available to the public at a very affordable price" (Miller, 2006).

The lack of strict government intervention due to the partial legality of many online poker sites has triggered instances of community self-regulation, such as the forums in online casinos such as *PokerStars* or comment threads in casinos' Facebook pages. In Australia, the legal framework that governs online gambling is determined by the Interactive Gambling Act 2011, which was subject to a review in 2011 to accommodate new technological and industry trends. However, the implementation of the recommendations emanating from this review has been inconclusive.

Generally, online communities are formed to tackle each one of these issues. Since the early days of online gambling in the early 1990s, forums have been created where players act as cyber-watchdogs of sorts, identifying malpractices and newly acquired skills to trick the machine and other players, which constitutes cheating or at least uneven competition. Casinos take advantage of one of the fundamental shortcomings of digital gambling – the uncertainty over the fairness of the games – to assert their trustworthiness. Casinos earn customer loyalty by acquiring industry-generated certifications.

Digital gambling networks provide gamblers with new forms of agency. Forums such as *Cards Chat: A Worldwide Poker Community* (www.cardschat.com) allow gamblers to disseminate tips and appraisals of online casinos outside of the official channels provided by casinos. It is unclear, however, if casino personnel are involved in these chat rooms as 'lurkers' or even as supposed gamblers. Websites such as *Casino Scam Report* (www.casinoscamreport.com) keep track of malpractices in the industry via crowdsourcing, and prevent gamblers from "being scammed by online casinos that don't pay out winnings to their players" (Casino Scam Report, 2013). Websites such as these establish new dynamics of accountability for casinos in which users help define how trustworthy each casino is.

The digital media practices described in this chapter reframe the routines associated with gambling and open up avenues for new modes of engagement, seduction and control.

Conclusion

The affordances of contemporary gamble-play platforms allow particular types of consumption that aid in the cultural normalisation of gambling as an acceptable form of digital entertainment. These affordances make evident the main cultural dynamic of gamble-play: promoting the fun aspects of gambling alongside the thrill of winning money.

There is an inherent contradiction in gamble-play consumption. On the one hand, the dynamics of gamble-play lead to the establishment of routinised behaviours that tighten the hold of operators over players and allow the pervasiveness of gambling in the player's overall digital media experience. On the other hand, players become co-producers of their gambling experience: they can create avatars, share their results through social networking sites and invite other friends to play.

References

Abarbanel, L., & Bernhard, B. J. (2012). Chicks with decks: The female lived experience in poker. *International Gambling Studies, 12*(3), 367–385.

Adams, G. (2013, December 15). Gambling on the Bitcoin? *IOL*. Retrieved from www.iol.co.za/scitech/technology/internet/gambling-on-the-bitcoin-1.162 2293#.Uq5VNGQW1vk

Adorno, T., & Horkheimer, M. (2000). The culture industry: Enlightenment as mass deception. In J. Schor & D. B. Holt (Eds.), *The consumer society reader* (pp. 3–19). New York: The New Press. (Original work published 1944)

Albarrán-Torres, C. (2016). Social casino apps and digital media practices: New paradigms of consumption. In M. Willson & T. Leaver (Eds.), *Social, casual and mobile games: The changing gaming landscape* (pp. 243–260). New York: Bloomsbury Publishing USA.

Arnould, E. J., & Thompson, C. J. (2005). Consumer culture theory (CCT): Twenty years of research. *Journal of Consumer Research, 31*(4), 868–882.

Arvidsson, A. (2006). *Brands: Meaning and value in media culture.* New York: Routledge.

Associated Press (2014, January 8). 76ers, Devils sign online gaming deal. *ESPN NBA*. Retrieved from http://espn.go.com/nba/story/_/id/10264922/philadelphia-76ers-new-jersey-devils-sign-online-poker-sponsorship-deal

Austin, I., & Smyth, M. (2013, November 19). "Our ferries are not riverboat casinos", NDP critic says in blasting BC Ferries slot-machines proposal. *The Province*. Retrieved from www.theprovince.com/health/ferries+riverboat+casinos+critic+says+blasting+Ferries+slot+machines+proposal/9181390/story.html

Baudrillard, J. (1998). *The consumer society: Myths and structures.* London: Sage.

Beer, D. (2008). Researching a confessional society. *International Journal of Market Research, 50*(5), Web 2.0 Special Issue, 619–629.

Beer, D. (2009). Power through the algorithm? Participatory web cultures and the technological unconscious. *New Media & Society, 11*(6), 985–1002.

Beer, D., & Burrows, R. (2007). Sociology and, of and in Web 2.0: Some initial considerations. *Sociological Research Online, 12*(5). Retrieved from www.socresonline.org.uk/12/5/17.html

Bjerg, O. (2009). Too close to the money: A theory of compulsive gambling. *Theory, Culture & Society, 26*(4), 47–66.

Bogost, I. (2006). *Unit operations: An approach to video game criticism.* Cambridge: MIT Press.

boyd, d., (2011). Social network sites as networked publics affordances, dynamics, and implications. In Z. Papacharissi (Ed.), *Networked self: Identity, community and culture on social network Sites* (pp. 39–58). New York: Routledge.

boyd, d., & Ellison, N. (2007). Social network sites: Definition, history, and scholarship. *Journal of Computer-mediated Communication, 13*(1), 210–230.

Campbell, C. (2005). The craft consumer: Culture, craft and consumption in a postmodern society. *Journal of Consumer Culture, 5*(1), 23–42.

CasinoScamReport.com (2013). *Casino Scam Report.* Retrieved December 2017 from www.casinoscamreport.com/

Chapman, G. (2013, November 5). New app blurs the line between real & virtual gambling. *The Times of India.* Retrieved from http://timesofindia.indiatimes.com/tech/personal-tech/gaming/New-app-blurs-line-between-real-virtual-gambling/articleshow/25261698.cms

Chesher, C. (2007). Neither gaze nor glance, but glaze: Relating to console game screens. *Scan Journal, 4*(2). Retrieved from http://scan.net.au/scan/journal/display.php?journal_id=19

Chon, B. S., Choi, J. H., Barnett, G. A., Danowski, J. A., & Joo, S. H. (2003). A structural analysis of media convergence: Cross-industry mergers and acquisitions in the information industries. *The Journal of Media Economics, 16*(3), 141–157.

Clarke, D. B. (2003). *The consumer society and the postmodern city.* London and New York: Routledge.

CMONEYMAKER (2009). Chris Moneymaker. Twitter.com/CMONEYMAKER.

Cooper, M. (2012, January 27). As states weigh online gambling, profit may be small. *The New York Times.* Retrieved from www.nytimes.com/2012/01/18/us/more-states-look-to-legalize-online-gambling.html?_r=0

Cosgrave, J., & Klassen, T. R. (2001). Gambling against the State: The State and the Legitimation of gambling. *Current Sociology, 49*(1), 1–15.

Cotte, J., & Latour, K. A. (2009). Blackjack in the kitchen: Understanding online versus casino gambling. *Journal of Consumer Research, 35*(5), 742–758.

Couldry, N. (2012). *Media, society, world: Social theory and digital media practice.* Cambridge: Polity.

Cowen, D. (2006). Hipster urbanism. *Relay: A Socialist Project Review, 13,* 22–23.

Deuze, M. (2006). Ethnic media, community media and participatory culture. *Journalism, 7*(3), 262–280.

Farnsworth, J., & Austrin, T. (2010). The ethnography of new media worlds? Following the case of global poker. *New Media Society, 12*(7), 1120–1136.

Finin, T., Joshi, A., Kolari, P., Java, A., Kale, A., & Karandikar, A. (2008). The information ecology of social media and online communities. *AI Magazine, 29*(3), 77.

Frank, K. (2007). Thinking critically about strip club research. *Sexualities, 10*(4), 501–517.

Gardner, J. (2013, November 18). Online Aussie casino start-up to offer real cash gambling. *Financial Review*. Retrieved from www.afr.com/p/technology/online_aussie_casino_start_up_to_e5XEqpOMVRZf2lAn5xO6gN

Good, K. D. (2013). From scrapbook to Facebook: A history of personal media assemblage and archives. *New Media Society, 15*(4), 557–573.

Grant, T. (2013, October 27). AFL clubs talk up community leadership while fostering pokie addiction. *The Age*. Retrieved from www.theage.com.au/afl/afl-news/afl-clubs-talk-up-community-leadership-while-fostering-pokie-addiction-20131026-2w8qe.html#ixzz2lEr5bC00

Griffiths, M. D. (2013). Social gambling via Facebook: Further observations and concerns. *Gaming Law Review and Economics, 17*(2), 104–106.

Hayatbakhsh, M. R., Clavarino, A., Williams, G. M., Bor, W., & Najman, J. M. (2012). Young adults' gambling and its association with mental health and substance use problems. *Australian and New Zealand Journal of Public Health, 36*(2), 160–166.

Hesmondhalgh, D. (2010). User-generated content, free labour and the cultural industries. *Ephemera, 10*(3/4), 267–284.

Hing, N., & Breen, H. (2002). A profile of gaming machine players in clubs in Sydney, Australia. *Journal of Gambling Studies, 18*(2), 185–205.

Hing, N., Russell, A. M., Gainsbury, S. M., & Nuske, E. (2016). The public stigma of problem gambling: Its nature and relative intensity compared to other health conditions. *Journal of Gambling Studies, 32*(3), 847–864.

Hope, J., & Havir, L. (2002). You bet they're having fun!: Older Americans and casino gambling. *Journal of Aging Studies, 16*(2), 177–197.

Humphreys, A., & Latour, K. A. (2013). Framing the game: Assessing the impact of cultural representations on consumer perceptions of legitimacy. *Journal of Consumer Research, 40*(4), 773–795.

Invendium Ltd (n.d.). Betting Billionaire. *bettingbillionaire.com*. Retrieved September 2014 from www.bettingbillionaire.com/

Ito, M. (2011). Machinima in a fanvid ecology. *Journal of Visual Culture, 10*(1), 51–54.

Jean, P. (2013, November 18). Gamblers 'blamed for addiction'. *The Sydney Morning Herald*. Retrieved from www.smh.com.au/national/gamblers-blamed-for-addiction-20131117-2xpg3.html

Jenkins, H. (2006). *Convergence culture: Where old and new media collide*. New York: New York University Press.

Kacapyr-Cornell, S. (2013, October 21). Why is online "gaming" fun but "gambling" is shady? *Futurity*. Retrieved from www.futurity.org/gaming-fun-gambling-seedy/

Kingma, S. F. (2010). Dutch casino space: The spatial construction of gambling pleasure. In S. F. Kingma (Ed.), *Global gambling: Cultural perspectives on gambling organizations* (pp. 144–170). London and New York: Routledge.

Kinnunen, J., Rautio, E., Alha, K., & Paavilainen, J. (2012). Gambling in social networks: Gaming experiences of Finnish online gamblers. DiGRA Nordic 2012 Conference: Local and Global-Games in Culture and Society.

Kücklich, J. (2005). Precarious playbour: Modders and the digital games industry. *Fibreculture, 5*. Retrieved from http://five.fibreculturejournal.org/fcj-025-precarious-playbour-modders-and-the-digital-games-industry/

Laquintano, T. (2010). Manufacturing scarcity: Online poker, digital writing, and the flow of intellectual property. *Computers and Composition, 7*(3), 193–201.

Liv_Boeree (2009). Liv Boeree. Twitter.com/Liv_Boeree

Livingstone, C., Adams, P., Cassidy, R., Markham, F., Reith, G., Rintoul, A., Dow Schüll, N., Woolley, R., & Young, M. (2017). On gambling research, social science and the consequences of commercial gambling. *International Gambling Studies*, 1–14. Retrieved from www.tandfonline.com/doi/abs/10.1080/14459795.2017.1377748?journalCode=rigs20

Lucas, A. F., & Spilde, K. (2017). Estimating the effect of Casino Loyalty Program offers on slot machine play. *Cornell Hospitality Quarterly*. doi: 10.1177/1938965516686113

Matthewson, D., & Diamond, A. (2005). *Winning poker: 200 rules, techniques and strategies*. New York: Black Dog and Leventhal.

McGandy, A. (2013, October 15). How you name it matters: 'gambling' vs. 'gaming'. *Cornell Chronicle*. Retrieved from www.news.cornell.edu/stories/2013/10/how-you-name-it-matters-gambling-vs-gaming

McMullan, J. L. (2012). Cyber fraud, online poker, and order-maintenance in virtual worlds. *Gaming Law Review and Economics, 16*(3), 100–113.

McMullan, J. L., & Kervin, M. (2012). Selling internet gambling: Advertising, new media and the content of poker promotion. *International Journal of Mental Health and Addiction, 10*(5), 622–645.

Meyer, G., Schwertfeger, J., Exton, M. S., Janssen, O. E., Knapp, W., Stadler, M. A., & Krüger, T. H. (2004). Neuroendocrine response to casino gambling in problem gamblers. *Psychoneuroendocrinology, 29*(10), 1272–1280.

Miller, E. (2006). Bots, cheating and online poker. *Noted Poker Authority*. Retrieved from www.notedpokerauthority.com/articles/bots-cheating-and-online-poker.html

Nguyen, T., & Davis, A. (2011). *The poker blueprint: Advanced strategies for crushing micro and small stakes NL*. Garden Grove, CA: DailyVariance Publishing.

Nomura Equity Research (2013, January 30). Australia Gaming and Leisure. Research analysts: Nick Berry, Emma Goodsell, Darina Farahbakhsh.

Ohtsuka, K., & Ohtsuka, T. (2010). Vietnamese Australian gamblers' views on luck and winning: Universal versus culture-specific schemas. *Asian Journal of Gambling Issues and Public Health, 1*(1), 34–46.

Owens, J. (2014, February 24). PokerStars hires W and targets arts in effort to widen appeal in UK. *PR Week*. Retrieved from www.prweek.com/article/1282157/pokerstars-hires-w-targets-arts-effort-widen-appeal-uk

Petticrew, M., Katikireddi, S. V., Knai, C., Cassidy, R., Hessari, N. M., Thomas, J., & Weishaar, H. (2017). 'Nothing can be done until everything is done': The use of complexity arguments by food, beverage, alcohol and gambling industries. *J Epidemiol Community Health, 71*(11), 1078–1083.

poker5videos (2013). Small Stakes Poker Strategy NL2 – Session 01. Youtube.com. April 21, 2013. Retrieved from www.youtube.com/watch?v=qeUGEHTIv8k

Raymen, T., & Smith, O. (2017). Lifestyle gambling, indebtedness and anxiety: A deviant leisure perspective. *Journal of Consumer Culture*. doi:10.1177/1469540517736559

Reckwitz, A. (2002). Toward a theory of social practices: A development in culturalist theorizing. *European Journal of Social Theory, 5*(2), 243–263.

Reith, G. (1999). *The age of chance: Gambling in Western culture*. London: Routledge.

Reith, G. (2007). Gambling and the contradictions of consumption. *American Behavioral Scientist, 51*(1), 33–55.

Renee (2011, June 2). What's left of US online poker after Black Friday and Black Tuesday. *Tight Poker*. Retrieved from www.tightpoker.com/news/what%E2%80%99s-left-of-us-online-poker-after-black-friday-and-black-tuesday-2592

Reuters (2014, March 11). Online casino RoyalPanda.com marks launch with Win-a-Space-Trip promotion. *Reuters*. Retrieved from www.reuters.com/article/2014/03/11/royal-panda-idUSnBw106436a+100+BSW20140311

Ricketts, T., & Macaskill, A. (2004). Differentiating normal and problem gambling: A grounded theory approach. *Addiction Research and Theory, 12*, 77–87.

Ritzer, G., & Jurgenson, N. (2010). Production, consumption, prosumption: The nature of capitalism in the age of the digital 'prosumer'. *Journal of Consumer Culture, 10*(3), 13–36.

Schüll, N. D. (2012). *Addiction by design: Machine gambling in Las Vegas*. Princeton: Princeton University Press.

Scull, S., & Woolcock, G. (2005). Problem gambling in non-English speaking background communities in Queensland, Australia: A qualitative exploration. *International Gambling Studies, 5*(1), 29–44.

Street, Z. (2013, December 2). Who will bring physical goods to mobile games? *Games Brief*. Retrieved from www.gamesbrief.com/2013/12/who-will-bring-physical-goods-to-mobile-games/

Stutz, H. (2012, May 28). Gaming companies place bets on social gaming sites. *Las Vegas Review-Journal*. Retrieved from www.lvrj.com/business/gaming-companies-place-bets-on-social-gaming-sites-154984755.html

Stutz, H. (2013, November 2). Nevadan at work: Veteran game designer is always creating. *Las Vegas Review-Journal*. Retrieved from www.reviewjournal.com/business/casinos-gaming/nevadan-work-veteran-game-designer-always-creating

Tanasornnarong, N., Jackson, A., & Thomas, S. (2004). Gambling among young Thai people in Melbourne, Australia: An exploratory study. *International Gambling Studies, 4*(2), 189–203.

Terranova, T. (2000). Free labor: Producing culture for the digital economy. *Social Text, 18*(2), 33–58.

Toffler, A. (1980). *The third wave: The classic study of tomorrow*. New York: Bantam.

Volberg, R. A. (2001). *When the chips are down: Problem gambling in America*. New York: Century Foundation Press.

Watts, J. M. (2013, December 3). Singapore looks to restrict online gambling. *The Wall Street Journal*. Retrieved from http://blogs.wsj.com/searealtime/2013/12/03/singapore-looks-to-restrict-online-gambling/

Webster, J. G. (2010). User information regimes: How social media shape patterns of consumption. *Northwestern University Law Review, 104*(2), 593–612.

Willingham, R. (2013, January 13). Fear that gaming apps will groom young gamblers. *The Sydney Morning Herald*. Retrieved from www.smh.com.au/digital-life/smartphone-apps/fear-that-gaming-apps-will-groom-young-gamblers-20130112-2cmre.html#ixzz2QVhYU1ns

Wulfert, E., Roland, B. D., Hartley, J., Wang, N., & Franco, C. (2005). Heart rate arousal and excitement in gambling: Winners versus losers. *Psychology of Addictive Behaviors, 19*(3), 311.

Zurcher, K. (1970). The "friendly" poker game: A study of an ephemeral role. *Social Forces, 49*(2), 173–186.

Zwick, D., Bonsu, S. K., & Darmody, A. (2008). Putting consumers to work: Co-creation and new marketing govern-mentality. *Journal of Consumer Culture, 8*(2), 163–196.

Digital Games Cited

Cassava Enterprises. (n.d). 888poker (Android version) [Mobile application software]. Retrieved from http://au.888.com/

DoubleDown Interactive (2010). Double Down Casino (Facebook version) [Mobile application software]. Retrieved from www.facebook.com/doubledowncasino

Playstudios (2016). *MyVegas*. Retrieved December 2017 from www.facebook.com/myvegas

Rational Entertainment Enterprises Limited (2014). PokerStars.com. *pokerstars.com*. Retrieved September 2014 from www.pokerstars.com/

Rovio Entertainment (2010). *Angry Birds*. Apple Store.

Zynga (2009). *Farmville*. Apple Store.

Zynga (2012). *BamPoker*. Retrieved December 2017 from https://apps.facebook.com/bampoker/

Part II
Gamble-Play Platforms

4 Gamble-Play and Popular Culture

When Slots Meet Hollywood

This chapter addresses one of the most culturally prominent forms of digital gambling: slot machines. Slot machines, which are part of the vast Electronic Gaming Machine (EGM) market sector, are gamble-play media because they digitally stage the process of risk-taking through complex gamelike interfaces. Slot machines are highly influential gambling media, as they establish procedures and cultural conventions that have been taken up by other gamble-play platforms, such as social casino apps. In this chapter, I argue that contemporary slot machines establish intense and intensive connections with users by appealing to their cultural sensitivity. I focus on how slot machine manufacturers use the popular culture strategies of exotica and kitsch, as well as Hollywood branding and storytelling techniques, to engage players. Slot machine designers also use other rhetorical tricks, such as the use of cute animals and objects, to engage players emotionally (Albarrán-Torres, 2016, p. 235).

Mechanical Gaming Machines (MGM) were first originated in San Francisco, United States, during the Gold Rush era of 1848–1855 and amid the expansion of traditional poker from the depths of the Mississippi River to the vastness of the West (Devol, 1887), across the Nevada desert and into the Pacific coastal towns (Findlay, 1986; Lears, 2003; Mazur, 2010). The origin of slot machines is located in an epoch associated with new beginnings and the foundational years of a nation, the United States, as well as the capitalist world view. It was also in this period that photography first and cinema later inaugurated new mediated ways of experiencing the world. Slowly but surely, gambling technologies adopted the affordances of these new entertainment technologies, culminating in the complex multimedia devices that we find in casinos today. Casinos are the pinnacle of capitalist entertainment (Christensen & Brinkerhoff-Jacobs, 2007).

Slot machines were introduced into the leisure market in 1887 as New Nickel Machines. To define winners and losers, randomness was then achieved mechanically through the spinning of reels and the arbitrary pairing of winning combinations. Today, by contrast, randomness is simulated through an algorithmic Random Number Generator (RNG). Just as contemporary slot machines provide multimedia experiences that go beyond mere gambling, their earliest predecessors offered perks that accompanied the consumption of bets. Griffiths (1993) points out in regard to early fruit machines,

> As early as 1902, some machines were designed to double up as a musical box, the thinking being that the person had to play the fruit machine to hear the music. Another marketing ploy which began to appear by the 1930's was the built-in vending machine. After playing the machine, players would receive items such as mints, bubble gum or candy.
>
> (Griffiths, 1993, p. 105)

Contemporary slot machines stage real-money gambling in interfaces that are technically and discursively complex, and that emphasise the playful aspects of wagering. Contrary to other gamble-play media, such as casino apps and online poker sites, slot machines do not invite user co-presence in the digital environment nor in-game socialisation. They promote a deep and sustained human-machine engagement. Most contemporary slot machines are designed with particular themes that connect with cultural meanings emanating from historical and aesthetic traditions, such as kitsch and exotica, or from other media assemblages, such as film, popular music and television.

On an operational level, however, slots are anything but simple as they are connected in an intricate network of machines that calculate winnings for the house. Schüll terms the configuration of play and risk in these machines "addiction by design" (2012). She stresses the fact that the structural characteristics and presentation of slots are conceived to promote compulsive play. The slot machine industry is commonly perceived as highly rationalised and predatory, and most academic research on these forms of gambling is dedicated to cases of problem gambling.

Slots are desiring-machines (Deleuze & Guattari, 2004a) and cross-platform media where digital gambling and video game conventions and procedures intersect, and where discourses of exotica and Hollywood narratives are enacted. Slots and gamblers form couplings that generate intimate assemblages that I call gambling-machines. These assemblages are fuelled by passion and composed of desire (Deleuze & Guattari, 2004a). Building on the concept of the procedure-image, I also argue that slots or 'pokies' share aesthetic and procedural similarities with digital games and that the gameplay's objective is not always merely to win money but to fulfil a desire to accomplish missions and embark on adventures (some echoing Hollywood storylines, like the TV show *The Walking Dead* and the *Star Wars* franchise).

The aesthetic and narrative components of poker machines are rarely studied. Fiona Nicoll (2014) is a pioneer in this field. In a paper that explores the representation of Native American peoples in slot machine design, she argues that

> To design and gamble on EGMs is very literally to play with cultural meanings. The development of EGM iconography and soundscapes over the past two decades has been exponential; in less than a generation EGM design has transformed from offering a basic digital representation of playing cards on what looked like small television screens to sophisticated haptic devices which employ state-of-the-art animations and literally vibrate when particular combinations of 'reels' occur.
>
> (Nicoll, 2014, p. 835)

Slot machines are more culturally significant than often acknowledged. EGMs are referred to in popular and academic literature in a variety of ways that reveal the conflicting nature of their consumption. For instance, the Japanese variety is called *pachislot*, a word that derives from the combination of *slot* and *pachinko*, a traditional Japanese game. *Pachislot* devices in Japan are similar to slot machines but have distinctive manga – and anime – inspired images as opposed to Hollywood branding. Most importantly, however, they require a degree of skill, much like the new and highly controversial skill-based slots (Toscano, 2017a):

> Pachislot is a fancier version of the classic slot machine. As with the one-armed bandit, the game starts when you pull a lever, but in Japan's version, you press buttons to stop the reels, adding an element of skill.
>
> (Iwatani Kane, 2005)

Even though gambling is illegal in Japan, *pachislot* is considered entertainment rather than gambling due to loopholes in legislation (Takiguchi & Rosenthal, 2011). In Spain and Latin America, slots are accusatorily referred to as *máquinas tragamonedas* or *máquinas tragaperras,* which translates as 'coin-eating machines' and 'peseta-eating machines'. In the United States. they have been baptised as 'fruit machines' and, most tellingly, as 'one-armed bandits', a pristine Wild West image. In Australia and New Zealand, slots are known colloquially as 'pokies'. I alternate between 'slot machines' and 'pokies', using the latter when referring specifically to the Australian or New Zealand context.

The affectionate terms indicate a playful relationship between players and the machines. We can deduce the presence of a flow, of human-machine negotiations in which machines are 'fed' with coins and machine bandits get consumers' money. Gamblers need to poke the machine to get its attention. Gamble-play in slot machines is an experience that engages users on a deep level, making them inhabit the moment of perpetual expectancy. Charles Livingstone describes slots as machines with which users develop attachments that are emotional and even irrational. The connection is deep, and users assign human qualities to gambling machines:

> In the long run, this stream of indeterminacy is determined, but the EGM gambler is concentrated in the immediate, and in the immediate moment of pushing the button indeterminacy, as it were, rules. No wonder the EGM is often misrecognised as a human subject, its reason viewed as capable of emotional influence, susceptible to belly-rubs, endearments, and deception.
>
> (Livingstone, 2005, pp. 529–530)

Slot machines have a particular cultural significance in Australia, perhaps more so than in any other country. Pokies were introduced in Australia in the early twentieth century. These devices were illegally imported and made available to New South Wales clubs in the 1930s (Lynch, 1990, p. 194). Caldwell (1972) argues, however, that their introduction could date back as far as the 1890s. Since their subsequent legalisation in 1956 (Con Walker, 2009), pokies have been both a cornerstone of the Australian leisure industry and, due to numerous cases of problem gambling, mainly among the working class (Breen et al., 2002), the focus of one of the most hotly contested policy issues in regard to consumption ethics. In other markets, such as the United Kingdom, slot machines have been linked to crime, with news reports placing them, for example, as the site of money laundering by drug dealers (Ramesh, 2013).

As technological artefacts, current slots are positioned at the centre of the mechanical/algorithmic spectrum. They require the physical action of the gambler and preserve the 'aura' (Benjamin, 2008) and cultural and aesthetic conventions of their earliest fruit machine versions, but they perform algorithmic operations to simulate randomness and establish the possibilities of winning. If we were to draw a timeline of the material development of gambling artefacts and devices, slot machines would sit at the middle of this spectrum. Slots are a connection between the mechanical past and the digital networked future in the material and historical trajectory of gambling cultures. As Richard Woolley and Charles Livingstone, two leading Australian scholars on pokie machine culture, wittily point out,

> These devices are a long way from the mechanical pokies they nostalgically invoke via their often quaint, folksy design. They are carefully constructed hybrids of sophisticated technology within a *présentement* of folksy familiarity – like a 1960s Volkswagen equipped with a Ferrari motor.
>
> (Woolley & Livingstone, 2010, p. 46)

This contradiction, being innovative and traditional at once, allows slot machine manufacturers and service providers to engage consumers by mobilising particular sociocultural discursive flows. These include, for instance, Hollywood franchises, the postcolonial ethos and Australian nationalism associated with the pioneering drive of the early mining industry. Manufacturers do this while keeping up with the latest technological developments, which guarantees fun for gamblers and an advantageous situation for operators.

The gamblers sitting in front of slot machines, perpetually chasing the coveted big win, are subject to forms of calculated "free-floating control" (Deleuze, 1992). The acquisition of bets in slots also connects with Baudrillard's theorisation of contemporary consumption as "the maximization of existence by the multiplication of contacts and relations, by the intensive use of signs and objects, and by the systematic exploitation of all the possibilities of pleasure" (Baudrillard, 1998, p. 48). In playing slots, gamblers engage with signs and objects intensively and, to the understanding of some gamblers who have the illusion of control over the machine, systematically.

The use of rhetorical strategies, such as the use of recognisable Hollywood franchises, in slot machine design and gameplay intensifies this engagement as signs and objects become familiar. Industry insiders have recognised that a player is more likely to play a branded machine because of familiarity with characters, fictional worlds and narrative plots (Gardner & Sun, 2017). As Parke and Griffiths argue in relation to *The Simpsons* themed slot machines,

> with an international quality brand such as *The Simpsons*, a player might think that they are unlikely to lose a lot of money. They might also think the jackpots are likely to be generous.
>
> (2006, p. 168)

In other words, in playing a *The Simpsons* slot machine, the affiliation that gamblers may have with the archetypical suburban American cartoon household and the archetypical American town (Springfield) makes gambling seem less harmful or potentially dangerous. By branding a slot machine with a show as popular as *The Simpsons*, which has had a continuous run of more than two decades, the global success of the slot machine is all but guaranteed. Anyone stumbling upon Homer's or Bart's iconic voices on a casino floor could feel that they are right in their living room. Through cross-industry branding, gambling is symbolically transported to the player's domestic space. Like gambling machines, *The Simpsons* is a cultural product that involves childlike play but can be read through an adult sensitivity (Figure 4.1).

Figure 4.1 The Simpsons slot machine video by Neily 777, JACKPOT HAND-
        PAY on THE SIMPSONS! Lots of slot machine bonuses and BIG
        WINS!, uploaded on July 26, 2017, accessed on November 15, 2017
        at www.youtube.com/watch?v=7NFNzCwz9Cs.

Contemporary slot machines have built-in structural characteristics
that encourage continuous play and increasing desire. Two of these characteristics are the systematic provision of 'near misses' when the gambler is just about to win (Billieux et al., 2012) and 'big wins' when the
user gets a considerable reward, which strengthen the idea that winning
to compensate for past losses is possible (Kassinove & Schare, 2001;
Weatherly et al., 2004). The idea that winning is possible is also emphasised through aural elements – enthusiastic and intense sound effects –
which "give the impression that winning is more common than losing"
(Griffiths, 1993, p. 112; see also Cummings, 2012).

How is desire automated? What do slot machines communicate? How
do EGMs allow the entering and exiting of flows in and out of structures?
Conceptualising the relationship between gamblers and EGMs as a
sociotechnical assemblage, the 'gambling-machine', shines some light on
these questions.

The Gambling-Machine: Slots and Gamblers as
Desiring-Machines

Slot machine markets can be conceptualised as what Deleuze and
Guattari call an assemblage of "desiring-machines" or *machines dé-
sirantes*. In *Anti-Oedipus* (2004a), the first volume of *Capitalism and
Schizophrenia*, Deleuze and Guattari lay out a challenging philosophical

idea that questions past notions of the relationships between humans and technology, and the ways in which these interlock and form chains of relationships, which they call assemblages or "compositions of desire". Bogard (2009) provides a useful interpretation of the Deleuzo-Guattarian assemblage, which is similar to the notion of assemblage that, based on DeLanda (2006), I use to analyse digital gamble-play markets. Bogard argues that an assemblage is

> a multiplicity which is made up of many heterogeneous terms and which establishes liaisons, relations between them, across ages, sexes and reigns – different natures. Thus, the assemblage's only unity is that of co-functioning: it is symbiosis, a 'sympathy'. It is never filiations which are important, but alliances, alloys; these are not successions, lines of descent, but contagions, epidemics, the wind' (Deleuze and Parnet 1987: 69). Assemblages can be anything from chemical bonds to cultural patterns. Assemblages in their machinic form, above all, are 'compositions of desire'.
>
> (Bogard, 2009, p. 30)

Assemblages in the Deleuzo-Guattarian imaginary are collections of organic and non-organic elements, of biological and technical machines that exist for the sake of connecting. Procedure-images in gamble-play media are one of these elements as they exist for the sake of interaction (with the user) and connection (with other images). A machine, in turn, can be considered an assemblage composed of smaller components and systems. In Deleuzo-Guattarian thought, a "machine" is "nothing more than its connections" (Colebrook, 2002, p. 56). A machine is symbiosis composed by desire. It is this desire to connect that defines the existence of the desiring-machine. Colebrook concludes that for Deleuze, "A machinic becoming makes a connection with what is not itself in order to transform and maximise itself" (2002, p. 57).

It is this desire for (incorporeal) transformation and maximisation that drives gamblers to form couplings with EGMs. Furthermore, this transformation is related to social class and the insertion in particular historical trajectories, such as the Australian myth of the Lucky Country or the sense of entitlement of the dominant postcolonial identity (Blunt & McEwan, 2002). The gambler connects to slot machines, as desiring-machines, to become something or someone different, and it is in this process of repetition (gambling) that they are also constructed as a subject. Medical literature has constructed the figures of the problem gambler and the pathological gambler based on the intensity of the gambler's desire and its subsequent search for fulfilment.

Deleuze and Guattari also define a machine as a "system of *interruptions* or breaks (*coupures*)" as every machine "is related to a continual material flow (*hylè*) that it cuts into" (Deleuze & Guattari, 2004b,

p. 38). If we extrapolate this notion to the study of digital gambling, we can theorise that both gamblers and slot machines transgress diverse flows through their coupling. Deleuze and Guattari also state that a machine "functions like a ham-slicing machine, removing portions from the associative flow" (2004b, p. 39). In gambling assemblages, this slicing through is defined by the cultural and procedural codes shared by the gambler and the slot machine. The slot machine cuts into the flow of the gambler's everyday experience and alters the position of the gambler in other assemblages – the household, the workplace, the financial system – as witnessed by Schüll in her ethnographic work in Las Vegas (2012). Slot machines also slice into communities and into the flow of aesthetic discourses, such as kitsch and exotica, which define the identities contained within these communities.

It is important to note that Deleuze and Guattari do not subscribe to the general notion of the "machine" as a technological artefact but consider all organic and non-organic entities to be part of mechanisms that, in turn, can be formed by smaller "machines", such as, for instance, the human organs. Humans are desiring-machines just as the artefacts – cars, computers, spoons, pencils – with which we form couplings are desiring-machines. For Deleuze and Guattari, everything, everywhere, is a machine. In this cosmology, nature is a collection of machines that have the sole purpose of producing for production's sake. The world itself is a "continual whirr of machines" (Deleuze & Guattari, 2004a, p. 2) that is never appeased.

This approach is philosophically challenging in that, like actor-network theory's attitude towards nonhumans (Cerulo, 2009), assemblages position humans and machines, as well as their organic and mechanic components, on the same ontological level (DeLanda, 2006). Therefore, assemblage theory calls for an understanding of couplings, of how desiring-machines interlock with other desiring-machines, as well as the social and cultural conditions in which these couplings occur. Communication is triggered by this succession of machines slicing through flows.

When a gambler and a slot machine interlock, something – a sociopolitical discourse, a monetary transaction, an aesthetic or bodily experience – is produced. Communication is shaped between the gambler and the flows (*hylè*) synthesised by the slot machine. When a gambler activates a slot machine, the human body functions as a desiring-machine that excretes stress hormones and sweat, and activates the slot-desiring-machine by 'poking' it, moving it to produce a random result. This coupling generates discursive, financial and aesthetic flows that are to be invoked, allowing simultaneous and collective couplings to happen.

In a gaming session, the gambler as a desiring-machine also becomes a body without organs, "*le corps disperse*" (Deleuze & Guattari, 2004a; Sasso & Villani, 2002, p. 244), experiencing a fluidity that intersects with other fluidities. Cook (2009) analysed internet gaming addiction through Deleuze and Guattari's notion of the body without organs, and concluded that this practice allowed gamers to extend their existence beyond the boundaries of their skin. Through an array of other machines (chair, desk, keyboard, joystick, controller) the player enters another world (a gaming-space) and establishes organism-configurations that they strive to come back to over and over again so they can experience the "limitlessness and intensity associated with becoming" (Cook, 2009, p. 196).

In his film *eXistenZ* (1999), Canadian filmmaker David Cronenberg provides a visual metaphor for such a coupling. The main characters immerse themselves in a gaming-space by literally connecting their machine-bodies to controller-bodies that have organic and non-organic components. This coupling provides them with the "limitlessness and intensity associated with becoming" (Cook, 2009, p. 196); through physical dispersion they acquire existential unity. The metaphor so vividly constructed in *eXistenZ* is also pertinent as a cinematic representation of the slot-desiring-machine and gambler-desiring-machine coupling, which I will from here onwards call 'gambling-machine'. The gambling-machine presumably allows the gambler (albeit, somewhat self-deceitfully) to become, to maximise themselves.

Roger Caillois's categorisation of ludic practices, which has been constantly referenced by video game theorists (Aarseth, 1997) and gambling researchers (Reith, 1999), is also useful for analysing gambling-machines. Two of his categories of play are particularly important in the analysis of pokies as desiring-machines: *alea* and *agôn*. *Alea* refers to games where chance defines the outcome. *Agôn* refers to practices that involve competition, skill and conflict.

During gambling sessions, there is often a negotiation between *alea* and *agôn*. These negotiations define both gameplay and discourse about gambling. Discussions about skill and chance in gambling are often related to the issue of problematic consumption. For example, anti-gambling advocacy groups are critical of mechanisms that lead gamblers to believe that skill is involved in slot machine outcomes. Slot machines "produce meaning" (Montfort & Bogost, 2009, p. 1) by triggering what Mazur calls "the gambler's illusion" (2009), the idea that consistent gambling will eventually lead to a 'big win'.

Through the 'fun' engagement with slot machines, gamblers experiment with a momentary change in how they perceive money. In a machine gambling session, money acquires a new dimension. Money is one of the main preoccupations in most gamblers' lives, but during their coupling with the gambling-machine, it acquires a ludic and procedural quality that eclipses its economic value. For example, Gabriela Byrne, an Australian gambler, narrates her experience in the parliamentary report *The Design and Implementation of a Mandatory Pre-Commitment System for Electronic Gaming Machines* (2011). She equates her pokie consumption to a split personality, referencing Robert Louis Stevenson's archetypical literary creature:

> I often compare it to the Jekyll and Hyde syndrome. I was still a responsible mother, wife, work colleague and friend when I was not gambling. The minute the urge hit me I switched and I became a person that had no values and no responsibilities and all I wanted was to feed the beast. In the time that I was a responsible mother, work colleague and friend, and whatever goes with that, I was able to make rational decisions and I looked for help. I was desperate for some kind of measure that would stop me from continuing the destructive behaviour.
>
> (*Proof Committee Hansard*, February 2, 2011, p. 17)

There are a variety of reasons that allow this transformation to happen. First, as in arcade games, money becomes a procedure-image that could potentially lose its economic value – at least momentarily – in the eyes of the gambler. Currency becomes a token, a gaming device. Recreational gamblers do not play *for* money: they play *with* money. During the human-machine coupling, losses are perceived as the price one has to pay to have a good time, to experience a relatively safe situation of risk epitomised in gamble-play. Baudrillard phrases the status of currency in gambling eloquently, concluding that in gambling, money is "no longer a sign or representation once transformed into a stake", and that "a stake is not something one invests" but "something which is presented as a challenge to chance" (1990, p. 139).

But what is the deep meaning that is attained by playing the slots? It is the pursuit of financial bonanza and class mobility though the fulfilment of missions, which could provide the individual with a new identity, a new life, a fresh start. Slots promise such incorporeal transformations (Deleuze & Guattari, 2004b, p. 89). That said, in EGM playing, money equals a stake, the token that is necessary to challenge chance.

As some (see Mazur, 2010; also Lears, 2003) have stated, this "challenge to chance" is embedded in social groups in which gambling has become one of the main drivers of the economy and one of the hubs for social interaction. Contrary to the limited and generally small amounts – as per the cost/gaming hours ratio – that video game and arcade game enthusiasts invest in their distraction, the amount of money a gambler can invest in playing the slots is unlimited in the long term and could represent a good portion of the player's income over time. The procedure-images are displayed in the same way (duration, design, brightness and so forth) regardless of who is sitting in front of the slot machine. EGMs do not discriminate. Most poker machines interact with a faceless, average gambler: they do not adapt to their interlocutor. This assertion might seem obvious, but it describes the asymmetrical nature of the interaction, of the communicative act that occurs in gambling-machine assemblages. This unequal relationship is made more prominent by the fact that the most sophisticated machines use loyalty cards to identify users, track their consumption patterns and sometimes respond in real time to a gambler's particular desires.

Exotica, Desire and the Australian Pokie Market

In both material and expressive terms (DeLanda, 2006) slot machines have undergone a dramatic change through the recent and increasingly complex digitisation of their procedures and the sophistication of their interfaces. They have morphed

> from simple stand-alone 'machines' to complex communicative and calculative 'devices' that are usually configured as nodes within a network.
>
> (Woolley & Livingstone, 2010, p. 45)

In gambling-prone countries like Australia, slot machines establish communication between the subject and institutional structures – the state, class divisions, the financial system – between humans and artificial intelligence agents and among gamblers as devices are generally installed in hubs for social interaction including pubs, clubs and casinos.

The mechanical or analogue gambling machine was first deterritorialised or uprooted from analogue environments and then, after its metamorphosis from a mechanical to a digital artefact, reterritorialised in diverse media landscapes of an increasingly digital and screen-based nature. Once reterritorialised, pokies fulfil the destiny of the Deleuzo-Guattarian machine: to be the place "where flows enter or leave structures" (Bogost, 2006, p. 143). Cultural, social, ideological and economic flows enter and leave the structures (social, cultural and financial) where pokies work as a *liaison* among other assemblages and humans, as the baby's mouth-machine that attaches itself to the mother's breast-machine in the Deleuzo and Guattarian metaphor (2004a).

This network or intricate mass of assembled desire works with algorithms that calculate wins and losses for the house, and establishes both short-term relationships – casual gambling – and long-term relationships – compulsive gambling – with punters. As Woolley states, a gambler "in the gaming room of clubs and hotels in Australia participates in a consumption market that is instituted through a systematic deployment of applications of science and technology throughout social space" (Woolley, 2007). These deployments of applications of science and technology are primarily built on desire, and this desire is made visible through designs that appeal to exotica and pre-existing cultural affiliations, such as film fandom.

For Deleuze and Guattari, this desire does not involve "natural or spontaneous determination" as there "is no desire but assembling, assembled desire" (Deleuze & Guattari, 1987, p. 399; as cited in Bogost, 2006, p. 143). In the case of pokie consumption, play is a ritual designed to urge constant engagement in search of transformation.

Since the 1980s, technological developments in slot machines have had deep repercussions in gambling markets. There is an added efficiency in their operation that leads to intensive and repetitive consumption. Their transformation from a "series of tumbling mechanical wheels" into a "communicative and calculative device" (Woolley & Livingstone, 2010, p. 59) that is available almost anywhere in places such as the Australian state of New South Wales, has reshaped their nature as a commodity. The conditions of their consumption are defined by the intensity of their couplings with the most avid gamblers, many of whom in Australia belong to vulnerable socio-economic sectors (Markham & Young, 2014).

Slot machine consumption in Australia is a political issue. The flows modulated by the gambler-pokie coupling and perpetuated through repetition are related to historical trajectories associated with the shaping of the Australian class system, the dominant postcolonial gaze and class mobility. Markham and Young (2014) argue that "Big Gambling" in Australia – pokie machines, horse race betting and now online and digital wagering – is an "ongoing class project" that "has transferred, with industrial efficiency, billions of dollars from the pay packets of the working classes to the bank accounts of a super-rich elite" (Markham & Young, 2014). They argue, additionally, that in Australia gambling is part of how individuals define themselves as consumers as wagering is inserted into everyday spaces and consumption practices. Critics have identified similar dynamics in countries such as the neighbouring New Zealand (Deane, 2013).

As desiring-machines pokies are communicative devices on two levels. On the surface, through their interactive audiovisual configurations – colours, sounds, themes, characters, gameplay – they stimulate the desire to win, have untamed fun, conquer the Other and to master destiny. Their "quaint, folksy design" (Woolley & Livingstone, 2010, p. 46) allows for swifter processes of reterritorialisation (DeLanda, 2006) as gamblers identify their own notions of entitlement, hope and aspiration in the fantastic universes displayed on pokie screens populated by procedure-images. On a second level, through the patterns of their consumption measured and anticipated by industry calculation (Schüll, 2012), they are situated within discourses of labour, class, money, luck and hope (Lynch, 1990).

I will now discuss the materiality and expressiveness of pokies in a particular market: New South Wales (NSW). NSW has an expanding gambling sector in the high-end tourism sector and extensive use of EGMs in everyday spaces including pubs and clubs. In 2009, there were almost

100,000 EGMs operating in NSW alone, out of a total of 197,820 in Australia (Parliamentary Joint Select Committee on Gambling Reform, 2011). By 2014, a report by the Gaming Technologies Association claimed that NSW held second place among the most gambling-machine packed jurisdictions in the world, second only to Nevada in the United States (Safi, 2013; Ziolkowski, 2017). In 2016, it held the 10th place with over 94,000 machines (Ziolkowski, 2017). What makes NSW different from a place like Nevada, though, is that the majority of consumers gamble in venues that are near their home or work, contrary to the US state, where the hubs of Las Vegas and Reno mostly attract a floating population of tourists.

Aristocrat Leisure Limited, an Australian company that sells EGMs primarily to the Australian, North American and Japanese markets, manufactures many of these devices. The company has reported a constant exponential growth since the early 2000s (Aristocrat Leisure Limited, 2011) and is one of Australia's most successful companies as it has a national and international captive market. Aristocrat is currently part of the convergence between the gambling and social casino industries. As previously mentioned, it bought a company called Product Madness in 2013, hoping to compete with the likes of social games developer Zynga (Kelly, 2013).

In NSW, clubs – a traditional Australian community institution – are organised around gambling as there are "no restrictions on the percentage of floor space that can be devoted to gambling (as opposed to catering or other recreational activities)" (Con Walker, 2009, p. 1). This reveals the emphasis that club owners give to the consumption of bets. In NSW, EGMs are not exclusive to casinos and large clubs, or to cities. In urban and rural environments, their presence is as ubiquitous as that of hotels and pubs as the majority of these establishments offer the possibility of gambling in their VIP lounges. Gambling revenue in the state will possibly increase with the opening of the new Crown Casino in Sydney, which hopes to attract overseas and local gamblers.

The Adventure of the Pokies: Just Like a Hollywood Movie

In casinos, clubs and VIP lounges avid gamblers embark on a sort of adventure, in what Simmel calls a voluntary "dropping out of the continuity of life" (1971, p. 187; cited in Reith, 1999, p. 126). Slot machines become a respite from the everyday. Lears (2003) recalls extreme cases of such "dropping out" in the North American context:

> In Niagara Falls, casino operators complain that slot machine players are urinating into the plastic coin cups supplied by the casino or onto the floor beside the machines. Some wear adult diapers. All

are reluctant to leave a machine they are hoping will soon pay off. And in Louisiana, video poker players report trancelike out-of-body experiences, the feeling of "being sucked into oblivion."

(Lears, 2003, p. 1)

Extreme cases such as these are the imagined scenarios that frame the discussion around EGM markets and consumption ethics. The frantic, narcotised state that some players seem to experience serves as a motivation for regulatory schemes and anti-gambling efforts. Policy discussions focus on the notion that EGMs are primarily sites where material goods are being exchanged – where people lose money consistently. There are, however, other aspects of EGM consumption that so far have been overlooked and that relate to the expressive capacities of slot machines. The use of exotica and Hollywood branding in the design of slot machine cabinets, as well as gameplay, is key in strengthening these expressive capacities.

In many pokie venues in NSW one encounters machines whose imagery resembles that of action-based digital games and Hollywood high-concept cinema. Punters engage in games in which missions need to be accomplished, adventures await and impossibly buff male characters, such as the comic book character *The Phantom*, fight side by side with anatomically generous female companions, such as the voluptuous protagonist of *Gypsy Moon*. Gamblers press buttons time and time again, courting their luck through repetitive actions, waiting for a thrilling experience. A jackpot will be announced by over-the-top animations and sounds, turning them into winners.

At first glance, the images and fictional environments that the visitor encounters on slot machines screens are not that different to what one would find in a video game store or a game arcade. The user is engaged, however, in what psychological studies have termed "continuous forms of gambling" (O'Connor & Dickerson, 2003), in which players establish an ongoing engagement with machines on short sessions or over many sessions in a prolonged period of time.

Most of the designs displayed on slots in NSW have an expressive particularity, which highlights the importance of graphic design in the coupling of gamblers and machines. Their design shows exotic landscapes that reveal cultures or natural environments foreign to what is generally considered as 'Australian' or 'Western'. There are exceptions, of course, some of which are described in this chapter. The nature of the images that embellish poker machines adds a layer of complexity to the analysis of both the procedures enacted in the interfaces and of the actual poker machine device – its physicality, graphics and interaction design.

Faux Chinese (Aristocrat's *Imperial House*, for instance) and aboriginal lore (*Big Red*), Gold Rush scenarios (*Where's the... GOLD*), exotic deserts, untamed African jungles and Arctic landscapes lie side by side in gambling venues. A postcolonial perspective informs these expressive particularities of pokie machine interfaces and design. When I talk about post-colonialism, I ascribe to the definition offered by Bhabha et al.:

> 'Post-colonial' as we define it does not mean 'post-independence,' or 'after colonialism,' for this would be to falsely ascribe an end to the colonial process. Post-colonialism, rather, begins from the very first moment of colonial contact. It is the discourse of oppositionality which colonialism brings into being.
>
> (Bhabha et al., 1995, p. 117)

This "discourse of oppositionality" (Bhabha et al., 1995, p. 117) sprouts from past and current historical trajectories in Australia and other markets, such as the United States, where many slot machines have been designed using a Native American theme (Nicoll, 2014). EGM design relies heavily on 'exotica', the discursive practice of making other cultures seem strange and uncanny, a curiosity, and sometimes an obscure object of desire. The *Tintin* comic book series, created by the Belgian artist Hergé and later adapted into a digital animation by Steven Spielberg and Peter Jackson, is an example of exotica. *Tintin* expresses a European-centred view of other continents and peoples. It has recently been deemed as a somewhat crude, uninformed view of the cultures that Europeans encountered during and after the processes of colonisation (Hunt, 2002; Matheson, 1996). The Hollywood genres of the Western and sci-fi cinema, heavily used in slot machine branding, traditionally mirror this "discourse of oppositionality" (Bhabha et al., 1995, p. 117), sometimes in a simplistic way.

The design of some slot machines follows this trend. As Nicoll contends,

> the iconography of some of the most popular poker machines implicitly references unresolved sovereignty struggles in nations built on white settler-colonisation.
>
> (Nicoll, 2008, p. 115)

Exotic slot machine design also brings to mind the simplistic 'good-conquers-evil' and 'civilisation-conquers-the-barbarian' plots of Hollywood mainstream cinema and television. This iconography is made culturally familiar through its association with the narratives of well-known action movies and video games, such as the *Indiana Jones* and *Tomb Raider* franchises, or cultural icons, such as John Wayne, all of which have been used to brand gambling machines.

EGMs intersect with the gambler's own sense of identity and assimilated historical trajectories. Exotic pokie design stimulates play by providing a familiar representation of the unfamiliar. A 2002 study that attempted to detect the main demographic patterns of poker machine players in New South Wales' largest metropolitan area, Sydney, concluded that

The most important results indicate that the best predictors of per capita poker machine expenditure in Sydney SLGs were high proportions of the resident population who were born in Malta, Greece, Lebanon, China, Italy, Vietnam, Yugoslavia, India or the Philippines; have no vocational or tertiary qualifications; or are unemployed. Also important is that the profile of Sydney populations which spend highly on poker machines broadly supports the lower socio-economic profile identified in previous Australian studies.

(Breen et al., 2002, p. 310)

Apart from the class and ethnic identity of gamblers, other historical factors contribute to this automation of desire. Pokies are also deeply embedded in the Australian fascination with leisure activities. For Con Walker, "gambling, drinking and sport" are "three of the most important forms of recreation in Australian history" (Con Walker, 2009, p. 3). At once deemed a social problem and glorified as a source of national identity and community building, Australia's relationship with gambling can be traced back – like its American counterpart (Findlay, 1986; Lears, 2003; Mazur, 2010) – to the pioneering spirit of the first European settlers, who tamed a foreign and often violent territory that later became the "Lucky Country" (Nicoll, 2008) (Figure 4.2).

Figure 4.2 YouTube video showing *Lucky Strike*, one of Aristocrat's pokie machines. Notice the mining theme, which resonates with Australian nationalism. Accessed November 17, 2017 at www.youtube.com/watch?v=7JZqZBNw3Jw.

Apart from pokies, other significant examples of gambling in Australian culture bring rituals of the exotic and the public together. We can think, for example, of the analogue game of Two-up, which is particularly noteworthy. In Two-up the punter tosses coins on a flat piece of wood and punters bet on the outcomes of each round of five tosses. Two-up is a heritage game associated with a national holiday, ANZAC Day, which commemorates Australia and New Zealand's participation in World War I, particularly the battle of Gallipoli, Turkey. ANZAC Day is a foundational myth, as Slade points out: "For many Australians and New Zealanders, Gallipoli has become the legendary place where their nations were conceived, albeit in a *de facto* sense" (Slade, 2003, p. 782).

Two-up can be legally played during this holiday basically anywhere: pubs, parks, corporate offices, government buildings, universities or domestic spaces. The prevalence of Two-up as a culturally accepted and encouraged form of gambling, even in morally innocent environments such as schools, talks of the significance of wagering and how it externalises myths of Australian-ness, such as mateship and the personal and communal histories of war and mining – arenas in which the game initially flourished.

Symbolically, exotica-themed Australian pokies also represent the conquest of a territory and its peoples. These pokies perpetuate various images of symbolic colonisation as well as discourses of hope. They also recall the taming of Fortuna: the imposition of human will over the uneasiness inspired by the unknown. In the 2011 report written by the Parliamentary Joint Select Committee on Gambling Reform (led by Andrew Wilkie MP), Livingstone briefly acknowledges the "symbolism on the machines":

> We know a machine with particular symbolism in the artwork will be very attractive whereas the same machine with different artwork will be less successful in the market. It is likely that some of the symbolism actually works to provide a greater incentive for people to play the machines.
>
> (Livingstone, *Proof Committee Hansard*, February 2, 2011, p. 34; as cited in *The design and implementation of a mandatory pre-commitment system for electronic gaming machines*, p. 41)

In many of the poker machines in NSW that I have observed, what Livingstone refers to broadly as "symbolism" (2011) are iterations of postcolonial tropes. These postcolonial representations are connected to the sense of a mission to conquer foreign, exotic environments through the pursuit of the big win and economic gain. By postcolonial tropes I mean that audiovisual constructions in pokies typically reference a sense of differentiation from the historical Other, or what Said has alternatively called "Orientalism", and which entails problems in the "representation of other cultures, societies, histories" that lead to "stereotypes" (Said, 1985, p. 1; see also Gruzinksi, 1996). Postcolonial aesthetics exteriorise the conflicts driven by historical colonisation and newfound relationships between peoples, and between humankind and the furtive, untamed natural world – a world of which chance is also part. In Australia, flows of postcolonial discourses and identities influence race, class and cultural relations. For immigrants and ethnic communities, postcolonial imagery in slot machines could also be a reminder or a shady representation of their historical and cultural past.

The procedure-images that seduce players with exotica or Hollywood themes turn poker machines into storytelling devices. Procedure-images add a layer of narrative complexity to the analysis of the discourse rooted in pokie machines: they are images that do not represent interaction but are interaction themselves. How and why procedures are enacted is as important as the procedure itself. The worlds represented on the slot machines, on the graphic design of the hardware, and on the screen interfaces influence the nature of the adventure upon which the gambler/player embarks.

The iconography that adorns pokies can be culturally specific (Nicoll, 2014). This is supported by evidence from the gambling industry itself in regard to the performance of culturally specific machines in other markets. In a statement that could be judged as borderline racist, Aristocrat's CEO Jamie Odell, for example, stated the following when discussing the placing of Australian-themed slot machines in Asian casinos:

> Many Asian people love gambling, but the great games there look and feel like Asian games: the graphics, the language, even the sounds. *Lucky Dragons* are common themes in Macau and Chinese character symbols like 'good fortune'. What didn't work for us was trying to take an Australian or American game, say *Outback Jack* with kangaroos and *Ayers Rock*, and stick that into Asia.
>
> (Odell, quoted in Kelly, 2013)

Interfaces such as *More Chilli*, *Jackpot Catcher* (Native American theme; on this trope see Nicoll, 2014), *5 Dragons* and *Mystic Panda* certainly reflect a particular view of the world defined by class and ethnicity. Riches are paired with the conquest of other cultures and territories through missions. Or they are coupled with the idea of a "big win", such as in slots with mining or Wild West motifs. The exotic tropes of these interfaces could also be related to recent migratory patterns to and from Australia, and the new cultural notions and discourses of oppositionality that sprout from these.

For instance, in the suburb of Cabramatta, NSW, the Vietnamese community is deeply invested in poker machine gambling. The Stardust Hotel is one of the highest-grossing venues in New South Wales (Vanda,

2010). Analysing the Fairfield EGM market, of which Cabramatta is part, Saulwick and Moore (2011) recall that

> The council estimates the area's unemployment rate is more than 10 per cent, double the state average. Fairfield residents are twice as likely to receive the disability support pension as others in NSW. On the Bureau of Statistics' measure, it is Sydney's most disadvantaged region. And yet Fairfield is at the heart of Sydney's poker machine industry and the licensed clubs that dominate it.
>
> (Saulwick & Moore, 2011)

Research on why migrants choose certain poker machines over others could complement studies, such as Scull and Woolcock's 2007 survey of gambling in Chinese, Greek and Vietnamese communities in Queensland. The authors identified culturally specific notions and practices, such as collectively trying to come up with strategies to "beat the system", which reportedly happens among the Vietnamese community (Scull & Woolcock, 2007). Other studies include Ohtsuka and Ohtsuka's study of Vietnamese-Australian gamblers (2010) and Tanasornnarong et al.'s research on gambling among young Thai people in Melbourne (2004).

The use of certain iconography in pokie gamble-play platforms appeals to the predilections of some players. In her testimonial for a government report, Julia Karpathakis recalled her ordeal as a problem gambler. Led by experience and intuition, she explained how the imagery influenced her choices:

> There is a lot of trickery. That is what it looks like now. But back then it had a romantic feel about it. The imagery is very romantic; I would play *Sweethearts*, *Cleopatra*, *Jewel of the Nile* and all of those kinds of machines. I hated *Shogun* – I was never attracted to the look of that one. So it was a bit romantic, not in a romantic-romantic way but dreamy, if you know what I mean.
>
> (Karpathakis, *Committee Hansard*, February 1, 2011,
> p. 15; as cited in *The design and implementation of a
> mandatory pre-commitment system for electronic
> gaming machines*, p. 10)

Karpathakis's testimonial serves as evidence that for certain gamblers the symbolic arrangements of interfaces – the "trickery", as Karpathakis calls it – is one of the factors that draw them to play or choose one pokie machine over another. She also describes the experience as "dreamy", which takes us back to the state that Reith described as "oneiric" (1999) and which is one of the defining particularities of the configuration of gambling-machines.

Alongside these "dreamy" images, pokie machines emit sounds akin to those of video games: explosions, high-octane rock 'n' roll music, and sound effects that would be at home in a Hollywood blockbuster. If some-one hits the jackpot, celebratory notes travel through the room, and punt-ers turn their heads momentarily to catch a glimpse of the lucky one who got to experience the much-sought-after "big win", the highlight of this form of consumption. Some particular slot machines are legendary as they accumulate jackpots that reach millions of dollars and make gamblers daydream – as is the case of the Lion's Share slot machine in the MGM Grand in Las Vegas and its USD $2 million-dollar prize (Leach, 2014).

I will now provide four examples of slot machines that have exotic designs and follow the cultural dynamic of gamble-play. Although not directly de-signed with a Hollywood franchise in mind, these slot machines use clichés derived from Hollywood genres. *Firelight*, one of Aristocrat's most popular pokies, which is offered in many pokie rooms across NSW and the rest of Australia, as well as in an app version, has been advertised as follows:

> Travel to an ancient civilization where magic and the powers of na-ture rule the world. The mystical Phoenix will cause your luck to rise as the volcano erupts with multiplied wins!
>
> (vShare, 2017)

In *Firelight*, the mission is not merely to make money but to make the volcano explode with multiplied wins. It is also about visiting an ancient civilisation and extracting resources, a theme constant in Hollywood epics, such as the sci-fi fantasy *Avatar* (1999). The advertisement could also have a gender-based connotation: winning is the equivalent of a py-rotechnic ejaculation. The sexualisation of gambling – meaning-making through appealing to the realm of the erotic – is a common practice among interface designers. Advertisements for online casinos, for in-stance, often show attractive women inviting potential clients. Similarly, Nicoll recalls merchandise that depicts pokie machines as ejaculatory devices, sex toys of chance:

> I also have a T-shirt purchased in Brisbane which displays a cartoon symbol in profile of two men each with the handle of a vibrating one-armed bandit or poker machine in his arse while coins pour out of his cock. Above the image are the words 'WARNING POKIES'. Two points that struck me about the image are: its very literal re-contextualisation of the 'money shot' with which traditional pornographic representations climax, and that its representation of poker machines erotically vibrating players is very close to the truth. I'm not sure when this image was produced but in the past five years pokies giving subtle vibrations timed to 'go off' with the animated and musical 'features' have been installed in most Australian gam-bling venues.
>
> (Nicoll, 2008, pp. 104–105)

In another famous pokie, *Love on the Nile,* Aristocrat pairs two of the main characters of its brand mythology, a practice that shares similarities with film, comic or video game cross-overs, high-concept franchises and practices of convergence (Jenkins, 2006). This pokie also uses an Egyptian theme, a common trope of gambling-related kitsch present in physical casinos, such as the Luxor Hotel & Casino in Las Vegas. The story is reminiscent of classic Hollywood and movies, such as *Cleopatra* (1963), famously featuring Elizabeth Taylor and Richard Burton, or DeMille's *The Ten Commandments* (1956). The Egyptian theme is also present in social casino app levels, such as *Cleopatra* in IGT's *Double Down Casino.*

Love on the Nile tells

> The love story between two of Aristocrat's most instantly recognizable game characters from the iconic games – *Queen of the Nile* and *King of the Nile.* The symbols in this 25 Line game are based on the original titles to provide the classic look and feel combined with an innovative feature extension. During the Feature when 2, 5 or 7 scatters are collected the BONUS WILD symbol is added to the reel, the BONUS WILD symbol combines the CLEOPATRA & PHARAOH WILD characters onto one symbols bringing these two characters together at last.

Stuntman Sam, another of Aristocrat's pokie machines, is not related to exotica but exemplifies the gamble-play qualities of EGMs. The interface presents an animated character that *performs* the outcomes of the player's forays with 'luck'. Stuntman Sam, a circus artist, enacts chance in a pyrotechnic way. His look reminds us of Evel Knievel, the stunt performer who became an icon of US popular culture worldwide. The game is advertised on the company's website as follows:

> In this daring new game, players meet Stuntman Sam, the latest hero from Aristocrat. Stuntman Sam attempts several heart-stopping, death-defying feats to give the player an entertaining gaming experience and a big win... This action packed game will have players cheering Stuntman Sam on as he attempts death defying stunts including getting shot out of a cannon, high dive, dodging the knife throw, bike jump and a risky plane stunt.

Finally, another one of Aristocrat's games, *Hillbillions* is advertised as follows: "Take players on an exhilarating journey celebrating the culture of mountain people with Billy, the Hillbilly". This constitutes another form of exoticism, one that represents a rural segment of the population (Green, 1965), and that also references Southern US culture and Americana, a common theme in slot machines and online gambling products.

By invoking particular visual and cinematic traditions through procedure-images, pokies strive to produce what Reith calls "sensory maelstrom" (1999, p. 128), where the perception of time and space changes, and the player can enter an oneiric state. The fantastic worlds represented in slot machines aid in inducing this oneiric state similar to the those experienced by video game players through their interactive attachment to the screen. It would be counterintuitive to think, therefore, that a gambler's experience remains the same regardless of the way in which the game is presented.

Just like exotica is used in the peculiar Australian pokie market, cinematic imagery is deployed worldwide to attract gamblers to slot machines distributed in casinos, cruise ships and other gambling venues as well as online spaces. Digital gamble-play is undergoing a process of cultural normalisation as it is being incorporated into popular culture by being fused with other media assemblages, mainly the dream factory of the Hollywood conglomerate. These dynamics allow gamble-play to emphasise the 'fun' aspects of gambling. Cultural normalisation happens when component parts of other assemblages are inserted into the digital gambling assemblages and vice versa through relations of exteriority (DeLanda, 2006).

Relations of exteriority are generated particularly through the licensing of film and television franchises in slot machines (both land-based and online, for real money and for virtual currencies), through celebrity endorsements of digital gambling platforms, mainly online poker, and through the appropriation of video game aesthetics and gameplay. Some gamble-play assemblages take shape by incorporating narratives and concepts from other media and cultural assemblages, such as mainstream Hollywood cinema. Industry professionals design contemporary digital gambling platforms incorporating video game procedures and pop culture iconography that ranges from Hollywood themes – *Sex and the City, Indiana Jones, Pink Panther* or John Wayne, to name a few – to, as we have seen, oversimplified representations of 'exotic' landscapes and peoples – China; pre-Columbian civilisations, including the Aztec and the Inca; Africa; the Australian outback; or Native American tropes (what Nicoll (2014) calls the "Indian sign"). There are intersections between gambling and mass media products, particularly those emanating from Hollywood and which represent the transnational entertainment complex.

When digital gamble-play establishes relations of exteriority with assemblages such as the Hollywood entertainment complex, it gains access to a vast pool of consumers formed around fandom and fan cultures. Gambling-machines are generated. This happens with products such as the *Star Wars Trilogy MultiPLAY Video Slots* machine manufactured by IGT and available in many casinos in the United States (Figure 4.3). On its website, the manufacturer promoted this product by emphasising the cultural relevance of the franchise, pointing out that

Figure 4.3 Star Wars themed slot machine. YouTube video "Star Wars Empire
  Strikes Back Cloud City Casino Slot Machine Game Bonus Round"
  uploaded by lathamfilm on August 9, 2012.
Image captured on October 30, 2017 from www.youtube.com/watch?v=warN_74OyAQ.

The film saga has created its own language, conventions, comic
book series and more; *Star Wars* has more than 9 million fans and
followers on social media channel; The *Star Wars* overture has become one of the most well-known pieces of modern, classical music.

Online, the real-money slots operator All Slots Australian Online Casino
offers a digital slot machine based on other high-concept films, including
the most recent incarnation of Warner Brothers' popular Christopher
Nolan *Batman* franchise.

Canadian journalist Bill Brioux described the convergence of gambling and popular culture during a visit to Las Vegas in 2013:

The Hangover, set in Vegas, has been immortalized in slots, as has
The Dark Knight Batman movies. Older films such as *Ghostbusters*
and *The Wizard of Oz* are also featured in casinos. Even popular
board game brands, such as *Clue* and *Monopoly*, are used to attract
players. There is also an obvious pitch to boomers through machines
with a '70s or '80s slant. Kiss slot machines sit next to Michael
Jackson terminals.

(Brioux, 2013)

The narrative structure of gamble-play media can also be shaped by
Hollywood professionals. For example, IGT's 2013 *Avatar*-themed slot
machine was created with the help of Jon Landau, the film's producer,
who told *The Hollywood Reporter*, "We're looking at the *Avatar* brand,
and how to build it as a global brand that lets people have the escape

they want, but also delivers to them things that are provocative in their everyday life" (Scheckells, 2013). The *Avatar* franchise, which originated with the 2009 film directed by James Cameron and will be followed by at least two more movies, is in itself a salient example of transnational convergence culture. It is a multi-platform, multimillion-dollar franchise that has expanded into video games, toys, pinball machines, merchandise, a theme park and cinematic blockbusters. The fact that the creators see slot machines as part of their branding efforts, as something that is "provocative" in the "everyday life" (Scheckells, 2013) of audiences, emphasises the prominent role that gambling is taking in the ecology of transnational entertainment media and reveals an orchestrated effort to use gambling as a gateway into other media consumption practices, brands and narratives. According to promotional material, the *Avatar* gambling-machine, which offers a multisensorial experience, with a vibrating cabinet and state-of-the-art graphics

> allows players to relive the magic of one of the most acclaimed movies of our time and experience the immersive, thrilling game content that players have grown to expect from IGT... players are put right in the middle of the struggles between humans and the Na'vi. With unlocked content, customizable options and never before seen bonuses, players will feel as though they have taken flight among the Na'vi warriors.

This example is evidence of the creative collaboration between film professionals and game designers in the creation of gambling experiences that are evocative of other media. Other Hollywood high-concept sci-fi franchises have followed suit. In January 2014, for instance, Microgaming signed a deal with Universal Partnerships and Licencing to develop a *Jurassic Park*-themed online slot machine. According to early reports, in the slot based on Spielberg's movie "the number of bonus levels will vary depending on the type of dinosaur selected at the beginning of the game" (Ancona, 2014). In this case, Hollywood narratives frame the staging of the bet, placing the consumer in a cultural space where gambling unashamedly becomes more like entertainment. In February 2014, Net Entertainment released an *Alien*-themed slot machine with three levels (The Search, The Encounter and The Hive) based on the 1979 space horror film directed by Ridley Scott. The machine was promoted by its manufacturer as follows, highlighting its aural elements:

> The film's sinister beauty is captured perfectly within the game, which is full of unique win sequences that will keep fans on the edge of their seats set against a horrifying soundtrack.
>
> (Net Entertainment, 2014)

The intersection between sci-fi and digital gambling is interesting as speculative fiction is key in shaping cultural imaginations concerning human-machine relations and the implications of technology in social life.

The stories and aesthetics of other fantasy worlds that are highly resonant with Hollywood fan cultures have been incorporated into slot machines, showing the adaptability and malleability of gamble-play. In 2014, for example, Konami Gaming launched two slot machines themed after the popular role-playing game *Dungeons and Dragons*, which include "glowing runes, faux stone design elements, hand painted 3D dragon toppers, and a variety of sign packages including one with a rotating red dragon" (Miozzi, 2014). *Dungeons and Dragons*, first released in 1974, brought card games from the depths of gaming subcultures to mainstream popular culture. This slot machine explicitly refers to the trope of magic and divination in gambling.

DoubleDown Casino has a social slot machine based on the classic board game *Monopoly*, which finds an intersection between play and finance, or finance as a game. This intersection is also evident in some recent Hollywood films whose narratives deal with how the financial system is based on dynamics similar to those of gambling, where negotiations between risk, loses, big wins and rewards work as narrative motors, and where informational networks work as the conduits for risk management (Brenner, 1990). We can think, for instance, of two high-octane and cynical dramas, Oliver Stone's *Wall Street: Money Never Sleeps* (2010) and Martin Scorsese's *The Wolf of Wall Street* (2013), or Leslie Cockburn's documentary *American Casino* (2009). The 2015 Oscar-nominated film *The Big Short* directly addresses the volatile nature of speculative markets and their gambling-like characteristics prior to the world financial crisis of 2008. The origins of modern finance are, in fact, closely related to the evolution of gambling and speculation (DeGoede, 2005).

The configuration of narratives around gambling in digital gamble-play products extends beyond the slot machine. The Facebook app *Poker Mafia* lures the player with the following promise:

> Think you have what it takes to make it in the mean streets? Put together the toughest crew and take over the family business. Play High Stakes Poker in the Mafia Underground as a Street Soldier and move your way up the ranks to become the next Don.

This gameplay recalls a classic genre in Hollywood film: the gangster movie. The typography is a clear reference to Coppola's *The Godfather* and the rags-to-riches narrative arc resembles those of Hawks and DePalma's *Scarface*, Scorsese's *Goodfellas* or the iconic HBO TV series *The Sopranos* (created by David Chase). Interestingly Mario Puzo, who wrote the novel on which the *Godfather* film is based, as well as the screenplay, authored a non-fiction book about gambling, *Inside Las Vegas*, published in 1977.

These examples reveal how pre-existing narratives and characters bring gambling platform design closer to Hollywood-themed video games, a long-standing genre (on the production dynamics of Hollywood-themed titles, see O'Donnell, 2011).

The intersection between the transnational entertainment complex and gambling industries has sparked some conflicts as real-money gambling opposes the family-friendly values and brand identity associated with some transnational media conglomerates. In 2013, after Disney acquired Marvel and Lucasfilm, and their collection of characters and franchises, it announced the discontinuation of the licenses for superhero and *Star Wars* themed slots, lotteries and online casinos (Alvarez & Snyder, 2013). Characters including Indiana Jones (formerly owned by Lucasfilm and now by Disney), Iron Man, the Hulk and Spider-Man are common in casinos and online slots, particularly in the US market, both in regulated and unregulated platforms. However, as Alvarez and Snyder point out,

> Disney is finding that keeping a constantly growing entertainment conglomerate completely removed from gambling is far more challenging than it used to be.
>
> (Alvarez & Snyder, 2013)

In the latest instalment of the *Star Wars* franchise, *The Last Jedi* (2017) director Rian Johnson created an interplanetary casino, Canto Bight, that accommodates the wealthy elites of the galaxy. The antigambling sentiment is clear in light of comments made by Johnson to *Vanity Fair*: "I was thinking, O.K., let's go ultra-glamour. Let's create a playground, basically, for rich assholes" (Kamp, 2017). Here, gambling is associated to class warfare, echoing the recent sociopolitical climate in the United States, including the #occupywallstreet movement and Bernie Sanders's political rise.

The convergence of digital gambling assemblages and popular culture is not exclusive to Hollywood and slots but extends to wider Western celebrity culture and other forms of gamble-play. In 2012, for example, British pop star Robbie Williams launched a social casino site and Facebook app. *Robbie Williams FUNPOKER* (www. robbiewilliamsfunpoker) was a cartoonish 3D environment where "you can play and be social", but "you can only win and play for fun money" (Robbie Williams FUNPOKER, 2013). Global superstar Madonna has also signed an agreement with Aristocrat to appear in a slot machine which will feature hit songs and videos (Gardner & Sun, 2017). Talk show host Ellen DeGeneres also has her very own Ellen-themed IGT machine, and even surprised players in the MGM casino in Las Vegas while they were playing it (Allison, 2017). Ellen has built a brand based on a feel-good mood and female empowerment, which makes it quite contradictory to promote a machine that is blatantly disempowering and that affects considerable numbers of women (Schüll, 2002). The TV show *The Voice*, a reality show based on a rags-to-riches narrative, also has its own slot machine (Schulte, 2017). Even minor celebrities, such as former boxing world champion Ray "Boom Boom" Mancini, who enjoyed modest mainstream popularity in the 1980s, have been immortalised on slot machines (WYTV, 2017). Celebrity culture has also been put to the service of other gamble-play practices. When discussing the "worldwide explosion in the participation and popularity of online poker", Wood and Griffiths point to an "increasing number of celebrities endorsing and playing poker; poker being shown via television (both terrestrial and cable channels) and the Internet" as possible factors (Wood & Griffiths, 2008, p. 81).

Mission: Chasing

Exotica and Hollywood branding mask the boredom inherent in slot machine playing. The procedures enacted in slot machine playing are seemingly simple, almost mechanical in nature: you insert a coin, press a button and hope that the right symbols align to your benefit. If you run out of money, you can get more cash from one of the ATMs that are generally installed in gambling venues – an arrangement that has sparked some controversy. In 2011, the activist group Just Act launched the "ATMs Away From Pokies campaign", claiming that the physical proximity of gambling devices to a source of money intensifies gambling. In 2013 there was further controversy as a new law, which established that there should be an AUD \$250 limit on cash withdrawals in pokie machine venues, was bypassed (Safi, 2013).

Woolley and Livingstone offer a concise explanation of the transaction involved in pokie machine playing:

> The contemporary poker machine can be understood as an industrial artefact, a device for staging the sale of a particular good or commodity – the 'bet'.
>
> (Woolley & Livingstone, 2010, p. 41)

They elaborate further, stating that EGMs are "hybrid devices, a composite of computer and video technologies, integrated alongside remnant mechanical components such as the coinbox" (Woolley & Livingstone, 2010, p. 45). The internal processes are digitised – the reels spin algorithmically rather than mechanically – but the experience preserves the aura of past devices while also providing the allure of interactivity provided by video games. Slots are cross-platform

media in which digital gambling interfaces and video game procedures intersect and trigger the player's desire. The staging of the bet,
however, involves increasingly complex images, sounds and procedures, as we have seen. Its design requires the work of professionals
who range from mathematicians to software engineers and computer
graphic artists.

Before exploring the procedural similarities between video games
and poker machines, we shall consider one basic question: what is the
key procedural particularity of basic video games? In a pioneering volume on platform studies, *Racing the Beam: The Atari Video Computer
System* (2009), Montfort and Bogost recall the dawn of arcade gaming
and establish a clear and relevant distinction between early titles, such as
Spacewar! (1962) and *Pong* (1972), and current video games: "The computer's ability to play against a person and to play somewhat like a person, rather than just serving as the playing field and referee" (Montfort &
Bogost, 2009, p. 5).

Today, they state, developments have led to the creation of "crafty
computer-controlled enemies" (Montfort & Bogost, 2009, p. 5). In
pokie machines, the crafty enemies are the algorithms that filter the values produced by the RNG and prevent the gambler from hitting the jackpot. The chances of a top jackpot in a typical machine are approximately
one in seven million. Journalist Bill Previtti described the computer chip
as "the little rascal that controls the random number generator, which
controls where and when the screen will project a winning array of symbols" (Previtti, 2006).

This "winning array of symbols" can correspond to two varieties of
bets: a three-reel single game or a five-reel 25-line game, that allows
multiple bets, a configuration that creates excitement and encourages
repetitive actions. Anti-gambling advocates have subjected this configuration to scrutiny.

Some gamblers play for hours on end, thinking that they have deci-
phered the code that defines the award patterns and that if they prolong
their session they will eventually hit the jackpot (Walker, 1992). This
is, however, highly improbable. As the materiality of slot machines has
evolved, so has the way in which randomness is achieved. Currently,
it is reproduced digitally through complex RNG. The following is a
brief explanation of how a RNG works. In a modern EGM, a central
computer controls the outcome of each 'pull' or 'push' (in old mechanical devices it was controlled by the motion of the reels). The computer
algorithm chooses one random number for each reel, maps the number
onto a position on the reel, then stops the reel at the appointed place
and scores the outcome. The outcome is predestined right from the moment when the player presses the button. The rolling of the reels is just
a representation of this automatic process – pure show – but it increases
the sense of expectation, the vertigo or *ilinx* (Caillois, 2001). It also

preserves the aura of the rituals associated with playing mechanical slot machines.

Slot machines are artefacts that have been provided with some structural features, such as gameplay and graphic design, of prevalent screen-based entertainment technologies. These features lead gamblers to believe that they are presented with a 'challenge', which in pokies is staged through the random appearance of jackpots. Gamblers face this challenge by chasing losses over time. In gamble-play pokies, the punter chases the computer, the aforementioned enemy represented by video game or Hollywood-like villains.

Livingstone points out that

> You have to remember that machines are around 100 years old. Aristocrat tells us in its annual report that it spends something like $120 million a year on research and development, which is a significant amount of money. I presume they are not wasting that money. We can presume that they are doing a lot of work on trialling features which they hope will have success in the marketplace. Remember that success in the marketplace for a gaming machine means getting people who play them to spend more time and more money on those machines.
>
> (*Proof Committee Hansard*, February 2, 2011, p. 34)

Vast quantities of money are being invested in the development of gameplay that guarantees the formation of gambler-pokie couplings based on continuous play, on the formation of the subject through repetition. "Chasing" is "the attempt to recover one's gambling loses by further gambling" (O'Connor & Dickerson, 2003, p. 360). This definition, informed by Lesieur's influential work *The Chase* (1984), sketches the prevalent cycle of gambling consumption: gamble, lose, gamble some more to recuperate your losses. Although there are many social, psychological and biological factors that contribute to "chasing" – such as the ones explored by Blaszczynski and Nower (2002) in their Pathways Model – both the interface and the gameplay are designed in such a way as to motivate the gambler to embark on "chasing" missions within one gaming session, which represents one step in the longer mission that envelops an ongoing relationship with the pokie machine. The inability of the gambler to refrain from repetition is known in the medical literature as "loss-of-control" (O'Connor & Dickerson, 2003, p. 361) but is encouraged by gambling venues and operators through bonuses and loyalty programs – an essential feature of gambling consumption.

Gamble-play slots offer a combination of audiovisual spectacle and gambling. Chasing losses is dramatised into narratives that might involve espionage, escaping enemies or racing against time. For example, another one of Aristocrat's EGMs is based on the movie and television franchise *Mission: Impossible*. It belongs to the entertainment-style video-slot category offered by the EGM manufacturer and is promoted with a trailer that resembles those of Hollywood blockbusters. In this pokie the bet is staged by using footage and characters from the movie franchise. It combines the universes of gambling and undercover agents. Its promotional materials read, "Espionage meets excitement with six great bonus features". The player literally chases the money with guns and helicopters, and by participating in showdowns with the series' villains.

There are other Hollywood slot iterations of the trope of chasing the money. In 2014 Aristocrat launched a slot machine themed after the hit AMC television series *The Walking Dead* (Figure 4.4). The gambler is witness to zombie attacks in realistic 3D graphics as well as bonus games with narratives, such as "Escape from Atlanta", with clear reference to the series' plotline, in which a random group of people try to survive a zombie apocalypse (Burkart, 2014). Likewise, in 2014, in preparation for the relaunch of the show, iSOFTBET and Twentieth Century Fox signed a deal to produce a slot machine based on Fox's wildly successful TV series *24*, where each episode is structured as a race against time. Michael Doyle, Vice President of Interactive Games at Fox Consumer Products, stated,

Figure 4.4 This YouTube video is the trailer for the Aristrocrat slot machine themed after the hit AMC series *The Walking Dead*. The player has to escape a horde of 'walkers' by engaging in constant, compulsive play (accessed on August 5, 2017 at www.youtube.com/watch?v=xWNHKtuUR4A).

This unique partnership with iSoftBet has resulted in an action-packed game recognizable to fans around the world featuring the twists and turns that kept viewers on the edge of their seats from week to week while watching *24*.

(iGamingBusiness, 2014)

In parallel to the procedural similarity of EGMs and video games, some argue that by also playing video games, gamblers can have false expectations of controlling outcomes. As King et al. point out, "it is possible that video game playing may influence some individuals' gambling knowledge, beliefs, attitudes, strategies and/or gambling behaviours" (King et al., 2012, p. 422).

Furthermore, they propose that this develops into false expectations:

> video game playing leads some people to develop false expectations about the amount of player control within gambling activities, particularly electronic forms of gambling. Because many video games require skill and strategy, some people may develop a belief that, with sufficient practice, they can overcome and master the challenges of the game.

(King et al., 2012, p. 425)

The commingling of digital gambling and video games extends beyond parallel consumption: video game-like gambling is not exclusive to slot machines but has extended into brick-and-mortar casinos, where, as if in scenes from a futuristic movie like *Blade Runner*, digital croupiers deal hands, or virtual hostesses spin the roulette. This adds to the culture of gamble-play, where the player establishes a relationship with a digital interlocutor and engages with interfaces that provide pleasurable gameplay.

By arguing that, just as in video games, there is an agonistic or competitive element in EGM playing, I am not saying that punters compete against each other, as happens in social casino apps. The gambler engages in an adversarial relationship with the machine, which in policy discourse has been perceived as a separate entity, with agency and the upper hand in its liaison with the player. Similar to the sentient machines found in many pieces of speculative fiction – from *2011: A Space Odyssey* and its resilient HAL, to the Skynet artificial intelligence in the *Terminator* saga and *The Matrix* in the Wachowskis cyber-noir fantasies – slot machines in general and Australian pokies in particular are presented in public discussions as separate entities, devices over which humans have no direct control.

In the media, and in policy discussions, pokies are often depicted as machines that motivate compulsive gambling. The title of an article published by the *Sydney Morning Herald* in October 2011 is revelatory: "The machines that are draining a city" (Saulwick & Moore, 2011). Government campaigns that promote responsible gambling stress the logic behind the assertion that the house always wins, and warn against optimistic expectations on the possibilities of defeating the system. For instance, the THINK! campaign launched by the NSW government, reads,

> THINK! WHAT ARE THE ODDS OF HITTING THE JACKPOT? Your chance of hitting the jackpot on a gaming machine is no better than a million to one.

In another Australian state, Victoria, the responsible gambling campaign launched by the state government also stresses the advantage that the machines have over gamblers. Its slogan would be fit for a Hollywood sci-fi movie: "In the end, the machines will win". The proposed solutions for problem gambling in Australia are generally not related to the transformation of the social conditions that generate problem gambling but to changes in the gameplay. These changes include solutions such as the pre-commitment scheme – which aims to allow gamblers to voluntarily set limits to their spending and losses (Dowling, 2013) – AUD $1 bets, or an expiry time for the opportunity to win the jackpot (Nogrady, 2014). The human-machine antagonism is further exacerbated by the "opposition between the happiness of *playing* and the unhappiness of *being played* by the machines" (Nicoll, 2008, p. 117), an ambivalent situation of pleasure and pain in risk-taking. Discussing the pleasure derived from winning, Lynch argues that

> the winning of money in either small or large amounts provides the player with at least a temporary sense of having beaten the system in which their life's struggle occurs and of gaining some respite from the struggle in the process.
>
> (Lynch, 1990, p. 200)

There is a widespread belief among digital punters that the machine can be controlled. This notion is exacerbated by the symbolism of the interfaces. If the machines are playing you, the machines could potentially be played by you: one only needs the sufficient will and strength of character to embark on a long, sometimes tedious mission towards transformation.

Conclusion

In this chapter, I have described and analysed the gambling-machine assemblage, providing examples of pokies available in a particular jurisdiction, NSW, Australia, as well as slots branded with Hollywood franchises, such as *Avatar, Star Wars, 24, The Walking Dead* and *The Ellen Show* (Figure 4.5). I have also pointed out how slot machine manufacturers such as Aristocrat and IGT design their interfaces in such a

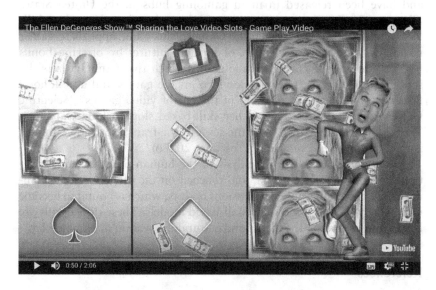

Figure 4.5 The Ellen DeGeneres slot machine (accessed on January 1, 2018 at www.youtube.com/watch?time_continue=117&v=Hv_PYYnrGOU).

way that they share structural and procedural similarities with video games and Hollywood storytelling.

Slot machines challenge the gambler to accomplish missions through chasing and other forms of procedural rhetoric that are associated with notions of class mobility. In Australia, pokies have been a federal and state issue since their introduction to the country in the beginnings of the twentieth century. Currently, the dominant discourses in policy making and academia focus on the figure of the pathological gambler and the repercussions that gambling has on communities and families, particularly in the lower rungs of the socio-economic ladder – some of whom are on a 'mission' to climb to the upper rungs.

Slot machines are strongly influenced by digital games. They automate repetitive action, providing excitement for an otherwise simple action in which the gambler has little agency beyond inserting coins and pushing buttons. Contemporary pokies sell the illusion of control over the outcome, presenting the gambler with gamelike features such as enemies and missions, narrative constants also in Hollywood cinema. In fact, as I write this book in 2017, various slot machine manufacturers are releasing new skill-based devices in an attempt to lure millennial gamblers. These machines

have more in common with video games and are aimed at drawing in a younger generation of gamblers who are not interested in the pokies. New machines include shooting games, racing games, card games, and can be single or multi-player, and have been released in main gambling hubs in the United States (Toscano, 2017a). Among these new machines is a *Space Invaders* skill-based model released by Scientific Games. This game appeals to gamer nostalgia (a distinctive element of hipster culture) by offering bonus free sessions of the classic arcade game, which the manufacturers describe as "one of the true classic video arcade games and a childhood favorite for many who grew up in the era of video games" (Scientific Games Corporation, 2017). Other skill-based slots include GameCo's *Terminator* slots (themed after the sci-fi movie franchise) and Gamblit's zombie-themed *Into the Dead* (Toscano, 2017b).

This chapter provided an analysis of the human-poker machine relationship understood as media, and touched on the often-overlooked audiovisual and iconographic dimensions of slots, which is bound to become increasingly complex with new skill-based models. These dimensions are key in understanding the media and cultural innovation of gamble-play.

References

Aarseth, E. (1997). *Cybertext: Perspectives on ergodic literature*. Baltimore: The Johns Hopkins University Press.

Albarrán-Torres, C. (2016). Kittens, farms and wild pandas: The impact of cuteness in adult gamble-play media. In J. P. Dale, J. Goggin, J. Leyda, A. P. McIntyre, & D. Negra (Eds.), *The aesthetics and affects of cuteness* (pp. 235–252). London and New York: Routledge.

Allison, K. (2017, September 21). Ellen DeGeneres surprises MGM Grand visitor playing celebrity-themed slot machines. *Casinopedia*. Retrieved from www.casinopedia.org/news/ellen-degeneres-surprises-mgm-grand-visitor-playing-celebrity-themed-slot-machines

Alvarez, L., & Snyder, M. (2013, October 26). Gambling debate entangles Disney in Florida. *The New York Times*. Retrieved from www.nytimes.com/2013/10/27/us/gambling-debate-entangles-disney-in-florida.html?pagewanted=1&_r=1&smid=tw-share

Ancona, J. (2014, February 1). Microgaming signs deal to develop Jurassic Park online slots games. *Online Casino Org*. Retrieved from www.onlinecasino.org/news/microgaming-signs-deal-develop-jurassic-park-online-slots-games-742#sthash.RtjysTqL.dpuf

Aristocrat Leisure Limited (2011). *HY2011 Market Presentation 25 August 2011*

Speaker Notes. Retrieved from http://ir.aristocrat.com/static-files/891e89b4-1a9c-4fb4-9d43-9fde04961d23

Baudrillard, J. (1990) *Cool memories 1980–1985*. London: Verso.

Baudrillard, J. (1998). *The consumer society: Myths and structures*. London: Sage.

Benjamin, W. (2008). *The work of art in the age of mechanical reproduction (Penguin Great Ideas)*. London: Penguin. (Original work published 1935)

Bhabha, H., Ashcroft, B., Griffiths, G., & Tiffin, H. (1995). *The post-colonial studies reader*. London and New York: Routledge.

Billieux, J., Van der Linden, M., Khazaal, Y., Zullino, D., & Clark, L. (2012). Trait gambling cognitions predict near-miss experiences and persistence in laboratory slot machine gambling. *British Journal of Psychology, 103*, 412–427.

Blaszczynski, A., & Nower, L. (2002). A pathways model of problem and pathological gambling. *Addiction, 97*(5), 487–499.

Blunt, A., & McEwan, W. (Eds.). (2002). *Postcolonial geographies.* New York and London: Continuum.

Bogard, W. (2009). Deleuze and machines: A politics of technology? In M. Poster & D. Savat (Eds.), *Deleuze and new technology* (pp. 15–31). Edinburgh: Edinburgh University Press.

Bogost, I. (2006). *Unit operations: An approach to video game criticism.* Cambridge: MIT Press.

Breen, H., Hing, N., & Weeks, P. (2002). Machine gaming in Sydney clubs: Characteristics of the supporting resident populations. *Journal of Gambling Studies, 8*(3), 293–312.

Brenner, R. (1990). *Gambling and speculation: A theory, a history, and a future of some human decisions.* Cambridge: Cambridge University Press.

Brioux, B. (2013, July 22). Gambling on show themes; colourful slot machines use images from TV and film to lure players. *Kamloops Daily News.* Retrieved from www.news1130.com/2013/07/19/colourful-slot-machines-with-tv-film-and-board-game-themes-lure-players/

Burkart, G. (2014, January 17). Try your luck against the zombie horde with the 'Walking Dead' slot machine. *Fear Net.* Retrieved from www.fearnet.com/news/news-article/try-your-luck-against-zombie-horde-walking-dead-slot-machine#sthash.vCzta8MX.dpuf

Caillois, R. (2001). *Man, play and games.* Urbana: University of Illinois Press.

Caldwell, G. T. (1972). *Leisure co-operatives: The institutionalization of gambling and the growth of large leisure organizations in New South Wales* (Unpublished doctoral thesis).Australian National University, Canberra.

Cerulo, K. A. (2009). Nonhumans in social interaction. *Annual Review of Sociology, 35*(1), 531–552.

Christensen, E., & Brinkerhoff-Jacobs, J. (2007). The relationship of gaming to entertainment. In W. R. Eadington & J. A. Cornelius (Eds.), *Gambling: Public policies and the social sciences* (pp. 11–47). Reno: University of Nevada, Reno Bureau of Business & Economic Research.

Colebrook, C. (2002). *Gilles Deleuze.* London and New York: Routledge.

Con Walker, B. (2009). *Casino clubs NSW: Profits, tax, sport and politics.* Sydney: Sydney University Press.

Cook, I. (2009). The body without organs and internet gaming addiction. In M. Poster & D. Savat (Eds.), *Deleuze and new technology* (pp. 185–205). Edinburgh: Edinburgh University Press.

Cummings, T. (2012). I'd lie awake, pokie music running through my head. *The Punch.* Retrieved from www.thepunch.com.au/articles/id-lie-awake-pokie-music-running-through-my-head/

Deane, S. (2013, August 27). Pokie cash: Robbing the poor to give to the rich. *The New Zealand Herald.* Retrieved from www.nzherald.co.nz/nz/news/article.cfm?c_id=1&objectid=11114737

DeGoede, M. (2005). *Virtue, fortune and faith: A genealogy of finance.* Minneapolis: University of Minnesota Press.

DeLanda, M. (2006). *A new philosophy of society: Assemblage theory and social complexity.* London and New York: Continuum.

Deleuze, G. (1992). Postscript on the Societies of Control. *October, 59,* 3–7.

Deleuze, G., & Guattari, F. (1987). *A thousand plateaus* (Trans. Brian Massumi). Minneapolis: University of Minnesota Press.

Deleuze, G., & Guattari, F. (2004a). *Capitalism and schizophrenia: Anti-Oedipus.* London: Continuum.

Deleuze, G., & Guattari, F. (2004b). *Capitalism and schizophrenia: A thousand plateaus.* London: Continuum.

Devol, G. H. (1887). *Forty years a gambler in the Mississippi.* Cincinnati: Devol & Haines.

Dowling, J. (2013, August 21). Limit your pokies spend... on your loyalty card. *The Age.* Retrieved from www.theage.com.au/victoria/limit-your-pokies-spend--on-your-loyalty-card-20130820-2s9lg.html

Findlay, J. M. (1986). *People of chance: Gambling in American society from Jamestown to Las Vegas.* Cambridge: Oxford University Press.

Gardner, R., & Sun, R. (2017, October 2). Hollywood is making millions off slot machines. *The Hollywood Reporter.* Retrieved from www.hollywoodreporter.com/news/hollywood-is-making-millions-slot-machines-1043343

Green, A. (1965). Hillbilly music: Source and symbol. *Journal of American Folklore, 78,* 204–228.

Griffiths, M. (1993). Fruit machine gambling: The importance of structural characteristics. *Journal of Gambling Studies, 9*(2), 101–120.

Gruzinksi, S. (1996). *La guerra de las imágenes: de Cristobal Colón a "Blade Runner" (1942–2019).* Mexico City: Fondo de Cultura Económica.

Hunt, N. R. (2002). Tintin and the interruptions of Congolese comics. In P. S. Landau & D. D. Kaspin (Eds.), *Images and empires: Visuality in colonial and postcolonial Africa* (pp. 90–123). Berkeley: University of California Press.

iGamingBusiness (2014, January 29). iSoftBet and Twentieth Century Fox Consumer Products unveil new online game featuring Fox's thrilling TV series 24. *iGamingBusiness.* Retrieved from www.igamingbusiness.com/press/isoftbet-and-twentieth-century-fox-consumer-products-unveil-new-online-game-featuring-fox-s

Iwatani Kane, Y. (2005, August 6). Not technically considered gambling, video-game like slot machines are a booming industry in Japan. *The Globe and Mail.* Retrieved from www.theglobeandmail.com/news/world/not-technically-considered-gambling-video-game-like-slot-machines-are-a-booming-industry-in-japan/article4119916/

Jenkins, H. (2006). *Convergence culture: Where old and new media collide.* New York: New York University Press.

Kamp, D. (2017, May 24). Cover Story: Star Wars: The Last Jedi, the Definitive Preview. *Vanity Fair.* Retrieved from www.vanityfair.com/hollywood/2017/05/star-wars-the-last-jedi-cover-portfolio

Kassinove, J. I., & Schare, M. L. (2001). Effects of the "near miss" and the "big win" on persistence at slot machine gambling. *Psychology of Addictive Behaviors, 15*(2), 155–158.

Kelly, R. (2013, August 25). Aristocrat Leisure hopes its bets pay off; Australian slot-machine maker's CEO Jamie Odell discusses the next growth phase and how the company is harnessing the popularity of social media. *The Wall*

Street Journal Online. Retrieved from http://online.wsj.com/article/SB10001 424127887323665504579028420024314700.html

King, D. L., Ejova, A., & Delfabbro, P. H. (2012). Illusory control, gambling, and video gaming: An investigation of regular gamblers and video game players. *Journal of gambling studies, 28*(3), 421–435.

Leach, R. (2014, February 19). The legend and cult of the $2.345 million Lion's Share slot machine at MGM Grand. *Las Vegas Sun*. Retrieved from http://lasvegassun.com/vegasdeluxe/2014/feb/19/cult-2345-million-lion-slot-machine-payoff-mgm-gra/

Lears, J. (2003). *Something for nothing: Luck in America*. New York: Viking.

Lesieur, H. R. (1984). *The chase: Career of the compulsive gambler*. Cambridge: Schenkman.

Livingstone, C. (2005). Desire and the consumption of danger: Electronic gaming machines and the commodification of interiority. *Addiction Research & Theory, 13*(6), 523–534.

Lynch, R. (1990). Working-class luck and vocabularies of hope among regular poker-machine players. In D. Rowe & G. Lawrence (Eds.), *Sport and leisure: Trends in Australian popular culture* (pp. 189–208). Sydney: Harcourt Brace Jovanovich.

Markham, F., & Young, M. (2014, March 6). Who wins from 'Big Gambling' in Australia? *The Conversation*. Retrieved from http://theconversation.com/who-wins-from-big-gambling-in-australia-22930

Matheson, D. (1996). Imperial culture and cultural imperialism. *European Journal of Intercultural Studies, 7*(1), 51–56.

Mazur, J. (2010). *What's luck got to do with it?: The history, mathematics, and psychology of the gambler's illusion*. Princeton: Princeton University Press.

Montfort, N., & Bogost, I. (2009) *Racing the beam*. Cambridge and London: MIT Press.

Net Entertainment (2014, February 5). Net Entertainment unleashes Aliens as latest branded slot. *The Wall Street Journal*. Retrieved from http://online.wsj.com/article/PR-CO-20140205-905577.html

Nicoll, F. (2008). The problematic joys of gambling: Subjects in a state. *New Formations, 63*(1), 102–120.

Nicoll, F. J. (2014). Indian Dreaming: Iconography of the zone/zones of iconography. *Continuum, 28*(6), 835–849.

Nogrady, B. (2014, July 8). 'Jackpot expiry' limits gambling losses. *ABC Science*. Retrieved from www.abc.net.au/science/articles/2014/07/08/4030031.htm

Miozzi, C. J. (2014, May 10). Dungeons & Dragons themed slot machines to be unveiled by Konami. *The Escapist*. Retrieved from www.escapistmagazine.com/news/view/134387-Dungeons-Dragons-Themed-Slot-Machines-to-Be-Unveiled-by-Konami

O'Connor, J., & Dickerson, M. (2003). Definition and measurement of chasing in off-course betting and gaming machine play. *Journal of Gambling Studies, 19*(4), 359–386.

O'Donnell, C. (2011). Games are not convergence: The lost promise of digital production and convergence. *Convergence: The International Journal of Research into New Media Technologies, 17*(3), 271–286.

Ohtsuka, K., & Ohtsuka, T. (2010). Vietnamese Australian gamblers' views on luck and winning: universal versus culture-specific schemas. *Asian Journal of Gambling Issues and Public Health, 1*(1), 34–46.

Parke, J., & Griffiths, M. (2006). The psychology of the fruit machine: The role of structural characteristics (revisited). *International Journal of Mental Health and Addiction, 4*(2), 151–179.

Parliamentary Joint Select Committee on Gambling Reform (2011, May). *First report: The design and implementation of a mandatory pre-commitment system for electronic gaming machines.* Canberra: Commonwealth of Australia. Retrieved from www.aph.gov.au/binaries/senate/committee/gamblingreform_ctte/precommitment_scheme/report/report.pdf

Pokermania GmbH (2014). *Robbie Williams FUNPOKER* (Facebook version) [Mobile application software]. Retrieved from www.robbiewilliamsfunpoker.com/

Previtti, B. (2006, November 4). Play video poker machines for winning bets. *Albuquerque Journal,* 10.

Ramesh, R. (2013, November 9). The gambling machines helping drug dealers 'turn dirty money clean'. *The Guardian.* Retrieved from www.theguardian.com/uk-news/2013/nov/08/gambling-machines-drug-money-laundering-bookies

Reith, G. (1999). *The age of chance: Gambling in Western culture.* London: Routledge.

Safi, M. (2013, December 13). Click "Yes" if you prefer not to comply with the law. *The Global Mail.* Retrieved from www.theglobalmail.org/feature/tick-yes-if-youd-prefer-not-to-comply-with-the-law/780/

Said, E. W. (1985). Orientalism reconsidered. *Cultural Critique, 1,* 89–107.

Sasso, R., & Villani, A. (2003). *Le vocabulaire de Gilles Deleuze.* Nice: Centre de Recherches D'Historie des Idées.

Saulwick, J., & Moore, M. (2011, October 14). The machines that are draining a city. *The Sydney Morning Herald.* Retrieved from www.smh.com.au/nsw/the-machines-that-are-draining-a-city-20111014-1lp52.html

Scheckells, M. (2013, September 24). 'Avatar' video casino games unveiled at Global Gaming Expo. *The Hollywood Reporter.* Retrieved from www.hollywoodreporter.com/news/avatar-video-casino-games-unveiled-635594

Schüll, N. D. (2002). Escape mechanism: Women, caretaking, and compulsive machine gambling. *Berkeley Collection of Working and Occasional Papers, 51.* Retrieved from http://hdl.handle.net/2345/4122

Schüll, N. D. (2012). *Addiction by design: Machine gambling in Las Vegas.* Princeton: Princeton University Press.

Schulte, S. (2017, December 6). 'The Voice' is coming to San Manuel Casino – As a slot machine. *The Orange County Register.* Retrieved from www.ocregister.com/2017/12/06/the-voice-is-coming-to-san-manuel-casino-as-a-slot-machine/

Scientific Games Corporation (2017, June 8). Scientific Games Debuts First Skill-Based Slot Machine with Classic Arcade Video Game Favorite – SPACE INVADERS™. *PR Newswire.* Retrieved from www.prnewswire.com/news-releases/scientific-games-debuts-first-skill-based-slot-machine-with-classic-arcade-video-game-favorite----space-invaders-300471194.html

Scull, S., & Woolcock, G. (2005). Problem gambling in non-English speaking background communities in Queensland, Australia: A qualitative exploration. *International Gambling Studies, 5*(1), 29–44.

Simmel, G. (1971). The adventurer. In D. N. Levine (Ed.), *On individuality and social forms.* Chicago: University of Chicago Press.

Slade, P. (2003). Gallipoli thanatourism: The meaning of ANZAC. *Annals of Tourism Research, 30*(4), 779–794.

Takiguchi,N.,&Rosenthal,R.(2011).ProblemgamblinginJapan.*ElectronicJournal of Contemporary Japanese Studies.* Retrieved from www.japanesestudies. org.uk/articles/2011/Takiguchi.html

Tanasornnarong, N., Jackson, A., & Thomas, S. (2004). Gambling among young Thai people in Melbourne, Australia: An exploratory study. *International Gambling Studies, 4*(2), 189–203.

Toscano, N. (2017a, July 15). Next-generation pokies: How casinos are luring Millennials with skill-based machines. *The Sydney Morning Herald.* Retrieved from www.smh.com.au/business/nextgeneration-pokies-how-casinos-are-luring-millennials-with-skillbased-machines-20170714-gxbtaf.html

Toscano, N. (2017b, July 25). 'Skill-based' slot machine maker GameCo has eyes on Australian gamblers. *The Sydney Morning Herald.* Retrieved from www.smh.com.au/business/skillbased-slot-machine-maker-gameco-has-eyes-on-australian-gamblers-20170724-gxh8tp.html

Vanda, C. (2010, November 15). Hotels reap rich pokie rewards for Woolworths. *Sydney Morning Herald.* Retrieved from www.smh.com.au/business/hotels-reap-rich-pokie-rewards-for-woolworths-20101114-17sr0.html

vShare (2017). Fire Light casino slot game. *vShare.* Retrieved from www.vshare. com/Fire-Light-casino-slot-game-download/

Walker, M. B. (1992). Irrational thinking among slot machine players. *Journal of Gambling Studies, 8*(3), 245–261.

Weatherly, J. N., Sauter, J. M., & King, B. M. (2004). The 'big win' and resistance to extinction when gambling. *The Journal of Psychology: Interdisciplinary and Applied, 138*(6), 495–504.

Wood, R. T., & Griffiths, M. D. (2008). Why Swedish people play online poker and factors that can increase or decrease trust in poker web sites: A qualitative investigation. *Journal of Gambling Issues, 21,* 80–97.

Woolley, R. (2007). "Conceptualising poker machine gambling as a technological zone" (conference paper). In *The Australian Sociological Association Conference* (4–7 December, Auckland, New Zealand). Retrieved from www. tasa.org.au/conferences/conferencepapers07/papers/168.pdf

Woolley, R., & Livingstone, C. (2010). Into the zone: Innovating in the Australian poker machine industry. In S. F. Kingma (Ed.), *Global gambling: Cultural perspectives on gambling organizations* (pp. 38–63). New York and London: Routledge.

WYTV (2017, December 22). Boom Boom Mancini celebrates new slot machine at Cleveland-area casino. *WYTV.* Retrieved from http://wytv.com/2017/12/22/boom-boom-mancini-celebrates-new-slot-machine-at-cleveland-area-casino/?preview_id=147555

Ziolkowski, S. (2017). *The World Count of Gaming Machines 2016.* Gaming Technologies Association. Retrieved from http://gamingta.com/wp-content/uploads/2017/05/World_Count_2016.pdf

5 Gamble-Play as *Second Life*
The Case of *PKR*

Remember, poker is all about getting information
—Slogan for the 3D online casino *PKR*

This chapter looks at the structural affordances that make the virtual world and online poker platform *PKR* a strong, pioneering example of gamble-play media. Even though *PKR* stopped operations in May 2017 due to financial difficulties, this gambling platform is a key, watershed example in the development of gamble-play media. Online poker platforms have come a long way since the first online casino, *Planet Poker*, dealt its inaugural hand on January 1, 1998. *Planet Poker* was a simple platform that presented a bird's-eye view of a poker table. Even though the game featured digital characters, their actions were limited, and play was constantly interrupted because of unreliable dial-up connections (Smith, 2011). Movement was cartoonish and sluggish.

Since the mid-2000s, digital gambling has appropriated the production processes and aesthetic qualities of mainstream video games. This has been made possible by better broadband and Wi-Fi connections, more powerful hardware and increasingly sophisticated game engines. These improvements can be seen in online casinos such as *PokerStars*, *888*, *Bodog* (poker.bodog.eu) and, most noticeably, the now defunct *PKR*. It is only fitting that poker would expand its possibilities through digital technology for, as Manovich puts it, "games are one cultural form which requires algorithm-like behaviour from the players" (2000, p. 180).

Poker has evolved through its digitisation. Gameplay has gone from being dependent on the materiality of cards and chips to being played on digital interfaces and through informational networks (Hoffer, 2007). Where early games were a lonely endeavour, online poker has become an increasingly participatory medium (Beer, 2009). From being played secretly or with an air of lawlessness, online poker has generated its own cultures of celebrity and aspiration. Because machines operate as both mediators and players, online poker has evolved from being a game predominantly defined by chance (even if skill is also involved) to one where skill is lauded. The complexity of online poker is defined by communicative acts that take place between humans brought together by non-human actors (machines) and between humans and machines. In complex online poker sites such as *PKR*, role playing has been core because gamblers are highly reliant on how their avatars express tells, bluffs and emotions.

The origins of modern poker lay in the pioneering drive of nineteenth-century America. Then, the Mississippi River served as a backdrop for a brewing gambling culture that was not devoid of certain drama. Fortunes were made and lost, and recently liberated slaves bet and lost their newly acquired freedom (Kelly, 2006). Much as on today's internet, some gamblers became professionals and established cultural and financial networks that ran parallel to mainstream cultural assemblages. Poker became a widespread cultural practice in the southern United States in the late nineteenth century, particularly via its dissemination through riverboats on the Mississippi (Humphreys, 2010, p. 494). Gamblers chose to bet on riverboats as they provided a jurisdictionally ambiguous space, much like the offshore physical location of the servers running today's online casinos (see Albarrán-Torres, 2017). Riverboats provide a powerful metaphor for understanding contemporary gambling assemblages such as *PKR*, which also navigate different types of ambiguity as hybrid media governed by changing legal regimes.

This chapter builds on the concepts developed in Part 1 of this book, "Digital gambling theory". It is a case study that analyses the real money online casino *PKR* (www.pkr.com), a state-of-the-art 3D immersive environment similar to video games and virtual worlds such as *Second Life* that, even though it was advanced in terms of technology, failed to sustain its business model. *PKR* was described in specialist publications as "a poker site with graphics and playability like a PlayStation video game but with real money up for grabs" (4kingbet, 2014); "not just an online poker room, it's a social networking hub, with a buzzing forum" (*Bluff Europe*, 2014) and comparable to console gaming. On its website, *PKR* also published enthusiastic testimonials in which players pointed to a technological shift in online poker that influenced the experience of play. Such is the case of a player called Jim:

> *PKR* has launched a poker site unrivalled by any of its competitors. It reminds me of when Pixar showed *Toy Story* to the film industry, every major studio realised that if they didn't change they would be out of the game. This site is so good that playing for fun is enjoyable and something you can do for hours without getting bored.
>
> (*PKR*, 2014)

Even though it was shut down due to bankruptcy, *PKR* is the epitome of digital gamble-play as the social and dramatic aspects of gambling were enhanced by the affordances of the platform. These features allowed actions akin to social networking sites, multiplayer video games and virtual environments. Through camera movements and cuts, action in *PKR* was presented in a dramatic fashion that emulated the format of televised poker tournaments (Schuck, 2010). *PKR* also generated its own celebrity culture around amateurs who had financial and reputational success in online poker and are now professional gamblers in both online and offline tournaments. When parent company Microgaming announced that *PKR* would cease operations in 2017 due to financial difficulties, players were unable to retrieve their balances immediately. Even though *PKR* had been in a slow decline for a few years, the player pool was still considerable. About 60,000 accounts had to be processed. In an unprecedented move, a rival casino, *Poker-Stars*, agreed to migrate these accounts, and their funds, to their own platform. By doing this, *PokerStars* gained access to 60,000 users and their balance information, potentially turning some of these into new *PokerStars* members. This transaction speaks of the social capital inherent in player profiles.

PKR is a classic example of a "spectacle" or "a social relation among people, mediated by images" (Debord, 1967, Chapter 1, Paragraph 4). In spectacles, the primary value is not assigned to the actual good – in this case, the consumption of bets – but its abstraction or visual representation (Debord, 1967; Kellner, 2004). This has ample political implications for the cultural practice of gambling as the basic "social relation" (Debord, 1967, Chapter 1, Paragraph 4), the winning and losing of money, is masked by mimicry and gameplay. *PKR* was branded as a product whose main asset was not the amount of pots or the frequency of wins but the formal and procedural features of the platform (which could perhaps explain its ultimate downfall). *PKR* brought out the inherent ludic aspects of gambling while generating other types of affects and sensations where winning and losing money was at times secondary to play, entertainment and technical innovation. As gamble-play media, *PKR* introduced users in new "intensive and extensive networks of enjoyment, production, and surveillance" (Dean, 2010, p. 4). Discerning the specific ways in which *PKR* generated social relations "mediated by images" (Debord, 1967, Chapter 1, Paragraph 4) will help us better grasp the cultural salience and innovation of digital gamble-play.

I support my argument by focussing on technical and cultural innovations that were involved in the remediation (Bolter & Grusin, 1999) of poker in *PKR*. The leisurely and social aspects of gambling came to the forefront through a visually and aurally rich interactive interface that was technically more complex than average online poker sites, such as *PokerStars*. *PKR* not only remediated the basic elements of a poker game but also the audiovisual tropes – close-ups of players' facial expressions, overhead cameras, infographics that reveal each player's standing in a particular hand – of televised poker tournaments, such as *World Series of Poker*, which is constructed following the conventions of sports broadcasting (Schuck, 2010).

In the *PKR* platform, gambling was further framed as play as it followed the hybrid logic of 'hypermediacy' and 'immediacy'. On the one hand, controls and infographics made users aware that they were attached to a state-of-the-art environment, leading them "to become aware of the new medium as a medium" (Bolter & Grusin, 1999, p. 6). They had to invest effort and creativity in the co-creation of the gambling experience. On the other hand, through realistic virtual environments, *PKR* introduced the player into a 'zone' (Schüll, 2012). In this 'zone', players abandoned themselves to actions that followed the logic of 'immediacy' (Bolter & Grusin, 1999, p. 6) (Figure 5.1).

As a spectacle, *PKR* contained key structural characteristics of video games, as recognised by King et al. (2010). Structurally, *PKR* can also be analysed as an assemblage made out of people, technology and the material and expressive goods they exchange (DeLanda, 2006). I identify some of these 'goods' and explain how they generated an immersive and novel experience in which gambling involved the manipulation of avatars and the navigation of virtual spaces.

Figure 5.1 The *PKR* interface. Note the different avatars, which include an alien and a player with a skeleton disguise.

PKR: Gamble-Play as Interactive Spectacle

At its peak, *PKR*'s reach within the online gambling community was vast. *PKR* was owned by PKR Limited. Both its headquarters and its game servers were located in the island of Alderney, a British Crown dependency near the coast of France and part of the Channel Islands. Most of *PKR*'s five million users came from the United Kingdom, but the player pool covered other European countries, including Germany, Finland, Greece, Norway, Portugal, Russia and Sweden. Due to regulations, *PKR* segregated websites in France (www.pkr.fr/fr/) and Italy (www.pkr.it/). It was not available in jurisdictions with tighter legal controls, such as the United States, Hong Kong, Israel, South Korea, Turkey and the Netherlands. Digital gambling has a global reach, but in legal terms, its practices are heavily bounded to locality (Albarrán-Torres, 2017; Hutto, 2005).

Unsurprisingly, *PKR* represented one of the most prominent partnerships between the video game and gambling industries when it comes to production processes. Jeremy 'Jez' San, an experienced video game developer, created this online casino. For decades, San has collaborated in the production of titles for platforms that range from the Commodore 64 (*Skyline Attack*, 1984) to Super NES (*Star Fox*, 1993) and PlayStation 3 (*Heavenly Sword*, 2007). The involvement of San in the creation of *PKR* exemplifies the convergence of the video game and gambling industries in the production of virtual environments and the formation of creative teams. Their expertise in creating engaging gameplay configurations in video games is imported to the production of gamble-play platforms. In an interview for *PKR*'s in-house magazine *Stacked*, which is not inaccessible after the site's downfall, San explained his motivations for creating the platform:

> I began to realise that the online versions of poker were not very good. They had the technical aspects without the fun aspects of the game. The cards were depicted as little icons, the bets by numbers, the players by text and if there was a picture it would be static with no representation of what they were up to.
>
> (*Stacked*, 2009)

PKR adapted to the technical affordances of desktop and mobile technologies while expanding its networks and infiltrating the spaces and flows of the everyday of its users. It could be played through a desktop program as well as in a mobile version for iPhone, iPad and Android. In both the mobile app and the desktop site, users could alternatively access a 2D version to have a swifter experience by saving memory and bandwidth, making player co-presence possible.

In *PKR*, the consumption of gambling was not only encouraged through repetition but also through the apparent uniqueness of each gambler's experience, which was achieved with game mechanics that allowed the user avatar and camera control. Contrary to other forms of machine-assisted gambling, such as slots, in which a repetitive action perpetually promises to result in a win, *PKR* seduced gamblers by making them co-creators of the gambling experience, a practice that superficially empowers users in other forms of interactive entertainment, such as massive multiplayer online role-playing games (MMORPGs) (Banks & Potts, 2010). Among some of the built-in affordances of *PKR*, which I detail later in this chapter, users could create a personalised avatar, send friend requests as on social networking sites such as Facebook, message other players, control a virtual camera, archive their learning process, convey different emotions at the table and buy both real and virtual items with their real-money winnings. As a gambling-machine (Albarrán-Torres, 2013), *PKR* strived to activate the desire to become someone else through the creation of an avatar and the desire to connect with others in a mediated space in order to 'have fun' and achieve reputational as well as financial success.

PKR was a digital version of what Ritzer calls "cathedrals of consumption" (1999), a term in which he groups sites of capitalist consumption, such as shopping malls, arcades and casinos. For Ritzer, "cathedrals of consumption" are highly rationalised settings destined for mass consumption and defined by several key mechanisms: simulation; the implosion or erosion of boundaries between two formerly distinct spheres, such as gambling and entertainment; and the manipulation of time and space (Ritzer & Stillman, 2001, p. 89). *PKR*'s main feature was online poker for real money, but following the casino model that privileges a variety of experiences contained in the same space (Ritzer & Stillman, 2001; Schüll, 2012), users could engage in other forms of entertainment and consumption, including shopping and side games, such as 3D blackjack, Caribbean stud poker, sports betting, European roulette, mini video poker, mini roulette, mini casino hold 'em and mini blackjack (Figure 5.2).

Figure 5.2 Promotional banner on *PKR*'s home page. The casino encouraged player engagement beyond the game (accessed on February 16, 2017 at www.pkr.com/en/community/). *PKR* is no longer in operation, and this web page is deactivated.

Like physical casinos, which generally have in-house restaurants and boutiques to keep money circulating within their confines (Fox, 2007; Jaschke & Otsch, 2003; Rotham, 2003), *PKR* encouraged its customers to spend their winnings in-house. In the *PKR* Shop, players were offered the possibility of exchanging their credits for a wide variety of products, which ranged from game consoles and TV screens to poker and soccer memorabilia, e-books, sunglasses and tickets to exclusive tournaments. *PKR* customers were also able to donate to a charity, *Ante up for Africa*, which has other corporate partners in the online casino industry, such as *PokerStars*. *PKR* was an expansive, engrossing experience. It followed the model of Las Vegas as a site of capitalist consumption, a model that Rotham has described as follows:

> Postmodern, postindustrial capitalism is about consuming experience, not goods, about creating insatiable desire that must be fulfilled in front of an approving audience. Las Vegas is geared to meet this challenge, to provide the audience, to deliver more than anywhere else and hold out the possibility of still more. The ability to quench desire brings people; the chance to dream of more brings them back again and again.
>
> (Rotham, 2003, p. 54)

As I have argued throughout this book, online casinos and other forms of digital gamble-play can be analysed through the lens of critical theory. For Debord, modern societies fetishise the representations of the real, privileging the symbolic over the material. That is the case of *PKR*, where the gameplay, as a representation of gambling mediated by avatars and other procedure-images, became at times more foregrounded than the act of wagering itself.

Debord is best known for *Society of the Spectacle*, published in 1967, long before the widespread dissemination of digital networked technologies. However, Debord's work is increasingly relevant when discussing digital communication and cultures generated by the digitisation of social practices that are highly reliant on images, as is the case in the media of digital gamble-play. Debord's ideas have been taken up recently by theorists of digital media, such as Italian philosophers Antonio Marturano and Sergio Bellucci, who argue that Facebook "is realising what Guy Debord calls 'the invasive forces of the spectacle'" (2009, p. 59). Similarly, Steven Best and Douglas Kellner contend that we are in a more advanced stage of the spectacle, "the *interactive spectacle*, that involves the creation of cultural spaces and forms that present exciting possibilities for creativity and empowerment of individuals, as well as novel forms of seduction and domination" (Best & Kellner, 1999, p. 144).

Digital gamble-play is a site of negotiation between individual empowerment and these "novel forms of seduction and domination" (Best &

Kellner, 1999, p. 144). Both new and reconfigured social relations are defined by the widespread use of digital media. "Interactive spectacles" (Best & Kellner, 2009) take the form of virtual worlds, video games, social media platforms, apps, interactive audiovisual content and other forms of computer-mediated communication (CMC) which influence the configuration of gamble-play.

We can also think, for instance, of the intricate set of relations established by MMORPGs, such as *World of Warcraft*, or virtual worlds, such as *Second Life*, both of which shared some key features with the online casino *PKR*, such as the creation of avatars and a system for exchanging virtual and real currency. They, too, empower players while at the same time seducing them in new ways (Best & Kellner, 1999) and generating new types of socialisation, production and consumption. Those interested in ethnographic studies on online realms should read Tom Boellstorff's *Coming of age in Second Life: An anthropologist explores the virtually human* (2008) and William Sims Bainbridge's *The Warcraft civilization: Social science in a virtual world* (2010). These books are pioneering academic explorations of the construction of identity, communities and cultural practices in virtual environments.

Debord begins *Society of the Spectacle*, an indictment of contemporary consumerist societies, with an all-encompassing decree:

> In societies where modern conditions of production prevail, all of life presents itself as an immense accumulation of spectacles. Everything that was directly lived has moved away into a representation.
>
> (Debord, 1967, Chapter 1, Paragraph 1)

As a Marxist theorist, Debord imagines a contemporary dystopia where social interactions are devoid of substance. 'Spectacles' can be understood as a modern equivalent to the flickering shadows that deceive the prisoners in Plato's allegory of the cave. For Debord, spectacles are "not a collection of images" but "a social relation among people, mediated by images" (Debord, 1967, Chapter 1, Paragraph 4). *PKR* could be read as a spectacle under this definition as the construction and management of procedure-images mediate social relations among gamblers and between gamblers and the house. Debord goes on to affirm that

> The spectacle grasped in its totality is both the result and the project of the existing mode of production. It is not a supplement to the real world, an additional decoration. It is the heart of the unrealism of the real society. In all its specific forms, as information or propaganda, as advertisement or direct entertainment consumption, the spectacle is the present model of socially dominant life.
>
> (Debord, 1967, Chapter 1, Paragraph 6)

PKR, as other gamble-play products, was "both the result and the project of the existing mode of production" (Debord, 1967, Chapter 1, Paragraph 6) in the gambling industry. As a collection of procedure-images – images that articulate particular types of procedural rhetoric – the sophisticated 3D environments in *PKR* were not a decoration but the cultural and media form itself.

The Debordian concept of the spectacular society has also been used elsewhere to describe gambling's place in contemporary capitalism. When analysing the gambling culture in Las Vegas, the epitome of spectacles and simulations, Robert P. Gephart states that a fundamental trait of the "spectacular society" is "the use of simulations to produce safe risk as a consumable service or commodity" (Gephart, 2001, p. 141). He also explores the relationship between risk and gambling:

> Financial safe risk emerges in images that depict organizationally produced financial or economic activities, services or products as safe, fun forms of entertainment and investment which can be legitimately pursued with limited concern for or likelihood of extensive problems or negative financial impacts.
>
> (Gephart, 2001, p. 146)

Gamble-play platforms such as *PKR* can be understood as an amalgamation of social relations that are mediated by complex visual mechanisms that involve risk that, seen as play or sport, is framed as "safe" or devoid of any substantial consequence (Gephart, 2001). This exchange is what sets real-money online gambling apart from most spectacles constructed through augmented or virtual reality representations: it involves the winning and losing of goods that are also valuable in real life. The consumption of bets in online casinos also has other implications, such as the risk of problem gambling derived from the always-on nature of gamble-play platforms as well as their playful sociotechnical dynamics.

How information is created, transferred and represented in poker – how the spectacle is constructed – is key to understanding the cultural dynamics of this practice, and how risk is sold as a form of entertainment. That is why the media in which the game is staged can generate new practices in terms of play, engagement and socialisation. As Hayano states in his study of analogue card games, poker is a game "of imperfect, or incomplete, information" where "players must form their own conclusions about what hands other players have, what betting decisions they may make, and what their behaviour means" (1982, p. 5; see also Billings et al., 2002). The interplay between subjects and the material and symbolic support through which they communicate, conceal and reveal information generates new cultural forms and practices.

In *PKR*, information was accumulated and shaped into a spectacle that drew from real-life, televised and cinematic representations of poker.

In this platform, information was selectively revealed through virtual camera movements and infographics that showed player statistics, card combinations and identity traits, such as each player's nationality. We can witness this dynamic in the games still published on *PKR*'s YouTube channel, PKRTV, which include a commentator's voiceover and showcase a variety of camera angles and movements that the gambler was able to control. Users also updated their own games (Figure 5.3).

How these exchanges of information came into being in *PKR* is defined by "the unnoticed technologies of the game, and the venue, from the cards to the chips and counting machines" that generated the gaming experience (Farnsworth & Austrin, 2010, p. 1125). In online poker, these "unnoticed technologies" are created by code and exteriorised by procedure-images. In virtual environments, such *PKR*, software serves as a cohesive force that brings the "assemblage of play" (Taylor, 2009) together. Software is "a kind of traffic between beings, wherein one sees, so to speak, the effects of the relationship" (Thrift & French, 2002, p. 311).

In regard to gambling, Martin Young is prompt to identify the fundamental role that software has "in the reconfiguration of the social relations of the game itself" (2010, p. 263). He argues, "human labour has been removed from the immediate production of gambling and replaced with linked random number generators, individually presented by electronic devices, in an increasingly private relationship between subject and machine" (Young, 2010, p. 263). However, *PKR* disrupted this

Figure 5.3 A 2016 YouTube video showing a real-money game in the online casino *PKR* (accessed on February 17, 2017 at www.youtube.com/watch?v=uJN9KLrVQ5g).

"private relationship" between the subject and the machine by shifting the emphasis from the production of random events to the staging of a spectacle.

Gamble-play products such as *PKR* are assemblages, "wholes characterized by relations of exteriority" (DeLanda, 2006, p. 203). As I explained in the Introduction, relations of exteriority establish that "a component part of an assemblage may be detached from it and plunged into a different assemblage", producing a different set of interactions (DeLanda, 2006, p. 203). In digital poker, the actions of human players and the procedures enacted by machines and made actual through procedure-images offer a multitude of inputs and outputs. Expressive components of other assemblages, such as the creation of realistic avatars in *Second Life* and other virtual environments, were plugged into the assemblage of gamble-play in *PKR*, generating a new media form and a new cultural form.

We can recall that DeLanda also points out that assemblages and their elements are defined along two dimensions: the material and the expressive. In the case of digital gamble-play, humans, machines and the cyborg-like actors composed of human and machine elements establish these relationships by alternating between material and expressive roles. Avatars, for example, mediate the material role of raising a bet or folding but also perform the expressive role of bluffing or showing preprogrammed emotions.

The *PKR* spectacle was an assemblage composed of human, non-human and hybrid actors that could in fact be defined as a "social relation among people, mediated by images" and destined for "entertainment consumption" (Debord, 1967, Chapter 1, Paragraph 6). Other new media theorists have offered alternate descriptions of similar assemblages where avatars have a key expressive role. In analysing the formation of normative frameworks in such visual-social spaces as *The Sims Online* and *Second Life*, Stromer-Gallet and Martey indicate that "the evolution of thinking about social norms online has moved from a mechanistic, somewhat technologically deterministic view to a systems view of humans and communication technology" (Stromer-Gallet & Martey, 2009, p. 1045). The authors explain that humans and technology are "intertwined" in a "complex system" that includes groups, identity, communication, norms and both offline and online contextual configurations (Stromer-Gallet & Martey, 2009). Similarly, in a paper that explores the challenges presented to ethnographic practice by the emergence of virtual worlds, Farnsworth and Austrin (2010) state that the construction of new media worlds involves

> numerous, often unnoticed intermediaries that link practices, entities, networks and even worlds together. They may work as individual agents but often they function in clusters – assemblages – to accomplish the work they do. Such assemblages are, commonly enough, a mixture of humans interacting with technologies.
>
> (Farnsworth & Austrin, 2010, p. 1125)

As an assemblage of "humans interacting with technologies" (Farnsworth & Austrin, 2010, p. 1125), *PKR* generated cultural spaces similar to other gambling environments, such as domestic environments, Las Vegas-like casinos and exclusive European betting rooms. As a 3D environment on par with *Second Life*, it achieved a high level of aesthetic and technical sophistication compared with other online casinos where the gameplay is carried out in a standard 2D representation, as in *PokerStars* or *888*.

What motivates gamblers to take risks in virtual spaces such as *PKR*? As Ferguson points out, gamblers' motivations cannot be understood on the basis of a "rational expectation" as they "lose repeatedly, so that any view of gambling which focusses directly on its outcomes confronts an essential contradiction" (Ferguson, 1999, p. xiii). This is where the play factor – the spectacular in gambling – takes prominence over winning and losing, where gamble-play opens up new sensations and new possibilities associated with the "limitlessness and intensity associated with becoming" (Cook, 2009, p. 196).

The Construction of the Spectacle: Structural Features in PKR

Caillois's typology of games, widely referenced in gambling studies (Reith, 1999; Young, 2010) and previously discussed in this book, can shed some light on how the ludic aspect of gambling gained prominence in *PKR*, and in gamble-play more generally. The video game features built into *PKR* presented different dynamics in Caillois's typology of games, as compared to traditional poker and online casinos with simpler interfaces. Let's recall that Caillois (1962) identifies four forms of play: *agôn* (competition), *alea* (chance), *mimesis* (mimicry, role playing) and *ilinx* (vertigo; a practice that alters sensorial perception). The ways in which analogue and digital gambling construct and exteriorise these forms of play through images, objects and procedures establish fundamental differences between these two cultural practices.

The staging of poker in *PKR* involved different mixtures of these types of play. In digital gamble-play, users need to acquire a particular literacy for the use of each platform. This knowledge adds an extra element of skill to games defined by chance or by traditional gambling skills. In the case of the remediation of poker in *PKR*, the ability to bluff, for example, translated into the capacity to communicate certain emotions through an avatar. *PKR* users were also offered the possibility of role playing or *mimesis* by creating avatars through which gamblers navigate visual-social spaces. The creation of avatars refashions one of the practices involved in analogue poker: the creation of a gambling persona as in real life, some poker players use props, such as sunglasses or headphones, to dumbfound their opponents.

PKR nourished a culture of *agôn* or competition through rankings as well as the formation of a celebrity culture around the brand. *PKR* required users to engage in *mimesis* through the creation of usernames and avatars. It also intensified *ilinx* or vertigo through the conflict-driven film and television tropes in the staging of digital poker games.

This online casino imported some of the main features of mainstream interactive entertainment. The following video game-like features, based on King et al. (2010), help us understand how *PKR* was constructed as a digital gamble-play assemblage and as an interactive spectacle. I will now explain how each of these features was built into the *PKR* platform. This analysis sheds light on how specific components of video game assemblages were plugged into the *PKR* assemblage to generate social relations mediated by procedure-images (Table 5.1).

Table 5.1 Structural characteristics in *PKR* that make it an example of digital gamble-play as it adapts structural characteristics of video games

Feature type	Sub-features	Features in PKR
Identity features	Avatar creation features	Complex avatar creation tools
		Emotes: exclusive tools to show emotions
Manipulation and control features	Player management features	Camera angles
		Dynamic view (virtual director, similar to televised poker games)
		First Person view (similar to First Person Shooter video games)
		Orbit camera
		Multi-tabling (users can play multiple games simultaneously)
Presentation features	Graphics and sound features	Complex virtual environments that recreate the aura of some cultural spaces of gambling: Atlantis, Basement Bar, Egyptian Casino, Monte Carlo, Home Game, Vintage Bar, Vegas Classic, PKR Studio, Zen Casino.
Social features	Social utility features	Team PKR Pro
	Social formation/ institutional features	PKR Social (offline meet-ups and tournaments)
	Leader board features	Social media accounts (Facebook, Twitter)
		Hall of Fame
		Player rankings
		Stacked magazine

Source: Table based on King et al. (2010, p. 93).

Identity Features

Gambling in *PKR* required the generation of a complex online identity that was more elaborate than the username and picture profiles found in most online casinos. How gamblers presented themselves at the poker table was central to the development, enjoyment and outcomes of the game. Identity features are "the ways in which the player can take on another identity in the game (as a fictional character or a construction of the self)" (King et al., 2010, p. 97). Identity features were fundamental in the construction of *PKR* as an interactive spectacle as they mediated the gambler's experience in ways that are exclusive to computer-mediated poker, and with a complexity then unique to *PKR*. As Hayano states, discussing traditional poker, "deception, miscommunication, and the analysis of the opponents' behaviour are important facets of the game" (1982, p. 4). The ways in which gamblers designed and manipulated their avatars were crucial to how they managed to deceive the rest of the players. Psychologists Galanxhi and Nah discovered in a study that compared user expression in text-based versus avatar-supported media, that avatars encourage deception, which "involves messages and information knowingly transmitted to create a false or misleading conclusion" (Galanxhi & Nah, 2007, p. 772). In *PKR*, this was mediated by emotes, discussed below.

Avatars are the most distinctive among the images that mediate "social relations among people" (Debord, 1967, Chapter 1, Paragraph 4) in *PKR* and other interactive spectacles. Much has been written, for example, about the expressive capacities of avatars in virtual environments (Bainbridge, 2010; Boellstorff, 2008). Söeffner and Nam describe avatars as "theatrical masks in a sense" (2007, p. 951), emphasising the performative capacities of computer-generated but user-manipulated mediators. In his ethnographic work in *Second Life*, Tom Boellstorff recalls that the term *avatar* is a "Sanskrit word [that] originally referred to the incarnation of a Hindu god (particularly Vishnu)" (2008, p. 128). He also points out that while historically the term has referred to incarnation or a transition from virtual to actual, in an online milieu "it connotes the opposite movement from actual to virtual, a decarnation or invirtualization" (Boellstorff, 2008, p. 128).

In *PKR*, gamblers played with real stakes through an avatar that could be either a direct representation of themselves or a character through which they performed. Performing with an avatar is an instance of *mimesis* or role playing (Caillois, 1962). The creation of virtual identities is also a manifestation of *presencing* or sustaining a public presence (Couldry, 2012), one of the digital media practices associated with the consumption of gamble-play products. Natasha Dow Schüll has argued that online poker is a technology of self (2016), which makes avatars even more important. *PKR*'s creator, Jeremy San, recognised the importance of avatars in generating emotional attachment in digital poker when recalling the production of the platform:

> There were even arguments that we weren't going to bother with avatars but coming from a design background I knew the emotional attachment of personalisation and there's almost a *Sims* (one of the biggest selling game series in the world) mentality.
>
> (Jeremy San quoted in *Stacked*, 2009, p. 22)

The *PKR* platform situated avatars according to class and gender identity. In *PKR*, through a complex avatar creation system, gamblers could develop characters by selecting gender, skin colour and body shape. They were able to manipulate the eyes, lips, nose and hair. At some point, gamblers could also pay to get a PKR Face, which was a 3D rendering of the player's face. The platform offered a wide variety of clothes and props to "perfect your poker personality" (PKR, 2014). Gamblers could use their real-money winnings to buy premium virtual items and even "celebrate in style with special seasonal costumes that are available for limited periods through Halloween, Christmas and Easter" (*PKR*, 2014). Seasonal promotions organised by gambling operators are constant in different forms of gamble-play, including social casino apps and online casinos, where other holidays, such as the Chinese New Year, are also used as promotional devices. This practice is also present in real-life gambling (Toby, 2013).

Through their avatars, gamblers could also use "specific emotes to let the table know if you're confident, nervous, thoughtful, aggressive, happy, indifferent or anything else" (PKR, 2014). Emotes in *PKR* were expressive goods borrowed both from common speech forms in internet culture (Crystal, 2001), and from gambling practices. In his foreword to Glenn McDonald's 2005 generalist book *Deal Me In! Online Cardrooms, Big Time Tournaments, and the New Poker*, poker world champion Chris Ferguson recognised the limitations of most online poker tables compared to real-life poker. He wrote,

> Since it isn't played face to face, it's impossible to see ones opponents' emotional reactions to different situations. Thus tells, though they still exist in a limited sense, don't have nearly the impact they do in the real world.
>
> (Ferguson in Foreword to McDonald, 2005, p. vii)

The designers of *PKR* tried to make up for this gap by programming a range of emotions that avatars could perform after the user typed particular kinds of emotions after the "/". According to *PKR*'s *Stacked* magazine, the most popular emotes were "Nice hand", "Clap", "Laugh My Ass Off", "Fresh Fish", "Good Luck", "Thank You", "Chuckle", "Cheer", and "Oh

My God" (*Stacked*, 2012). The ways in which gamblers configured their avatars affected the dynamics of their interactions with other players and, in turn, the approach that other players would take towards them (Figure 5.4).

Manipulation and Control Features

Manipulation and control features are functions that relate to the sense of mastery or control that the player feels over the game (King et al., 2010, p. 93). The sense of mastery or agency over the device is one of the fundamental traits of gamble-play, and what distinguishes it as a new media form. Gambling is predominantly defined by chance, but particular gameplay configurations and features allow gamblers to control the tempo of the gambling experience, creating the illusion of control over the outcome. However, the sense of control was provided in *PKR* through the manipulation of what the user saw and how they saw it.

Two of the most important expressive components in *PKR* were the virtual camera and real-time editing. Alexander Galloway has identified the expressive power of the virtual camera in video games and its affinities with cinema. He argues that "video games and film are influencing and incorporating each other in novel ways" (Galloway, 2006, p. 39). *PKR* brought the expressive power of the virtual camera to the realm of digital gamble-play, making the gambler a co-creator of the experience, exacerbating the feeling of control over the dynamics of play and, falsely, the outcome.

Figure 5.4 Avatar configuration in an earlier version of *PKR*. The player could choose from a variety of objects and features.

Image captured from www.youtube.com/watch?v=c4othsDp2Os.

In *PKR*, gamblers were provided with a sense of mastery over the experience by controlling the way in which the action was shown. As in mainstream console video games, they could choose different camera angles and viewing modes. In the Dynamic Mode, for example, gamblers were offered the possibility to be "the star of your own poker TV show with a 'director' automatically delivering all the best angles and following the action as it happens" (PKR, 2014). The Dynamic Mode generated real-time editing that resembled the fast-paced cuts in televised poker. The camera moved, shifted focus, circled the opponents and provided the gambler with aerial shots and first-person point-of-view takes. Crisp sound effects accompanied the dealing of hands and the accumulation of chips. The camera also panned and tilted in crane shots that would be impossible to replicate in real-life gambling without greatly interfering with the game. The camera became both the extension of the player's eyes and the tool through which space was constructed and navigated. On the other hand, editing blended together the camera shots and sound effects and, through real-time montage, refashioned the narrative of a poker game as dramatic storytelling.

Editing also controlled the tempo of the game and homogenised the perception of time to allow players' co-presence in the virtual environment. The ways in which the virtual camera and real-time editing created a coherent sequence of images and sounds was influenced by the aesthetics and grammar of other spectacles, such as television and film. Hayano identified this dynamic in the early 1980s, arguing that television shows

> may be partially responsible for feeding this interest by providing 'action' in gamble like games of luck and knowledge and by generating feverish levels of excitement for both contestants and viewers.
>
> (Hayano, 1982, p. 3)

These "feverish levels of excitement", of *ilinx*, were reproduced in *PKR* (Figures 5.5 and 5.6).

In his 2008 book *Video Game Spaces: image, play and structure in 3D worlds*, video game theorist Michael Nitsche writes about the construction of video game spaces following cinematic conventions. In video games, he states, "dynamic movements of the camera are used to dramatize the events and the spaces in which the actions unfold" as movement "defines the role of the camera as both spatial and spatializing entity" (Nitsche, 2008, p. 83). Nitsche conceives video game spaces as a "hybrid between architectural navigable and cinematically represented space", arguing that "the necessary eye of the virtual camera makes these spaces cinematic and the interaction makes them accessible

Figure 5.5 A bird's-eye view shot that shows the cards being dealt and establishes the placement of players in space. In the Dynamic mode, a "virtual director" chooses what the gamblers see.

Image captured on September 17, 2014 from www.pkr.com/en/game-info/viewing-options/.

Figure 5.6 The virtual camera in First Person perspective shows other players' emotions and provides information about the other players in the manner of televised poker tournaments.

Image captured on September 17, 2014 from www.pkr.com/en/game-info/viewing-options/ [Note: PKR declared bankruptcy in 2017, web page inactive].

much like architectural structures" (2008, p. 83). The virtual camera also establishes a video game subjectivity, which, as Chesher (2007) has pointed out, establishes a new type of relationship between the player and the world that reveals itself on the screen. Chesher defines this relationship as glaze – a concentrated vision, the hold of the game over the player and the sense of identification with the game world. He states that one of the elements of this subjectivity is sadomasochistic fetishism, which has also been related to the gambler's pleasure in losing and inflicting defeat on others (Bergler, 1957).

Poker gameplay is defined by the concealment and revelation of information. In *PKR*, the virtual camera chosen by the player selectively revealed information in the visual-social space. The space of gamble-play was actualised as the player navigated through it. Another viewing option, the First Person view, similar to those of mainstream First Person Shooter video games, allowed users to view the action through the eyes of their in-game character or avatar. First Person views in video games provide the user with a sense of control over the environment and a more intense sensation of embodiment (Barlett et al., 2007; Galloway, 2006). Other options included the Orbit camera, which was suspended over the virtual table and could be easily controlled with the mouse, showing the action from every possible angle, and the Overview camera, which provided a more traditional bird's-eye view of the action.

The platform provided other manipulation features, such as multi-tabling, which allowed the user to play multiple poker hands at the same time – a practice adopted by seasoned gamblers that has recently become institutionalised and is now one of the main differentiators between amateur and professional players (McCormack & Griffiths, 2012). Until multi-tabling was officially supported, players would find their own ways of playing multiple games simultaneously. At this point, multi-tabling was a form of what Salen and Zimmerman call transformative play, "when the free movement of play alters the more rigid structure in which it takes shape" (2003, p. 12). Multi-tabling is generally practised by gamblers who prefer to accumulate small wins in low-stakes tables, rather than risk larger amounts of money in high-stakes games (Griffiths et al., 2010). Multi-tabling was built into the *PKR* platform: "you can now play up to nine tables in separate windows! Cascade, tile, resize or arrange your table windows, lobby and mini games to suit your preference" (*PKR*, 2014). Multi-tabling is a feature that allows gamblers to experience control and increased agency over the platform. By allowing the player to be involved in various games at a time, the software expanded the spatial possibilities of poker compared to analogue gambling.

Presentation Features

Presentation features define how a game is constructed by images and sound (King et al., 2010, p. 97). In the case of *PKR*, these features were identified as the selling point and as the competitive advantage over other online casinos. Digital gamble-play media designers strive to replicate shared Western imaginations of the cultural spaces of gambling and how they should look.

The look and feel of online poker sites such as *PKR* are designed to recall a sense that Benjamin defines as "aura", the "uniqueness of a work of art", that which is "inseparable from its being imbedded in the fabric of tradition" (Benjamin, 2008). Benjamin coined this term to describe how the reproduction and mass production and distribution of works of art diminished or destroyed their aura. Even more, in the age of digital media, artefacts lose their aura. However, designers aspire to reinvesting artefacts with new forms of aura. As Bolter et al. argue, the question of loss of aura is particularly relevant for technologies

> which combine the physical and the virtual and therefore exist at the boundary between reproductive technologies and older forms, to which Benjamin ascribed aura.
>
> (Bolter et al., 2006, p. 21)

The way in which particular configurations of interactive images try to connect with aesthetic traditions in gambling cultures is significant in understanding gamble-play. Online poker tables actualise tradition, recalling the aura of traditional gambling. As Friedberg notes, when

> new media are introduced, metaphor functions as accommodation, wrapping the newly strange in the familiar language of the past ... In the culture of interface, we live in the realm of metaphor.
>
> (Friedberg, 2006, p. 12)

Digital poker interfaces such as *PKR* wrap the "newly strange" (Friedberg, 2006, p. 12) procedures with the familiar aura and *ethos* of traditional gambling practices. For Benjamin, the aura of the original undergoes a metamorphosis through its reproduction by mechanical means. This metamorphosis is also apparent in the digital, as is the case in the media shift currently experienced by gambling platforms. Benjamin's work has been influential in new media and digital art scholars (Cameron, 2007; Cavanagh, 2008; MacIntyre et al., 2004). Bolter et al. (2006) argue that digital technology "increases the options for designers and allows the invocation of aura in new ways" (p. 36). The mass customisation in digital technologies makes it pertinent to extend Benjamin's ideas for evaluating what is lost – and gained – through digitisation in gamble-play.

Benjamin argues that technical mass reproduction distorts the spatial relationship between the spectator and the original work of art. Technical reproduction can "put the copy of the original into situations which would be out of reach for the original itself" (1935/2008, p. 214). In digital poker, what is digitally reproduced is not a work of art per se (as in Benjamin's original approach) but a commodified experience that, just like art, introduces spectators into a world isolated from their own. In digital gamble-play, poker escapes the confinement of the gambling space (casinos, cruise ships, underground high-stakes gambling circles) and becomes available virtually everywhere, anytime through fixed and mobile digital screens. However, digital gamble-play is a move away from identical reproduction and towards customised experiences. In *PKR*, for example, users could manipulate their own avatars in great detail. Allowing more user control, however, does not stop online casinos from designing gameplay that strategically captures players.

In *PKR,* poker's fabric of tradition was invoked through the recreation of gambling spaces that recalled the look and feel of diverse gambling environments ranging from sophisticated casinos to domestic spaces and hypermediated settings such as TV studios – similar to the *World Series of Poker* video games designed by Activision for the PlayStation 3 and Xbox 360 consoles. Unlike most online poker platforms that offer limited environment options, in *PKR*, gamblers experienced not only Las Vegasian scenarios but also less glamorous settings, such as home games (with props that included pizza boxes and beer bottles), traversing a wide spectrum of gambling venues. As in mainstream console video games in the vein of *Grand Theft Auto, PKR* inserted players in virtual spaces that evoked real-life spaces.

These environments were filled with detail and distractions that emulated the hubbub of real-life gambling venues. A spokesperson for *PKR* explained the ways in which virtual environments were created in the platform:

> There's a fine line between adding depth and overloading the game so much that it distracts from the cards. That's why most of the features are sneakily awesome – subtle touches like the background characters.
>
> (Marketwired, 2014)

Gamblers could enter representations of diverse spaces that evoke particular gambling cultures. The underground high-stakes room Atlantis and the speakeasy-inspired Basement Bar related back to the origins of poker as a secretive, illegal activity. The Egyptian Casino evoked the Luxor casino in Las Vegas, a site of spectacular simulation where "designers have exhibited a consummate dedication to Egyptian art, architecture and cultural custom at every level" and where "ritual objects of veneration… have been transposed to the modern sphere" (Meskell, 2005, pp. 67–68). Meskell further describes the Luxor as a "heterotopic space where time and space have collapsed" (Meskell, 2005, p. 68).

Social Features

PKR players could access social features to communicate with other players online and offline. These social features "create a cooperative and competitive community of players" (King et al., 2010, p. 93). These features included social media channels, such as Facebook and Twitter; a Hall of Fame showcasing the highest ranked players; and offline meet-ups and tournaments.

These types of features are a constant in social casino apps but less common in online poker sites, where the competitive nature of play is emphasised. Research conducted by Kinnunen et al. among Finnish on-line poker players concluded that online gambling has evolved from an "asocial to a social activity" and that platforms have made interaction an essential part of the gaming experience (Kinnunen et al., 2012, p. 1).

Poker playing in *PKR* was designed to be a more social activity: "Poker's more than just a card game, it's a people game" (*PKR*, 2014). Upon sign-up, gamblers were given a MyPKR account, through which they could track their progress, maintain a friend list and manage their *PKR* money. Through these activities, users constructed a personal story of their gam-bling experience over time. The interface resembled player profiles in video games and social networking sites.

Ritzer and Stillman describe the erosion of boundaries between gam-bling and other activities, such as tourism and shopping, in Las Vegas:

> One of the interesting things about the use of implosion in Las Vegas is the way in which it has confounded the meanings associated with gambling.
>
> (Ritzer & Stillman, 2001, p. 93)

In *PKR*, gambling was associated with computer-mediated socialisation, which complicated the relationship among gamblers, who are conceived as 'friends' in many other gamble-play platforms, following the conven-tions of social media. By imploding the spheres of gambling and online friendship, gamble-play turns a relationship that is traditionally based on anonymity (in casino gambling, offline and online), to one where gamblers are amicable. *PKR* also ran Facebook and Twitter accounts (@pkrpokerpro) through which players could find out about tourna-ments, learn playing methods or organise meetings with other gamblers, both online and offline. At its peak, *PKR* has more than 25,000 fans on Facebook and more than 10,000 followers on Twitter. The company also published a magazine, *Stacked*, that revolved around the PKR cul-ture and generated brand awareness and consumer loyalty.

Through offline tournaments and meetups, *PKR* promoted brand affil-iation through the configuration and maintenance of groups of poker en-thusiasts who shared a geographical location in the United Kingdom. This was done through PKR Social, which offered users to "Meet your PKR buddies and put names to faces..." (PKR, 2014). PKR Social organised poker tournaments as well as other activities including golf games and pool tournaments. In a process counter to the "decarnation" (Boellstorff, 2008) experienced by players through avatars, avatars are incarnated when gamblers meet up in real life. *PKR* established its position on the formation of communities through its official communications:

> Playing poker online is our first love, but hanging out, competing and living it up with our poker mates is a very close second... Apart from amazing gameplay, one thing that has always set PKR apart from the competition is the awesome sense of community among our players. And now there is even more chance to get involved and meet your poker buddies at a series of kick ass events across the UK!

Online, *PKR* constructed a cooperative yet competitive environment. It used devices similar to leader boards in video games and other gamble-play media referenced earlier in this book, enhancing the reputational value of winning. As explained in Chapter 3, gamble-play platforms expand their networks by adding socialising features that highlight the social and competitive aspects of gambling. In *PKR* one of these features was the creation of a system in which amateur players could become professionals and ultimately be part of *PKR*'s Hall of Fame. There were also player rankings where customers could "Check out the *PKR* poker rankings to sort out the best from the rest and see how you compare with other *PKR* tournament players" (PKR, 2014). The ranking system highlighted gamblers' nationalities, which further bridged the online and offline environment, as well as the gambler's avatar and real-life identities.

The gambler progresses through a poker career in a similar way to levels in a competitive video game. The goal is to become famous. *PKR* incorporated the cultural dynamics of the celebrity culture present in global poker, which is "richly populated with its own celebrities and celebration of success, both financial and reputational" (Austrin & Farnsworth, 2012, p. 337) and is "a central celebration of contemporary capitalism" (Austrin & Farnsworth, 2012, p. 339).

The competitive features in *PKR* exemplify how this and other online casinos (most saliently *PokerStars*) nourish a culture in which amateur players can become professionals. What professionalism entails in gambling can be explained through David Hayano's 1982 pioneering anthropological work on poker players, *Poker Faces: The Life and Work of Professional Card Players*. After observing gamblers in card rooms in California, Hayano developed a typology of professional poker players based on the role that gambling plays in their lives.

Hayano states that for a poker player to be considered a professional, they have to derive "all or a significant chunk of his [*sic*] income by playing poker as a sole or in some cases a subsidiary livelihood" (1982, p. 20). The types of professional poker players identified by Hayano are: 1. *Working professional*, who works full-time, part-time or sporadically and earns a substantial amount of money from gambling regularly on the side; 2. *Outside-supported professional*, where the gambler possesses a pension, retirement or trust fund as main form of income; 3. *Subsistence Professional*, a retiree or younger man or woman who chooses not to work for others. In order to survive, this pro must play poker and win consistently; and 4. *Career professional*, who lives almost entirely off poker winnings (Hayano, 1982, pp. 20–24).

PKR built a culture of competition that consistently encouraged players to aspire to become career professionals. Austrin and Farnsworth (2012) argue that offline poker has generated a culture of celebrity with its own score of success stories that solidifies the collective identity of poker enthusiasts. *PKR* strengthened its brand by creating an explicit meritocracy around it. Online poker champions are transnational celebrities who aid in the normalisation of poker as an acceptable pastime and a new sport. Consider, for example, the case of Adrien Allain or "zlatan35", a consummate "career professional" (Hayano, 1982). Allain is a French player who became part of PKR Team Pro in 2010 after building an online reputation in *PKR* and winning USD $391, 000 in a real-life tournament, the Asian Poker Tour in Macau (a buoyant gambling economy which has surpassed Las Vegas as the main gambling hub in the world). Allain created and nourished an online identity and then succeeded in the global poker circuit, working as one of *PKR's* ambassadors. He was part of the PKR Hall of Fame. The economies of celebrity in online gambling are similar to those of video games, where the most successful players become online celebrities in their own right by broadcasting their games through platforms such as Twitch (Dredge, 2014; Groen, 2012; Keogh, 2014; Sherr, 2013).

Other members of Team PKR Pro included Eleanor Gudger or "Elz442", an English player who in seven years of online playing amassed USD $225,000 in winnings (PKR, 2014) and Steven Richner or "Stevee6666", a chef turned poker pro who after two years of online play joined the live tournament circuit. Members of Team PKR Pro also worked as brand ambassadors and promoters, keeping various channels open to communicate with gamblers. They held institutional Twitter accounts through which they commented on current events, such as the *World Series of Poker*, and shared personal moments from their everyday lives, such as photographs of a beer drunk after a game. They also shared the joys and vicissitudes of a professional gambler's life:

> Darn ran into the embodiment of the downside of live poker @ LeicesterPoker slow rolling loud mouth, bust MTT n skipping cash #moodkiller.
>
> (@Elz442, August 31, 2014)

In their social networking accounts, professional gamblers experienced what Wesch calls "context collapse" (2009). Professional players performed as brand ambassadors for *PKR*, sharing intimate moments to generate "a sense of closeness and familiarity between themselves and their followers" (Marwick & boyd, 2011, p. 147). This also produced brand affiliation. By providing inside knowledge of the world of poker, they promoted

> the process of publicly performing a connection between practitioners and fans using language, words, cultural symbols, and convention.
> (Marwick & boyd, 2011, p. 147)

Celebrity culture in online spaces such as *PKR* is one of the ways in which gambling enters domestic and social spheres previously foreign to it. It also shifts the perception of poker in moral terms. Gambling was one of the pioneering practices of an underground and untaxed online economy – alongside pornography, for instance. The internet provided a safe haven for cultural practices that carried the stigma of taboo, which was a feasible option thanks to the possibility of anonymity in online spaces. Just as traditional poker flourished in the isolated, outlaw river culture of the Mississippi and then became normalised as it spread inland (Findlay, 1986; Lears, 2003), digital poker first prospered in shady internet enterprises and is now becoming normalised by creating new experiences. Online poker has acquired an allure that encourages social cohesion among gamblers. High-profile players live their own rags-to-riches journey and reach the status of stardom. Skill and persistence are required in order to be a global poker superstar like the Team PKR Pro members Allain, Gudger and Richner.

Conclusion

PKR is a strong example of the cultural form of online gamble-play, where gambling is experienced as play. As interactive spectacles more closely associated with video games than gambling, gamble-play platforms mark a significant media change that reframes gambling's positioning in popular culture and entertainment markets.

In this chapter, I have explained how *PKR* was a salient form of gamble-play and why it could be categorised as a spectacle (Debord, 1967) as well as the political and cultural implications of this media and cultural change. As an interactive spectacle, *PKR* foregrounded the play aspect of gambling over the consumption of bets, which has repercussions in how gambling is perceived as a cultural form and how it is consumed.

References

4kingbet (2014). PKR Poker Review. 4kingbet. Retrieved from http://www.4kingbet.com/poker/reviews/pkr/ [the URL is no longer active]

Albarrán-Torres, C. (2013). Gambling-machines and the automation of desire. *Platform: Journal of Media and Communication, 5*(1). Retrieved from https://platformjmc.com/2013/10/01/vol-5-issue-1/v5i1_torres/

Albarrán-Torres, C. (2017) Where the stakes are higher: Transnational labor and digital gambling media. In Goggin, G. and McLelland, M. (Eds.), *The Routledge Companion to Global Internet Histories* (pp. 425–435). London, New York: Routledge.

Austrin, T. & Farnsworth, J. (2012). Celebrity, infamy, poker. *Celebrity Studies*, 3(3), 337–339.

Bainbridge, W. S. (2010). *The Warcraft civilization: Social science in a virtual world.* Cambridge: MIT Press.

Banks, J., & Potts, J. (2010). Co-creating games: A co-evolutionary analysis. *New Media & Society, 12*, 235–270.

Barlett, C. P., Harris, R. J., & Baldassaro, R. (2007). Longer you play, the more hostile you feel: Examination of first person shooter video games and aggression during video game play. *Aggressive Behavior, 33*(6), 486–497.

Beer, D. (2009). Power through the algorithm? Participatory web cultures and the technological unconscious. *New Media & Society, 11*(6), 985–1002.

Benjamin, W. (2008). *The work of art in the age of mechanical reproduction (Penguin Great Ideas)*. London: Penguin. (Original work published 1935).

Bergler, E. (1957). *The psychology of gambling.* New York: International Universities Press.

Best, S., & Kellner, D. (1999). Debord, cybersituations, and the interactive spectacle. *SubStance, 28*(3), 129–156.

Billings, D., Davidson, A., Schaeffer, J., & Szafron, D. (2002). The challenge of poker. *Artificial Intelligence, 134*(1), 201–240.

Bluff Europe (2014) PKR.com – Bonus and Promotions. *Bluff Europe*. Retrieved from www.bluffeurope.com/reviews/en/PKR-com_3735.aspx.

Boellstorff, T. (2008). *Coming of age in Second Life: An anthropologist explores the virtually human.* Princeton: Princeton University Press.

Bolter, J. D., & Grusin, R. (1999). *Remediation: Understanding new media.* Cambridge: MIT Press.

Bolter, J. D., MacIntyre, B., Gandy, M., & Schweitzer, P. (2006). New media and the permanent crisis of aura. *Convergence: The International Journal of Research into New Media Technologies, 12*(1), 21–39.

Caillois, R. (1962). *Man, play and games.* Urbana: University of Illinois Press.

Cameron, F. (2007). Beyond the cult of the replicant: Museums and historical digital objects–traditional concerns, new discourses. In F. Cameron & S. Kenderdine (Eds.), *Theorizing digital cultural heritage: A critical discourse* (pp. 49–75). Cambridge: MIT Press.

Cavanagh, T. (2008). The work of art in the age of mechanical production. *International Journal of Technology and Human Interaction, 4*(3), 27–42.

Chesher, C. (2007). Neither gaze nor glance, but glaze: Relating to console game screens. *Scan Journal, 4*(2). Retrieved from http://scan.net.au/scan/journal/display.php?journal_id=19

Cook, I. (2009). The body without organs and Internet gaming addiction. In M. Poster & D. Savat (Eds.), *Deleuze and new technology* (pp. 185–205). Edinburgh: Edinburgh University Press.

Couldry, N. (2012). *Media, society, world: Social theory and digital media practice.* Cambridge: Polity.

Crystal, D. (2001). *Language and the Internet.* Cambridge: Cambridge University Press.

Dean, J. (2010). *Blog theory: Feedback and capture in the circuits of drive.* Cambridge: Polity.

Debord, G. (original 1967). *Society of the Spectacle.* Marxists.org. Retrieved from www.marxists.org/reference/archive/debord/society.htm

DeLanda, M. (2006). *A new philosophy of society: Assemblage theory and social complexity.* London, New York: Continuum.

Dredge, S. (2014, June 3). Professional video gaming becoming global spectator sport. *The Guardian.* Retrieved from www.theguardian.com/technology/2014/jun/02/professional-video-gaming-global-spectator-sport-study

@Elz442 (2014) Darn ran into the embodiment of the downside of live poker @ LeicesterPoker slow rolling loud mouth, bust MTT n skipping cash #moodkiller. *Twitter.com.*

Farnsworth, J., & Austrin, T. (2010). The ethnography of new media worlds? Following the case of global poker. *New Media Society, 12*(7), 1120–1136.

Ferguson, H. (1999). Preface: Gambling, chance and the suspension of reality. In G. Reith (Ed.), *The age of chance: Gambling in western culture* (pp. xiv–xix). London: Routledge.

Findlay, J. M. (1986). *People of chance: Gambling in American society from Jamestown to Las Vegas.* Cambridge: Oxford University Press.

Fox, W. L. (2007). *In the desert of desire: Las Vegas and the culture of spectacle.* Reno: University of Nevada Press.

Friedberg, A. (2006). *The virtual world: From Alberti to Microsoft.* Cambridge: MIT Press.

Galanxhi, H., & Nah, F. F. H. (2007). Deception in cyberspace: A comparison of text-only vs. avatar-supported medium. *International Journal of Human-Computer Studies, 65*(9), 770–783.

Galloway, A. (2006). *Gaming: Essays on algorithmic culture.* Minneapolis: University of Minnesota Press.

Gephart, R. P., Jr. (2001). Safe risk in Las Vegas. *M@n@gement, 4*(3), 141–158.

Griffiths, M., Parke, J., Wood, R., & Rigbye, J. (2010). Online poker gambling in university students: further findings from an online survey. *International Journal of Mental Health and Addiction, 8*(1), 82–89.

Groen, A. (2012, September 29). How video games are becoming the next great North American spectator sport. *Ars Technica.* Retrieved from http://arstechnica.com/gaming/2012/09/how-video-games-are-becoming-next-great-north-america-spectator-sport/

Hayano, D. M. (1982). *Poker faces: The life and work of professional card players.* Berkeley: University of California Press.

Hoffer, R. (2007). *Jackpot nation: Rambling and gambling across our landscape of luck.* New York: Harper-Collins e-books.

Humphreys, A. (2010). Semiotic structure and the legitimation of consumption practices: The case of casino gambling. *Journal of Consumer Research, 37*(3), 490–510.

Hutto, J. (2005). What is everybody else doing about it? A foreign jurisdictional analysis of Internet gaming regulation. *Gaming Law Review, 9*(1), 26–34.

Jaschke, K., & Ötsch, S. (Eds.) (2003). *Stripping Las Vegas: A contextual review of casino resort architecture* (Vol. 7). Weimar: University of Weimar Press.

Kellner, D. (2004). Media culture and the triumph of the spectacle. *Razón y Palabra*. Retrieved from www.gseis.ucla.edu/faculty/kellner/essays/mediaculture triumphspectacle.pdf

Kelly, J. (2006). Poker: The very American career of the card game you can learn in 10 minutes and work on for the rest of your life. *American Heritage, 57*(6). Retrieved from https://www.americanheritage.com/content/poker

Keogh, B. (2014, June 3). The virtual grandstands of professional video gaming. *ABC the Drum*. Retrieved from www.abc.net.au/news/2014-06-03/keogh-video games-as-a-spectator-sport/5495870

King, D., Delfabbro, P., & Griffiths, M. (2010). Video game structural characteristics: A new psychological taxonomy. *International Journal of Mental Health and Addiction, 8*(1), 90–106.

Kinnunen, J., Rautio, E., Alha, K., & Paavilainen, J. (2012). Gambling in social networks: Gaming experiences of Finnish online gamblers. DiGRA Nordic 2012 Conference: Local and Global-Games in Culture and Society.

Lears, J. (2003). *Something for nothing: Luck in America*. New York: Viking.

MacIntyre, B., Bolter, J. D., & Gandy, M. (2004). Presence and the aura of meaningful places. *Presence: Teleoperators and Virtual Environments, 6*(2), 197–206.

Manovich, L. (2000). Database as a genre of new media. *AI & Society, 14*(2), 176–183.

Marketwired (2014) Have You Spotted the 'Sneakily Awesome' Gameplay Features in PKR's TV Ads? Marketwired.com Retrieved December 2017, from www.marketwired.com/press-release/have-you-spotted-the-sneakily-awesome-gameplay-features-in-pkrs-tv-ads-1870220.htm

Marturano, A., & Bellucci, S. (2009). A Debordian analysis of Facebook. *ACM SIGCAS Computers and Society, 39*(3), 59–68.

Marwick, A. E. & boyd, d. (2011). I tweet honestly, I tweet passionately: Twitter users, context collapse, and the imagined audience. *New Media & Society, 13*(1), 114–133.

McCormack, A., & Griffiths, M. D. (2012). What differentiates professional poker players from recreational poker players? A qualitative interview study. *International Journal of Mental Health and Addiction, 10*(2), 243–257.

McDonald, G. (2005). *Deal me in: Online cardrooms, bigtime tournaments, and the new poker*. San Francisco, London: Sybex.

Meskell, L. (2005). Objects might appear closer than they are. In D. Miller (Ed.), *Materiality* (pp. 51–71). Duke: Duke University Press.

Nitsche, M. (2008). *Video game spaces: Image, play and structure in 3D*. Cambridge: MIT Press.

Reith, G. (1999). *The age of chance: Gambling in Western culture*. London: Routledge.

Ritzer, G. (1999). *Enchanting a disenchanted world: Revolutionising the means of consumption*. Thousand Oaks: Pine Forge Press.

Ritzer, G., & Stillman, T. (2001). The modern Las Vegas casino-hotel: The paradigmatic new means of consumption. *M@n@gement, 4*(3), 83–99.

Rotham, H. (2003). The shape of the city: Money and the visual face of Las Vegas. In K. Jaschke & S. Ötsch (Eds.), *Stripping Las Vegas: A contextual review of casino resort architecture* (Vol. 7). Weimar: University of Weimar Press.

Salen, K., & Zimmerman, E. (2003). *Rules of play*. Cambridge: MIT Press.

Schuck, R. I. (2010). The rhetorical lines on TV's poker face: Rhetorical constructions of poker as sport. *American Behavioral Scientist, 53*(11), 1610–1625.

Schüll, N. D. (2012). *Addiction by design: Machine gambling in Las Vegas*. Princeton: Princeton University Press.

Schüll, N. D. (2016). Abiding chance: Online poker and the software of self-discipline. *Public Culture, 28*(380), 563–592.

Sherr, I. (2013, November 24). Video games become a spectator sport. *Wall Street Journal*. Retrieved from https://www.wsj.com/articles/videogames-become-a-spectator-sport-1385339390

Smith, E. (2011, August 10). Planet Poker Era. *Poker History*. Retrieved from www.pokerhistory.eu/history/planet-poker-first-online-poker-room

Söeffner, J., & Nam, C. S. (2007). Co-presence in shared virtual environments: Avatars beyond the opposition of presence and representation. In *Human-computer interaction: Interaction design and usability* (pp. 949–958). Berlin: Springer Berlin Heidelberg.

Stacked (2009). Behind the Avatars. *Stacked*, Issue 4, Spring 2009. Retrieved from www.pkr.com/en/community/stacked/?stackedId=9 [Note: PKR declared bankruptcy in 2017, web page inactive].

Stacked (2012)./Express yourself. *Stacked*, Issue 16, Spring 2012, 42–45. Retrieved from www.pkr.com/en/community/stacked/?stackedId=20#page=42 [Note: PKR declared bankruptcy in 2017, web page inactive].

Stromer-Gallet, J. and Martey, R.S. (2009). Visual spaces, norm governed places: The influence of spatial context online. *New Media Society, 11*(6), 1041–1060.

Taylor, T. L. (2009). The assemblage of play. *Games and Culture, 4*(4), 331–339.

Thrift, N. & French, S. (2002). The automatic production of space. *Transactions of the Institute of British Geographers, New Series, 27*(3), 309–335.

Toby, X. (2013, November 13). Chasing the dragon: The gambling ad con. *The Sydney Morning Herald*. Retrieved from www.smh.com.au/entertainment/about-town/chasing-the-dragon-the-gambling-ad-con-20131112-2xdup.html

Wesch, M. (2009). Youtube and you: Experiences of self-awareness in the context collapse of the recording webcam. *Explorations in Media Ecology, 8*(2), 19–34.

Young, M. (2010). Gambling, capitalism and the State: Towards a new dialectic of the Risk Society? *Journal of Consumer Culture, 10*(2), 254–273.

Online casinos cited

PKR Limited (n.d.). PKR Let's Play. *pkr.com*. Retrieved September 2014, from www.pkr.com/en/ [Note: PKR declared bankruptcy in 2017, web page inactive].

Rational Entertainment Enterprises Limited (2014). PokerStars.com. *pokerstars.com*. Retrieved September 2014, from www.pokerstars.com/

6 Mobile Gamble-Play Apps
A Casino in Your Pocket

With the *Slots Journey* application you'll experience the full scale of uplifted emotions just like a real casino player but at the same time, you won't risk losing a single cent!

—*Slots Journey,* promotional slogan

Gamble-play is a malleable cultural form that has found its way to millions of mobile screens, mainly smartphones, forming new techno-social assemblages. In the social casino market, users play apps in which they cannot win or lose real money but pay for enhanced experiences. These apps expand available spaces and opportunities for gambling-like practices, adapting to regulatory restrictions and finding new avenues for revenue, such as the 'freemium' model inaugurated by pioneering companies like Zynga (Albarrán-Torres & Goggin, 2014). Gamble-play app designers adapt to the affordances of mobile devices while reframing the procedures and conventions of previous gambling media, such as slot machines, a long-standing technology.

The relationship between mobile technology and gambling started in the early 2000s, when cell phones' capabilities were found to be "fine for such things as lotteries, sweepstakes, and sports betting (without streaming video)" (Owens, 2010, p. 172). These market segments were quickly adopted in countries such as the United Kingdom, the Netherlands and Australia (Owens, 2010), where, for example, mobile sports betting is a burgeoning industry (Gainsbury et al., 2012). Early on in the development of mobile technology, however, the remediation (Bolter & Grusin, 1999) of other forms of gambling, such as poker and slots, remained elusive due to technical limitations.

With the advent of the smartphone in the late-2000s and its increased capacities in graphics, speed and screen space, other gambling products, such as duplicate versions of poker and blackjack, made their way onto mobile screens through apps (Owens, 2010). The technocultural dynamics established by the mobile phone expand the possibilities of gamble-play by allowing people and operators to be co-present in new ways. They also expand the possibilities for managing social relationships (Licoppe, 2004) around gambling rituals, as we will see.

However, gambling for real money in mobile poker and slots is still somewhat limited. This is due mainly to restrictive regulatory frameworks based on geographical location and jurisdiction. For example, gambling companies in New Jersey, one of the first US states to legalise online gambling, operate mobile apps but can only offer them to users who live in the state *and* access the app from within its borders (Parry, 2014). Another blockage is the difficulty of devising mechanisms to stage transactions in a purely mobile space whereby "the payment solution of mobile gaming is not organic to participation" (Owens, 2010, p. 172). As the apps market is administered and controlled by tightly managed companies such as Apple (through its App Store) and Google (Play Store), which comply with local and transnational gaming regulations, historically unregulated gambling is not as adaptable to mobile markets as it has been to the internet (Hörnle & Zammit, 2010). Although there are apps that allow real-money gambling, they have been in effect mobile extensions of well-established online operators, such as *PokerStars*, *888* and the ill-fated *PKR*.

This chapter examines slot or pokie apps that operate on the 'freemium' model in which players cannot win real money. Mobile devices turn gamble-play into an experience that is at the same time more intimate and increasingly collective. Pokie apps are slot machine apps used in mobile devices, mainly smartphones and tablets, but are also accessible through social media platforms such as Facebook and the Chinese platform Tencent – users can generally move across platforms with the same profile, keeping a portable archive of their wins. Pokie apps are mobile applications that involve wins in play currency, and build on the structural characteristics and cultural meanings of both slot machines and mobile phones.

Pokie apps include *Slots Journey*, *Slots by Zynga* and *Slotomania*, which are analysed in this chapter, but also many others, such as IGT's *Double Down*, *Big Fish Casino* (now owned by Aristocrat), *Hit It Rich* (also developed by Zynga), *Slots Craze*, *House of Fun Slots*, *Best Casino Slots Bingo and Poker*, and *Caesars Slots*, which is operated by Caesars Entertainment, a long-standing institution in the real-money gambling industry, with venues in Las Vegas and Atlantic City.

Pokie apps take on the affordances of social networking sites and invite users to engage in the digital media practices that Couldry (2012) identifies and that I discuss in Chapter 3, such as creating a public profile, inviting other social media users to join, sharing and archiving. Pokie apps also recontextualise some rhetorical procedures of video gaming, particularly those related to the quest and skill-based movement through levels.

I use the nomenclature 'pokie apps' because I situate this analysis in the Australian context, where this new cultural form has generated public concerns and brought vested interests involving the gambling industry to light. Concerns and interests are stirred because pokie apps remediate (Bolter & Grusin, 1999) particular aspects of pokies, a controversial gambling platform in Australia, the market on which some of the main arguments of this book focus. The ubiquitous placement of traditional slots in urban and rural spaces has caused significant anxieties derived from concerns about the problematic consumption of gambling. The portability and ubiquity of mobile devices have propagated and rekindled these preoccupations. Pokie apps reveal some of the ways in which the technologies of digital gambling, social gaming apps and pokies interact both as media and as manifestations of traditional gambling cultures.

This chapter is structured in five sections, which show how mobile gamble-play media remediate previous gambling media, such as slot machines, and how they establish complementary relations with other cultural forms, such as social games. First, I situate pokie apps within the social casino games industry and describe the ways in which they modify slot machine play in their spatial and temporal dynamics. Second, I discuss a telling cultural juncture between social casino apps and social games: the critiques that claim the structures of social games are based on similar reward and punishment mechanisms (King et al., 2010) to those in slot machines. This indicates that, as a long-standing ludic media form, gambling has also influenced social games, the larger market segment in which social casino apps are categorised. Third, I discuss the social imaginaries and cultural anxieties generated around the ubiquitous placing of pokie machines in Australia and the ways in which pokie apps appropriate their cultural meanings and instances of procedural rhetoric (Bogost, 2007). Through assemblage theory (DeLanda, 2006), I then analyse three popular pokie apps – *Slotomania*, *Slots by Zynga* and *Slots Journey* – and the ways in which they synthesise discourses associated with slot machines through the appropriation of their procedures, audiovisual design and iconography. To conclude, I discuss three cases in which gambling apps generated controversy in Australia as hybrid media that exist in the liminal space that separates gambling and play. These controversies are indicative of the disruptive nature of gamble-play.

Social Casino Apps: Gambling for Nothing on Mobile Phones

The first vignette in Chapter 1[1] helped illustrate a fundamental shift that gamble-play practices are undergoing through the widespread use of 'social casino gaming'. Social casino gaming establishes new economic dynamics that correspond to my conceptualisation of 'gamble-play media', whereby users pay for gambling or gambling-like experiences not only with money but also with *playbour* (Kücklich, 2005), time and social media influence and reach. Business analysts describe the social casino gaming revenue model as games that are "not considered gambling chiefly because players can put money into a game but never take it out" and where "players use real money to buy virtual credits, then use those credits to buy virtual goods" (GamblingData, 2012). The revenue model of social casinos is based on the 'freemium' model, where play is free, but players have the ability to use real money to purchase additional 'credits' or features that would otherwise be earned through extended gameplay.

(Dayanim, 2014, p. 31)

Social casino apps are a culturally complex and economically profitable phenomenon. Pokie apps are a particular form of 'social casino gaming' or what, alternatively, Albarrán-Torres and Goggin (2014) have theorised as Mobile Social Gambling, an evolving sociotechnical assemblage and

> a new form of media and cultural practice that fuses gambling (a longstanding social practice), social networking (in both the older pre-Internet and newer online forms), and 'social gaming' (the new social media form, popular especially on Facebook), together with the affordances of mobile media devices, networks, applications, and touchscreens.
>
> (Albarrán-Torres & Goggin, 2014)

Mobile social gambling aids in the cultural normalisation of gambling-like procedures, bringing them closer to the realm of casual social gaming, which is already widely played. Apps make possible the continuous availability of gamble-play beyond desktop computers. According to Goggin, apps are a "new cultural platform" that reveal how the "intersection of mobile technologies and ubiquitous computing is already resulting in profound socio-cultural ramifications" (Goggin, 2011, p. 149). The expansion of digital gambling practices is one of these "profound socio-cultural ramifications" (Goggin, 2011, p. 149). Both the gambling and the social gaming industries have closely monitored the expansion of this immensely profitable market (Streitfeld, 2013). This has resulted in mergers and acquisitions that have seen power players in the video game and real money gambling industries (Atari and Aristocrat, respectively) place their bets on social casino games, with varying levels of success.

Throughout its recent history, gambling has had a strong, complementary relationship with contemporary media ecologies and information and communication technologies or ICTs. People's familiarity with screen-based technology has aided in the cultural normalisation of gambling (Schüll, 2012, p. 5). As we have seen in the preceding chapters of this book, the technical affordances of networked digital media, including mobile capacities, aid in the cultural normalisation of gambling and in the commingling of gambling with mainstream entertainment. This happens by means of convergence in production processes as well as publics, practices and branding efforts, such as the licensing of Hollywood franchises and celebrities in state-of-the-art slot machines (Figures 6.1 and 6.2).

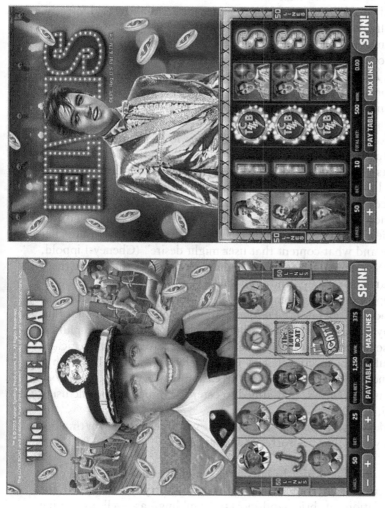

Figure 6.1 (Left) Level themed after the TV show *The Love Boat* in the social casino app *Slotomania*.
Image retrieved on June 7, 2014 from Google Play: https://play.google.com/store/apps/details?id=air.com.playtika.slotomania.

Figure 6.2 (Right) Level themed after pop star Elvis Presley in the social casino app *Slotomania*.
Image retrieved on June 7, 2014 from Google Play: https://play.google.com/store/apps/details?id=air.com.playtika.slotomania.

Like land-based slot machines, pokie apps have been branded with Hollywood concepts directed to demographic groups that might not be familiar with gambling but that have other brand affiliations. For example, the pokie app *Hit It Rich* (developed by social gaming giant Zynga) features *Ted*, a beer-drinking, foul-mouthed teddy bear from the film by *Family Guy* creator Seth MacFarlane. The *Ted* level includes clips from the film and movie dialogue. Game designer Joe Kaminkow told *Variety*, "*Ted* is really popular with people in their 20s... It's part of their pop-culture vernacular" (Spangler, 2014). By incorporating the *Ted* brand, as well as others, including *Magic Mike XXL*, *The Real Housewives of Atlanta*, *Bridesmaids*, *Terminator* and the cult B-movie and internet phenomenon *Sharknado* (Jain, 2014; Zynga, 2014) *Hit It Rich* strives to expand its network of users. The *Sharknado* level was promoted as follows in Zynga's press release: "With beautiful artwork, authentic sounds and core slots gameplay, *Hit It Rich! Sharknado* blends the *Sharknado* brand with a slots experience that brings to life the fun and excitement of playing slots on a casino floor" (Zynga, 2014). These branding strategies also expand the network of mobile devices in which the app is installed. These devices produce significant amounts of information, which aids in the generation of a new subjectivity that Cheney-Lippold calls "algorithmic identities" (2011). Algorithmic identities define "who the user is believed to be and what content that user might desire" (Cheney-Lippold, 2011, p. 168). Companies are able to build user profiles that allow them to target particular groups and individuals.

Pokie apps appropriate some of the tools of seduction put into place by slot machine operators. Following the design approach of other gamble-play forms, such as traditional slot machines, companies, including social casino start-up High 5 Games, have also strategically included culturally specific themes in their slot apps. In 2013, High 5 Games launched *Shake the Sky*, a social casino with Asian-themed products, such as *Zen Panda*, that aimed to cater to ethnically specific users (Takahashi, 2013).

Mobile devices rearticulate the place of gambling in the rhythms of the everyday; as Albarrán-Torres & Goggin state,

> As devices that aspire to encourage intensive real-time gameplay, the expansion of the mobile gaming industry has allowed for a translation of brick-and-mortar gambling, as well as online gambling, into mobile screens characterized by ubiquity, personalization, and sociability. The player does not go to the casino, but carries the casino around in their pocket.
>
> (Albarrán-Torres & Goggin, 2014, p. 103)

Mobile devices transform the cultural form of pokies in at least three ways. First, they allow for co-presence in play. Second, they afford play in times that were not associated with this activity. Third, they allow for ubiquitous opportunities to gamble-play.

Co-presence in some slot apps is made possible through profile pictures of the user's contacts as well as by the reward mechanisms that provide users with extra credits when they share their results or invite other users to play. Leader boards are also a common feature, adding an element of competition, or *agôn* (Caillois, 2001), to slots.

Mobile technology disrupts the temporal dynamics of gamble-play, allowing it to enter the rhythms of everyday life and breaking the Magic Circle of play (Albarrán-Torres & Goggin, 2014; Huizinga, 1955; Moore, 2011; Salen & Zimmerman, 2003). Gamble-play through mobile media is also a way of claiming back instants of leisure in the intensity of modern everyday life. Moments that are 'lost', such as waiting for a bus or killing time in a café, are transformed into what Arvidsson refers to as the "'Lazarus time' resurrected by the mobile" (2006, p. 118), which

> is put to work in producing a kind of sociality that centres on informational networks rather than on physically anchored communities and that is over-layered on, and made to interact with (relatively) fixed social interaction systems of the offline world.
>
> (Arvidsson, 2006, p. 118)

Larissa Hjorth has explained how mobile media invite us to think differently about place, asserting that mobile, networked technologies "not only transform how we understand place in everyday life, they also remind us that place is more than just physical geographic location" and that "places are constructed by an ongoing accumulation of stories, memories and social practices" (Hjorth, 2011, p. 85). As symbolic spaces, pokie apps become sites where stories and memories are accumulated through archiving. Archives come in the form of player history and profiles as well as posting on the player's behalf on social networking sites such as Facebook, a condition that the user agrees to in the Terms and Conditions of most apps.

The relevance of archiving in pokie apps is not only related to gameplay but also to the ways in which the player provides operators with information that can be used for marketing and design purposes. In her paper "Digital Gambling: The Coincidence of Desire and Design", Natasha Dow Schüll discusses the ways in which slot machine designers and operators gather information about individual player preferences and consumption patterns.

> For the gaming industry, gambling machines function not only as individual play boxes but as "electronic surveillance devices" whose internal monitors track a player's game preferences, wins and losses, number of coins played per game, number of games played per

minute, number of minutes or hours of play, number of visits to the casino, number of drinks consumed, and more. Individual machines perform these recording functions within a larger network of units controlled by a central computer.

(Schüll, 2005, p. 72)

Pokie apps follow the same information-rich model and work in conjunction with other digital media, such as social networking sites, to generate precise snapshots of consumption trends, individually as well as collectively. As Gainsbury et al. state, the outcomes in social casino games

are not always based on predetermined odds or randomly determined by chance; instead, game mechanics respond to individual users and playing behaviour to increase player engagement and game satisfaction.

(Gainsbury et al., 2014, p. 8)

As they are not regulated in the same way as pure gambling (Rose, 2014), outcomes in pokie apps are not entirely dependent on chance but on analysing individual consumption patterns. As Gainsbury et al. also state, "it is possible for social casino games to use algorithms that produce different outcomes in response to user behaviours to encourage continued play and in-game purchases" (2016, p. 60). Users are rewarded at appropriate moments through extra credits, new levels or special in-game moments, such as the display of celebratory graphics after a big win.

By being portable and ubiquitous, mobile technologies subvert the spatial relationships required in traditional slots. Traditional pokies in Australia must be placed in a discrete space where gambling can be offered legally. Pokie apps on mobile devices, by contrast, are accessed in indeterminate spaces including work, public spaces and domestic environments.

Gambling-Like Features in Social Games

Pokie apps are part of a larger media segment: social games. Social games have recently been compared to gambling as they operate through gameplay that allegedly stimulates compulsive engagement. This comparison points to further complications in the relationship between gambling and mobile games.

Social games generally operate in social media settings and apps, and typically use virtual currencies (Schneider, 2012, p. 711). Titles such as *Candy Crush* (King), *Angry Birds* (Rovio Entertainment), *Words with Friends* (Zynga), *Farmville* (Zynga), *Draw Something* (Omgpop) and *Mafia Wars* (Zynga) are already part of global popular cultures.

Derivatives or spin-offs of poker have surfaced, such as *Poker Pals*, an iPhone application that brings together letter games such as *Words with Friends*, and traditional poker. The virtual economies market is expected to reach USD $40 billion dollars by 2019 (Chayka, 2014). Some social games, such as *Angry Birds*, have been adapted in cartoons, Hollywood movies, merchandise and fan art. Social games are an integral part of the media consumption habits of millions of smartphone, tablet and social media users. Icon Group International reports that global usage of mobile games doubled in the decade following their boom in 2003, going from USD $43.17 million to USD $90.52 million per annum in 2014 (Parker, 2008, p. 13).

All around, gaming is an important part of contemporary media assemblages. For Hjorth, it is "a vehicle for understanding new media more broadly" (Hjorth, 2011, pp. 1–2). Hjorth expands on the technocultural changes associated specifically with mobile games:

> Through the lens of paradoxes that encompass virtual and actual, online and offline, haptic and visual, delay and immediacy, some lessons about twentieth-century media and gaming practice can be learnt.
>
> (Hjorth, 2011, p. 100)

Like gambling platforms, social games have faced cultural regulation. Media reports have described these games as a potentially addictive form of consumption (Dockterman, 2013). News stories, such as "This is what *Candy Crush* does to your brain", published by the globally available *TIME* magazine, establish a direct relationship between the intensive gameplay in these apps and the compelling nature of poker machines (Piotrowski, 2013). Some bloggers have been highly critical of the social games industry, with Dowling, for example, comparing them to slot machines and claiming that they are "Devious, parasitic little games so brazenly and unashamedly aiming straight for your wallet – this is a business model based almost entirely on exploitation" (Dowling, 2014).

Griffiths has explained how the procedural similarities between social games and gambling work:

> ... social gamers know that they are spending money as they play with little or no financial return. They are buying entertainment, and the intrinsic play of the game itself is highly psychologically rewarding. Like slots players, social network gamers love playing the game itself; money is simply the price of entry, which they are willing to pay. However, unlike those involved in social gaming, gamblers do at least have an outside chance of getting (some of) the money they have staked back. Therefore, allowing those who play

social games the chance to actually get their money back (or gain more than they have staked) is why companies currently operating social games want to get into the pure gambling market.

(Griffiths, 2013, p. 105)

Griffiths identifies how the reward and punishment features of social games resemble the gameplay of gambling machines in that they keep the player on a loop of desire. Video game theorist Ian Bogost wrote an opinion piece in the digital magazine *The Baffler* that critiques the cultural dynamics of social games. In it, he claims that as a relatively new platform, gaming apps provide an experience that is "designed to offer players a potentially toxic brew of guilty pleasure spiced with a kind of extortion" and that by doing so "they profit by stoking addiction" (Bogost, 2014). Bogost's appraisal of gaming apps reminds us of Schüll's (2012) work on land-based slot machines in Las Vegas in its recognition of a calculated effort to generate and sustain addictive consumption. Bogost compares social gaming users to gamblers in that they experience an illusion of control over the machine:

Like most gamblers, players believe they are exceptions who will resist being duped into spending money on in-game items or energy, or else they'll be especially market-savvy entrants who will rationalize small payments as a reasonable concession after being backed into a corner.

(Bogost, 2014)

Although on a scientific or medical level the link between social gaming and addiction might be inconclusive, current critiques show conflicting views on mobile social gaming as a new cultural form. This link has been pointed out by commentators such as Gail Collins, who in a *New York Times* op-ed equalled the high intensity of *Candy Crush* play to the liberalisation of the online gambling market in jurisdictions, such as the state of New Jersey in the United States (Collins, 2013). Here, we see how two media assemblages, namely mobile social gambling and the larger segment of social games, influence each other in how they "capture their users in intensive and extensive networks of enjoyment, production, and surveillance" (Dean, 2010, p. 4).

I will now discuss the cultural particularities of another techno-cultural form, pokies. I will show how these stand-alone machines translate into pokie app design, and how these two media forms coexist in complementary ways. I focus this analysis on the Australian context.

Pokies and Pokie Apps: Gamble-Play in the City

Slot machines and pokie apps are widely used in the Global North and form complex transnational markets. However, the Australian case provides insight into the controversies generated by the introduction of social casino apps in the context of wider debates about gambling technologies.

Even before pokie apps began to appear on people's mobile devices, the gambling experience was never far from those who lived in urban Australia. Picture a contemporary Australian urban setting. Pyrmont is similar to many suburbs in Australia. It is located near Sydney's CBD and metres away from the luxurious casino The Star, which hosts hundreds of pokie machines. Pyrmont is a recently gentrified, vibrant hub consisting of cafés, ethnic restaurants, apartment buildings and gourmet shops. Yet, alongside the stretch of Harris Street, as in countless streets in Australia, dozens of pokies are readily available to any adult who wishes to gamble. Electronic Gaming Machines or EGMs are located in the VIP Lounges of numerous pubs, such as The Dunkirk, The Quarryman Hotel and The Harlequin Inn. These EGMs or pokies are a ubiquitous technology in most of Australia, where in any given year at least 70 per cent of the population engages in some form of gambling (Commonwealth of Australia, 2013). Many pubs also offer digital bingo and wagering in events such as Australian Football League, National Rugby League, greyhound and horse racing (both traditional and simulated through 3D graphics).

The contemporary ubiquitous pokie is an outcome of a series of technological developments that started with mechanical slot machines and the legendary Liberty Bell model launched in 1899. This development continued with the move to electromechanical technology in 1963, went on with the appearance of digital microprocessors in 1978 and is regenerated with the introduction of increasingly complex RNG, algorithms and network capacities (Schüll, 2012, pp. 80–81). Pokie apps are a ramification of these technological developments; their cultural uses and meanings, nonetheless, vary as they are intermeshed with mobile cultures of gaming and play.

The ubiquitous placing of pokies is an important element of contemporary life in most Australian jurisdictions. Pokies were introduced into Australian pubs starting in the 1980s in New South Wales, and, with the exception of Western Australia, continuing in the 1990s in Victoria, Queensland, South Australia and Tasmania, taking over spaces previously designed to host other leisure activities, such as concerts.

The discussion around the availability of pokies across geographies has been the focus of many public policy debates at both state and federal levels. Pokies are also a key element of a sort of 'gambling nationalism' in Australia. Campaigns trying to limit their use, which are constantly associated with concerns over problem gambling and addiction, are deemed by the gaming sector as un-Australian, as evidenced by the *It's Un-Australian* campaign (www.its-unaustralian.com.au).

Physically, pokies are similar to other ever-present machines, such as vending machines or ATMs, which are part of contemporary everyday life in the Global North, as noted by Schüll (2012, p. 80). They are also one of the types of screen with which the contemporary Australian *flâneuse/flâneur* – "the viewer who takes pleasure in abandoning himself [herself] to the artificial world of high capitalist civilization" (Lauster, 2007, p. 140) – engages on a continuous basis, either actively or passively. For instance, not far from Harris Street, in the Harbourside shopping mall of Darling Harbour, metres away from both the world's largest IMAX screen and close to the Crown Casino development of Barangaroo (Hasham, 2014), a VIP Lounge lies hidden amid fast food restaurants and souvenir shops (Figure 6.3). This VIP Lounge belongs to Margaritaville, a Tex-Mex restaurant chain that also owns casinos in Las Vegas and Biloxi, Mississippi, the birthplace of contemporary North American gambling cultures (Lears, 2003; Longstreet, 1977).

The deregulation of pokies in Australia altered the social dynamics of these and other spaces, further expanding gambling practices into the everyday. Pokies can be considered as intrusive machines that cut into normalised social and cultural flows (Albarrán-Torres, 2013a). The establishment of new cultural spaces of gambling has had enduring effects, as Nicoll recalls,

> Although New South Wales clubs and casinos in other Australian capital cities had provided spaces of pokie play from the mid 1970s, the pokie lounge was uniquely grafted onto the existing social institution of the suburban pub. The transfer and perversion of the

Figure 6.3 VIP Lounge at the Margaritaville restaurant in the Harbourside shopping mall in Sydney, Australia.
Photo by the author.

pub's previous cultural meanings and uses has been the source of considerable disquiet, as we will see in the case of pub-rock, which was displaced by the arrival of pokies.

(Nicoll, 2011, pp. 223–224)

Contemporary media landscapes are many faceted. Alongside Harris Street there are also dozens of people using their mobile devices, which are perceived by some as yet another disruptive technology (Turkle, 2011). They use their mobiles while having lunch, waiting for the bus or having a beer in the local pub. Through these devices, mostly high-tech smartphones and tablets, it is also possible to engage in pokie playing for play money or virtual currency. Pokie apps remain one of the most sought after mobile game genres in Australia, with *Slotomania* being the most downloaded product in the iTunes store in 2012 (Willingham, 2013b).

Both pokies and the mobile devices used to access pokie apps are part of what Greenfield presciently termed "everyware", objects with which we interact daily as "sites of processing and mediation" (Greenfield, 2006, p. 1). However, pokies and pokie apps do not process or mediate the exact same things: one is almost purely gambling, the other almost exclusively play. The key word is "almost": both exist in the crevices of that zone of indeterminacy where the concept of 'digital gamble-play' gains currency and relationships are articulated among gambling, social gaming and everyday media consumption.

The cultural figure of the *flâneur*, famously invoked by Walter Benjamin, remains relevant in contemporary mediascapes and cities, where pokies and pokie apps are available. As de Souza e Silva and Hjorth state,

> One hundred years on from the time of the *flâneur*, the spirit of modernity has dramatically transformed while still haunted by the specters of the spectacle.
>
> (de Souza e Silva & Hjorth, 2009, p. 607)

As I have previously stated, gamble-play platforms can be theorised as "spectacles" (Debord, 1967) where the social relation of gambling is mediated by audiovisual interfaces populated with procedure-images. However, mobile technology reframes the relationship between the city wanderer and these spectacles.

Whereas the wanderers of the modern city, those involved in *flânerie*, play traditional pokies, pokie apps are accessed by a player Luke calls a *phoneur,*

> the cell phone sporting, incessantly talking, e-urbanite whose identity is articulated within the mediated space of the mobile phone and the ensuing enculturation processes of the wireless web.
>
> (Luke, 2006, p. 187)

De Souza e Silva and Hjorth describe the main differences between the modern *flâneur* and the contemporary phoneur:

> Unlike the *flâneur* that was ordered by the visual, the phoneur is structured by the information city's ambience, whereby modes such as haptic and aural override the dominance of visual.
>
> (de Souza e Silva & Hjorth, 2009, p. 607)

Pokies and pokie apps present a combination of haptic, aural and visual stimuli that generate new types of sensations, affects and desires. One of the main concerns for opponents of pokies is that during play, money acquires a different meaning. Money becomes part of the procedure-image by momentarily being devoid of its real value. Baudrillard, a key figure in understanding the dynamics of capitalist consumption, argues that in gambling, money is "no longer a sign or representation once transformed into a stake" and that "a stake is not something one invests" but "something which is presented as a challenge to chance" (Baudrillard, 1990, p. 139; also cited in Reith, 1999, p. 143). In gambling, as in other realms, such as the stock market – which is often compared to gambling and I explore in Chapter 7 – the *expressive* and symbolic qualities of money make themselves evident, but its material qualities are momentarily suspended. Presenting money as a game item is one of the rhetorical tools mobilised in both slot machines and pokie apps.

By playing pokie apps, players may feel they are presenting a challenge to chance, but the programming of these apps means that outcomes are often engineered towards enhancing the user experience. If gambling practices involved rituals that summoned chance or fortune, current forms of gamble-play involve digital make-believe. For, as Schüll notes, "the sense of magic and wonder that gambling machines provoke in their users has a great deal to do with the hiddenness and the opacity of the 'means and calculations' by which they mediate chance" (Schüll, 2012, p. 78).

Just like slot machines, smartphones and tablets are, by all accounts, black boxes: devices that require inputs and generate outputs but whose inner workings are, for the most part, unknown but alluring to the lay player. Hence, "the sense of magic and wonder" (Schüll, 2012, p. 78) comes to light.

As opposed to online or mobile poker, or previous digital card games, such as solitaire, there is no real skill involved in playing pokies. Whatever control over the computer that gamblers think or wish they have is merely an illusion. In computerised slot machine gambling "players quite literally become catalysts for autonomous machine processes" (Schüll, 2012, p. 82). Even though some gamblers have the illusion of controlling the outcome, the fact is that the game mechanics are not influenced by a player's decisions. Unlike in other forms of gambling that require human-to-human interaction, in playing the pokies gamblers engage solely with the machine and with the mechanisms of surveillance and control that operate in pubs and other venues.

Pokies and pokie apps constitute two distinct but complementary and parallel screen cultures in which gamble-play procedures are carried out. What we see is cross-pollination between these and other media forms, such as video games, in their use of procedures and audiovisual tropes. We are also witnessing the insertion of pokies and pokie apps into the realm of the everyday in a country such as Australia, where the prevalence of gambling is high and where cultural and political discourses are articulated around the media panics generated around these forms of gamble-play media.

Apps are now being used with the goal of encouraging gamblers to use self-control. For example, the North East Primary Care Partnership, the Victorian Local Government Association and the Moreland City Council launched the app *Quit Pokies* in early 2014. Based on users' location, the app triggers a warning to problem gamblers if they step into a venue where pokies are available. The alert is repeated every ten minutes until the person leaves the venue. The app also alerts them if there are other pokie venues nearby. Additionally, the app recommends other leisure activities, such as seeing friends (Schetzer, 2014), emphasising how gambling can replace socialisation for some individuals.

The NSW government also launched an anti-pokie app in 2013, *Gambling Terminator*, which runs on Apple and Android and detects when a person is inside a gambling venue in New South Wales. The app requires users "to perform 'acts' of physical and affective labour aimed at behaviour change and developing the skills of self-control" (Humphry and Albarrán-Torres, 2015). Apps like these exemplify how the online and offline "universes of reference" (Guattari, 1995) of digital gambling overlap and produce new meanings, practices and negotiations among the state, industry and neo-liberal subjects (in the case of problem gambling apps, a new subjectivity, the 'neo-liberal addict'). The spatial dynamics of play are altered with the use of locative media (Farman, 2012) as the player's location opens and closes possibilities for action.

Pokie App Platforms: Reterritorialising Slots

Pokie apps are a reterritorialisation of slot machines. The identity of slot machines is destabilised by the technical affordances of mobile media. When the assemblage of the pokie app is formed, the previous order is not annihilated. It is not an absolute reterritorialisation (DeLanda, 2006, p. 19). Pokies and other prior forms of gambling have not lost their identity or currency but coexist with pokie apps.

The meanings associated with pokie apps have complicated the older discourses around gambling. Most academic and public discussions around the implications of pokie consumption, predominantly problem gambling and addiction, focus on the material goods that are lost by consumers and won by the manufacturers and owners of pokie machines. However, there are other values being exchanged, such as hope, aspiration and class mobility. These are fundamental processes in the reterritorialisation of EGM playing into pokie apps. When you detach one from an assemblage and place it into another, something new emerges: that is the case in pokie apps. Bogost's concept of "procedural rhetoric" (2007) is useful in establishing the similarities between pokies and pokie apps. This kind of rhetoric is "the art of persuasion through rule-based representations and interactions rather than the spoken word, writing, images, or moving pictures" (Bogost, 2007, p. ix).

The procedural rhetoric of traditional pokies and pokie apps involves persuading the gambler to engage in repetitive play. Slot machines are devices that instigate an intensive, draining form of consumption associated with the hope for the big win. In turn, pokie app designers mix quests and levels into slot playing, generating a hybrid gameplay order, which makes them a salient example of digital gamble-play.

In parallel, pokie apps also preserve the *aura* of EGMs through the use of certain iconography, most of which has a postcolonial visual style associated with particular geographies (Albarrán-Torres, 2013a) but also themes that are historically associated with gambling, such as the Wild West.

Pokie apps remediate (Bolter & Grusin, 1999) the basic procedures of slot machines and add more elaborate gameplay. Developers interpret the procedural and audiovisual text of pokies and render their translations, which take advantage of the affordances of mobile platforms. The tactile dimension in smartphones, for instance, is similar to the tactile dimension in contemporary slot machines: the gambler touches a button, reels roll and excitement arises. Pokie app designers mobilise the device's haptic capacities by generating vibrations when the player hits a jackpot.

Slot machine gambling involves losing and sometimes recuperating money in an endless cycle known as 'chasing'. Pokie players cannot get better (or richer) through a continuous repetition of the procedure, at least not without hacking the machine.

In turn, while pokie apps only simulate wins and losses, they sometimes require players to pay to engage in continuous play, a procedure similar to 'chasing'. Pokie apps operators, moreover, "are not required to be transparent about how games work, it is difficult to clarify how outcomes are determined" (Gainsbury et al., 2014, p. 8).

The lack of regulation gives operators free rein to design products that make use of procedural devices of traditional gambling, such as 'near misses' and 'big wins' (Kassinove, & Schare, 2001), to foster continuous play. Pokie apps are structured in levels and provide rewards and punishments that follow the conventions of both video games (King et al., 2010) and slot machines (Schüll, 2005, 2012). However, through the design of quests, leader boards and levels, players get a sense of accomplishment.

Pokie apps refashion the cultural signifiers of slot machines and cultural spaces of gambling, such as the VIP Lounge, and allow gambling-like practices to enter the spaces and rhythms of the everyday in particular ways. We can discern the nature of the pokie app assemblage by describing some of the key affordances and dynamics of three examples. Pokie apps carry out a translation of pokies in three main ways: by simulating the spatial logic of VIP Lounges (as seen in *Slotomania*), by enacting the main procedure of slot playing (press the button, the reels will align) and by using similar iconographic tropes.

Slotomania

Slotomania is historically the most popular pokie app in Australia. It is owned and operated by Playtika, a subsidiary of Caesars Entertainment Corporation, and was the most downloaded app in the iTunes Store in Australia in 2012. Caesar's Entertainment Corporation is an important player in the brick-and-mortar gambling industry. It owns resorts and the *World Series of Poker* brand, with its strong online and TV presence. Caesar's Entertainment Corporation has expanded further into the social casino app market. In February 2014, it acquired the Israeli social gaming company Pacific Interactive, which owns the slot machine app *House of Fun* (Stutz, 2014).

Playtika promotes *Slotomania* as follows: "Enjoyed by millions worldwide; *Slotomania* is the favorite social slots game online providing unlimited FREE entertainment for double the fun, top-tier graphics, and high-quality sound effects" (Playtika, n.d.).

The app is also available in the Google Play store and in Amazon apps. The game is promoted less like gambling and more like online shopping or investing in entertainment. The app does not offer wins in real money but requires the user to buy credits with real money to engage in continuous play. Even though the game is intended for people over 21 years of age, it is likely that underage players engage in this form of gamble-play, which has raised moral concerns among opponents of gambling in countries including Australia, where problem gambling is a pressing political issue.

Slotomania appropriates the space of the VIP Lounge (Figure 6.4). The loading screen shows a cartoon character – a voluptuous hostess –

Figure 6.4 Slotomania's loading screen, which recalls the cultural space of the VIP Lounge.

Image captured on April 16, 2013 from the author's Android device.

playing the slots. The dimly lit room sports a star-pattern carpet: the setting is familiar to anyone who has set foot in an Australian VIP Lounge. Brick-and-mortar VIP Lounges are assemblages composed of machines, workers, gamblers, alcoholic drinks, social links, computer code and audiovisual discourses. The VIP Lounge also expresses socio-economic class, as explained by Nicoll:

> The choice of the term 'lounge', rather than 'room' to promote and describe spaces in Australian pubs which house pokie machines is significant. It simultaneously evokes luxuriousness and an earlier cultural configuration of the pub in which the 'ladies lounge' was a small space segregated from the large bar area where men drank in a sparsely furnished and functional environment that was sometimes tiled for ease of cleaning.
>
> (Nicoll, 2011, p. 227)

In the image, we can also perceive a segregated space lit by a spot-light. The rest of the world does not seem to exist: the female player sits alone with her machine, immersed in "the zone", a state demar-cated from the everyday, yet embedded in the gambler's daily activities (Schüll, 2012).

Slotomania is also accessible through Facebook, a sign that social networking, social gaming and gambling are venues for gamble-play assemblages. *Slotomania* welcomes the player by offering two options: connect with your Facebook account now, or connect later.

Slotomania borrows from other forms of interactive entertainment, such as console video games and social games in the vein of Zynga's *Farmville*. In its themed pokies, *Slotomania* showcases cartoon-like characters that range from dogs, cows and scarecrows to vampires, and pharaohs. Users can also play with cowboys and mafia crooks, mythologies historically related to gambling, particularly in the United States.

Slots by Zynga

Slots by Zynga is a pokie app produced by Zynga, one of the main actors in the mobile social gambling market. Zynga, initially a social gaming company, has attempted to expand into real-money online gambling with the launch of its Zynga Plus Casino in the United Kingdom, an initiative that turned out to be short lived. This move is an exemplar of the partial convergence of social gaming and gambling industries.

In *Slots by Zynga*, players are offered bigger jackpots if they connect and play with their Facebook friends. In a pop-up window, we can see three plastic cups overflowing with golden coins, an image that resonates with the scenes one might witness in an Australian VIP Lounge. This image is interesting as it represents money as a fetish object. It is a representation of virtual currency for which users can play if they connect through their Facebook profile.

Slots by Zynga also offers different settings, evocative of geographical locations related to traditional gambling enclaves: The Strip (simulating Las Vegas), Jade Harbour (Macau), Bayou Bay (New Orleans, the birthplace of poker) and The Oasis (Egypt, a recurring gambling trope, as seen in the Luxor hotel in Vegas or *The Queen of the Nile* pokie in the Australian market). These representations add a sense of luxury and class exclusivity that is also present in the VIP Lounge. In these settings, the player can engage with different slot machines that can be accessed only through winning points by constant play. Among these we can find *Zombie Dash*, *Farmville Frenzy* (a cross-platform iteration of the popular social game), *Slots with Friends* (it recontextualises the icons of the social game *Words with Friends*), the western *Bullseye Saloon* and *Wings of Freedom*.

The user is sent 'push notifications' to her smartphone, reminding her that the opportunity to gamble is always waiting to be taken, and luring her with bonuses and credits. This further pushes the game space into everyday spaces and promoting the formation of a habit.

Other slot machine procedural tropes are present. In the *Alice in Wonderland*-themed pokie, the White Rabbit runs horizontally as the reels roll vertically, emphasising a sense of urgency and vertigo.

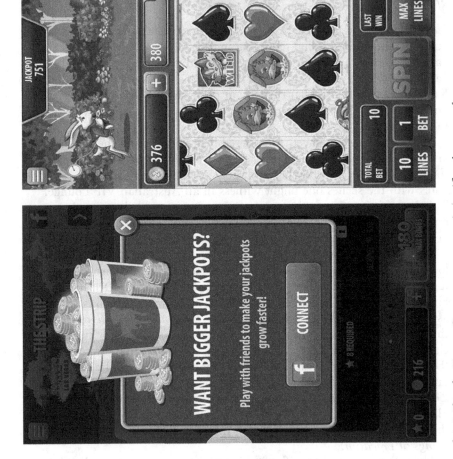

Figures 6.5 and 6.6 Slots by Zynga. Constant movement intensifies the sense of urgency. Images captured on April 16, 2013 from the author's Android device.

The White Rabbit is the "chasing" procedure personified. This two-directional movement represents the repetitive actions needed in slot machine playing (Figures 6.5 and 6.6).

Slots Journey

Slots Journey constructs a narrative of quest and adventure around pokie playing. The player travels through virtual space by unlocking levels when hitting jackpots. The gameplay is also a race against time as players have to complete levels in under an hour. It is promoted in Google's Play Store as follows:

> Dive into the flow of luck and fortune and complete your unforgettable quest with a brand-new slot machine simulator *Slots Journey*! / With the *Slots Journey* application you'll experience the full scale of uplifted emotions just like a real casino player but at the same time, you won't risk losing a single cent!

This product description is the epitome of gamble-play: it invites the user to "dive" into a flow of fortune while not risking real money. However, the user is constantly invited to connect to their social networks via Facebook. The player does not pay with money but with social influence in sociotechnical networks.

Slots Journey's visual style resembles the adventure genre in other media forms, such as video games and film. One of the fonts, for instance, replicates the iconic logo from the *Indiana Jones* movie franchise. Similarly, the overall design seems to derive from social games targeted to children in the vein of *Angry Birds*.

The game is structured in levels, and the gambler/player can only advance to the next one after completing the previous journey. The following sequence is available, with a Coming Soon icon promising a new adventure: Egypt→ China→ Islands→ Greece→ Transylvania→ Texas→ Australia→ North Pole→ France. The player needs to engage in constant play in order to 'travel' through these real and imaginary landscapes, which remind us of those showcased in popular pokies, such as *Queen of the Nile*, *Mystic Panda*, *Five Dragons* and *Artic Treasure* (Albarrán-Torres, 2013a). These visual tropes (pyramids, Chinese temples, deserts) are elements extracted from other assemblages that are woven into the fabrics of history and culture, such as that of the postcolonial gaze, and inserted in the assemblage of digital slot betting, mobile and otherwise.

The narrative of mobility mirrors the mobility of the device and its owner, the *phoneur*. It is also a sort of gambling channel-surfing (Figures 6.7 and 6.8).

Figure 6.7 Slots Journey: the mobile app has a narrative of mobility, echoing both city dwelling and traditional gambling practices.
Images captured on April 15, 2013 from the author's Android device.

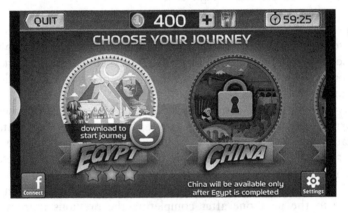

Figure 6.8 Slots Journey: the mobile app has a narrative of mobility, echoing both city dwelling and traditional gambling practices.
Images captured on April 15, 2013 from the author's Android device.

Conclusion: Social Casino Apps and Cultural Regulation in Australia

As a new media form, social casino apps are scrutinised and culturally regulated, particularly in countries with a high incidence of problem gambling, such as Australia. The popularity of *Slotomania* and other pokie apps has raised concerns among the Australian public. The assemblages of gambling and social games are coming together, creating and regenerating meanings, norms and practices. Other forms of screen-based gambling, such as online poker and traditional pokies, have been

long debated by public commentators, including politicians and jour-
nalists. These controversies frame the current discussion around social
casino apps. In early 2013, Senator Nick Xenophon, a long-standing
advocate for increasing government intervention in gambling practices,
was quoted as saying, "It is laughable to say it's not gambling because
you can't take your winnings out, even though you can lose buckets of
money" (Xenophon, as quoted in Willingham, 2013a).

In 2013, Xenophon tried to introduce a bill that would classify
gambling-like social games as gambling. Ironically, one of Xenophon's
political opponents, the organisation Clubs Australia, shared his concerns. This industry body represents the interests of licensed clubs across
Australia and New Zealand. The organisation is also responsible for
ensuring that the interests of clubs are represented in dealings with par-
liamentarians and that clubs are informed of key policy developments.

Clubs Australia has conducted a campaign for the regulation of gambling apps, perhaps sensing a disruption in the economic balance of
gambling markets. This brings vested interests into the light. Clubs are
one of the main hubs for pokie playing in Australia but also an institution where community ties are solidified through socialisation.

This industry body, which represents the interests of club owners, has
called for the formation of a panel that "will investigate every aspect
of social gaming in the hopes of developing codes of practice that will
dictate how social gaming must operate in Australia" (Scimia, 2013).
Anthony Ball, Clubs Australia's executive director, called for legislative
standards for digital gambling that are similar to traditional gambling
standards. He is reported as saying,

> We've long called for similar standards to be applied to online gambling
> and these social gaming apps. The guidelines that our expert working
> group develop will provide a policy for clubs to abide by if they con-
> sider entering the social media space in the future and make sure that
> clubs continue to be leaders when it comes to... responsible conduct.
>
> (Ball, as quoted in Scimia, 2013)

This quote evidences a degree of confusion regarding the nature of each market, the nuances of two dissimilar cultural practices (online gambling and
social gaming apps) and lack of specificity regarding users and audiences.

Social casino apps have also caused concern in state and local governments. The South Australian government, for instance, launched its
own campaign in December 2013, Gambling Is No Game (nogame.com.
au). This campaign aimed to warn parents and educators about the risks
involving what they call "simulated gambling".

This campaign also seeks to "add MA15+ classification to games that
contain simulated gambling", which would mean that "it would be illegal
to sell games with slot machine or card game mechanics to those under

15" (Byrne, 2013). As part of the campaign, billboards were placed in public spaces. These billboards showed a young girl with a tablet device surrounded by gambling items and the slogan "GAMBLING starts with GAMES". The Interactive Games & Entertainment Association (IGEA), which represents the interests of the video game industry, launched a formal complaint. IGEA claimed that the billboard misrepresented the relationship between video games and gambling, and argued there is no definite evidence to support the notion that video games lead to problem gambling (Interactive Games & Entertainment Association, 2013). In parallel, multiple memes were generated, showing the young girl playing poker with James Bond in the film *Casino Royale*, in an iPad ad or in a setting of the movie *The Matrix* (Serrels, 2013). Online commentators in video game blogs and forums were equally harsh. Hopewell, for example, wrote, "if you are an adult gamer, it will probably see you spit out your corn flakes" as "it demonises games and gamers alike, especially those who encourage their kids to play games" (Hopewell, 2013). The billboards were eventually taken down after these efforts (Scurry, 2013).

In 2013, the Victorian government launched a satirical ad campaign titled KidBet (http://kidbet.com.au/) under the slogan "They should never go together". In a TV ad campaign, we can see a young boy playing a fake sports betting app with his tablet, in an attempt to emphasise the threat of gambling addiction to savvy but vulnerable young mobile media users (Stravopoulos, 2013). In the KidBet website, the Victorian Responsible Gambling Foundation states that "Community concern is growing over the impact gambling is having on young people, particularly through sport, advertising, online games and social media".

The CEO of the foundation, Serge Sard, told the ABC at the launch of the campaign that the ad "is deliberately provocative because there appears to be a misplaced complacency around the issue" (Stravopoulos, 2013). He also stated, "There's saturation of free game apps that encourages kids to gamble... Social media promotes media activities, and gambling simulation games, that essentially teach kids how to gamble" (Stravopoulos, 2013).

This campaign is an example of how meaning is negotiated when a new form of consumption of gamble-play emerges, informed by digital media practices. Similarly, in November 2013 the then Premier of South Australia, Jay Weatherill, called for new regulations on gambling-like apps (Albarrán-Torres, 2013b). He sought the cooperation of Apple to "make it an offence to supply gambling apps or games to minors" (AAP, 2013). He was forceful in saying, "I won't stand back and watch a new generation of gambling addicts emerge" (Weatherill, as quoted in AAP, 2013).

These examples of cultural regulation show how social casino apps are a media form that has significant political and social implications. Social casino apps are associated with pokies in how they are perceived culturally. They revive worries about the conflicting relationship between users and gambling technologies. This chapter contributes to a field that is largely unexplored. Pokie apps are a hybrid media form in which the gambling and entertainment industries converge. Cultural analysis can inform further discussions around gambling and gaming, two overtly contested aspects of contemporary media landscapes. This understanding can go beyond social panics or utopian celebrations around interactive digital media, such as pokie apps, and inform academic and policy discussion.

Note

1 "New York, 9 am Samantha is waiting for the bus, which has already been delayed for 20 minutes. She is getting anxious, as she has an important business meeting in half an hour. She takes out her Android smartphone and texts her colleague to say she is running late. Then, to pass the time before the bus arrives, she accesses *Hit It Rich*. She likes playing slots on her mobile, even though she is not making or spending real money. Samantha finds the cartoonish characters appealing and enjoys the vibrant graphics, encouraging messages and vigorous sounds, particularly the ones in the level themed after her favourite childhood movie, *The Wizard of Oz*. As a financial advisor, she deals with risk all day long, so she enjoys gambling for nothing. Risk with no stakes is liberating. Before her bus finally arrives, she has a big win (10,000 credits!) and shares it with her Facebook friends (this will give her a few more extra credits)".

References

AAP (2013). SA to set new rules around gambling apps. *The Australian*. Retrieved from www.theaustralian.com.au/news/latest-news/sa-to-set-new-rules-around-gambling-apps/story-fn3dxiwe-1226762668354

Albarrán-Torres, C. (2013a). Gambling-machines and the automation of desire. *Platform: Journal of Media and Communication, 5*(1). Retrieved from https://platformjmc.com/2013/10/01/vol-5-issue-1/v5i1_torres/

Albarrán-Torres, C. (2013b, November 28). Big money made on social apps as gambling and gaming collide. *The Conversation*. Retrieved from http://theconversation.com/big-money-made-on-social-apps-as-gambling-and-gaming-collide-20546

Albarrán-Torres, C. & Goggin, G (2014). Mobile social gambling: Poker's next frontier. *Mobile Media & Communication, 2*(1), 94–109.

Arvidsson, A. (2006). *Brands: Meaning and value in media culture*. New York: Routledge.

Baudrillard, J. (1990). *Cool Memories 1980–1985*. London: Verso.

Bogost, I. (2007). *Persuasive games: The expressive power of video games*. Cambridge: MIT Press.

Bogost, I. (2014). Rage against the Machines. *The Baffler*. Retrieved from http://thebaffler.com/past/rage_against_the_machines

Bolter, J. D., & Grusin, R. (1999). *Remediation: Understanding new media*. Cambridge: MIT Press.

Byrne, S. (2013). Gambling starts with games, says SA Government. *C/Net Australia.* Retrieved from www.cnet.com.au/gambling-starts-with-games-says-sa-government-339346186.htm

Caillois, R. (2001). *Man, play and games.* Urbana: University of Illinois Press.

Chayka, K. (2014, June 25). Virtual economies are the future of consumption. *Pacific Standard.* Retrieved from www.psmag.com/navigation/business-economics/angry-birds-smartphones-virtual-economics-future-consumption-84353

Cheney-Lippold, J. (2011). A new algorithmic identity: Soft biopolitics and the modulation of control. *Theory, Culture & Society, 28*(6), 164–181.

Collins, G. (2013, December 18). Candy Crush and Mr. Christie. *The New York Times.* Retrieved from www.nytimes.com/2013/12/19/opinion/collins-candy-crush-and-mr-christie.html?_r=0

Commonwealth of Australia (2013). Problem gambling: Facts & myths. Retrieved from www.problemgambling.gov.au/

Couldry, N. (2012). *Media, society, world: Social theory and digital media practice.* Cambridge: Polity.

Dayanim, B. (2014). Social casino gaming: An evolving legal landscape. *Gaming Law Review and Economics, 18*(1), 30–36.

Dean, J. (2010). *Blog theory: Feedback and capture in the circuits of drive.* Cambridge: Polity.

Debord, G. (original 1967). *Society of the Spectacle.* Marxist.org. Retrieved from www.marxists.org/reference/archive/debord/society.htm

DeLanda, M. (2006). *A new philosophy of society: Assemblage theory and social complexity.* London and New York: Continuum.

de Souza e Silva, A. & Hjorth, L. (2009). Playful urban spaces: A historical approach to mobile games. *Simulation & Gaming, 40*(5), 602–625.

Dockterman, E. (2013). Candy Crush Saga: The science behind our addiction. *Time.* Retrieved from http://business.time.com/2013/11/15/candy-crush-saga-the-science-behind-our-addiction/

Dowling, H. (2014). 10 soulless video games that are just slot-machines. *What Culture.* Retrieved from http://whatculture.com/gaming/10-soulless-games-that-are-just-slot-machines.php#O8KWl4p4KLIxOW9t.99

Farman, J. (2012). *Mobile interface theory: Embodied space and locative media.* New York, London: Routledge.

Gainsbury, S., Hing, N., Delfabbro, P. H., & King, D. L. (2014). A taxonomy of gambling and casino games via social media and online technologies. *International Gambling Studies,* (ahead-of-print), 1–18.

Gainsbury, S. M., Russell, A. M., King, D. L., Delfabbro, P., & Hing, N. (2016). Migration from social casino games to gambling: Motivations and characteristics of gamers who gamble. *Computers in Human Behavior, 63,* 59–67.

Gainsbury, S., Wood, R., Russell, A., Hing, N., & Blaszczynski, A. (2012). A digital revolution: Comparison of demographic profiles, attitudes and gambling behavior of Internet and non-Internet gamblers. *Computers in Human Behavior, 28*(4), 1388–1398.

GamblingData (2012). GamblingData Social Gaming White Paper. Retrieved from http://www.gamblingdata.com/files/SocialgamingDataReportOct2012.pdf

Goggin, G. (2011). Ubiquitous apps: Politics of openness in global mobile cultures. *Digital Creativity, 22*(3), 148–159.

Greenfield, A. (2006). *Everyware: The dawning age of ubiquitous computing.* Berkeley: New Riders Press.

Griffiths, M. D. (2013). Social gambling via Facebook: Further observations and concerns. *Gaming Law Review and Economics, 17*(2), 104–106.

Guattari, F. (1995). *Chaosmosis: An ethico-aesthetic paradigm.* Sydney: Power.

Hasham, N. (2014, May 30). Crown casino to dominate shrunken cove. *The Sydney Morning Herald.* Retrieved from www.smh.com.au/nsw/crown-casino-to-dominate-shrunken-cove-20140529-3976t.html

Hjorth, L. (2011). *Games & gaming: An introduction to new media.* London: Berg.

Hopewell, L. (2013, December 11). Why is South Australia still demonising video games? *Gizmodo.* Retrieved from www.gizmodo.com.au/2013/12/why-is-south-australia-still-demonising-video-games/

Hörnle, J., & Zammit, B. (2010). *Cross-border online gambling law and policy.* Camberley: Edward Elgar Publishing.

Huizinga, J. (1955). *Homo ludens: A study of the play-element in culture.* Boston: Beacon Press.

Humphry, J., & Albarrán Torres, C. (2015). A tap on the shoulder: The disciplinary techniques and logics of anti-pokie apps. *M/C Journal, 18*(2). Retrieved from http://journal.media-culture.org.au/index.php/mcjournal/article/view/962

Interactive Games & Entertainment Association (2013). IGEA letter to Strategic Communications Unit Website, SA. Retrieved from www.igea.net/wp-content/uploads/2013/12/IGEA-letter-to-Strategic-Communications-Unit-Website.pdf

Jain, A. (2014, July 29). Zynga Inc (ZNGA) adds Sharknado to hit it rich: Casino Slots. *Value Walk.* Retrieved from www.valuewalk.com/2014/07/zynga-adds-sharknado-hit-it-rich/

Kassinove, J. I., & Schare, M. L. (2001). Effects of the "near miss" and the "big win" on persistence at slot machine gambling. *Psychology of Addictive Behaviors, 15*(2), 155–158.

King, D., Delfabbro, P., & Griffiths, M. (2010). Video game structural characteristics: A new psychological taxonomy. *International Journal of Mental Health and Addiction, 8*(1), 90–106.

Kücklich, J. (2005). Precarious playbour: Modders and the digital games industry. *Fibreculture, 5.* Retrieved from http://five.fibreculturejournal.org/fcj-025-precarious-playbour-modders-and-the-digital-games-industry/

Lauster, M. (2007). Walter Benjamin's myth of the "flâneur". *The Modern Language Review, 102*(1), 139–156.

Lears, J. (2003). *Something for nothing: Luck in America.* New York: Viking.

Licoppe C. (2004). 'Connected' presence: The emergence of a new repertoire for managing social relationships in a changing communication technoscape. *Environment and Planning: Society and Space, 22*(1), 135–156.

Longstreet, S. (1977). *Win or lose: A social history of gambling in America.* Indianapolis: Bobbs-Merrill.

Luke, R. (2006). The phoneur: Mobile commerce and the digital pedagogies of the wireless web. In P. Trifonas (Ed.), *Communities of difference: Culture, language, technology* (pp. 185–204). Palgrave: London.

Moore, C. (2011). The magic circle and the mobility of play. *Convergence, 17*(4), 373–387.

Nicoll, F. (2011). On blowing up the pokies: The Pokie Lounge as a cultural site of neoliberal governmentality in Australia. *Cultural Studies Review, 17*(2), 219–256.

Owens Jr, M. D. (2010). There's an app for that (or soon will be): Smart phones, social networking, and Internet gaming. *Gaming Law Review and Economics, 14*(3), 171–174.

Parker, P.M. (2008). *The 2009–2014 world outlook for mobile games.* Las Vegas, NV: Icon Group International, Inc.

Parry, W. (2014). New Jersey online gambling sees 1st monthly revenue decline $11.4 million in April. *The Republic.* Retrieved from www.therepublic.com/view/story/e2b47e7a357a4c269a2f9296670c47ac/NJ--Casino-Revenues

Piotrowski, D. (2013, November 3). This is what Candy Crush does to your brain. *NEWS.com.au.* Retrieved from www.news.com.au/technology/gaming/this-is-what-candy-crush-does-to-your-brain/story-fn81y8rt-1226752241164

Playtika Ltd (n.d.) Play Slotomania – The #1 free slot machine game! Come play with us. *slotomania.com.* Retrieved, September 2014, from www.slotomania.com/

Reith, G. (1999). *The age of chance: Gambling in Western culture.* London: Routledge.

Rose, I. N. (2014). Should social casino games be regulated? *Gaming Law Review and Economics, 18*(2), 134–137.

Salen, K., & Zimmerman, E. (2003). *Rules of play.* Cambridge: MIT Press.

Schetzer, A. (2014, February 15). App triggers warning to problem gamblers. *The Sydney Morning Herald.* Retrieved from www.smh.com.au/technology/technology-news/app-triggers-warning-to-problem-gamblers-20140215-32sp2.html

Schneider, S. (2012). Social gaming and social gambling. *Gaming Law Review and Economics, 16*(12), 711–712.

Schüll, N. D. (2005). Digital gambling: The coincidence of desire and design. *The Annals of the American Academy of Political and Social Science, 597*(1), 65–81.

Schüll, N. D. (2012). *Addiction by design: Machine gambling in Las Vegas.* Princeton: Princeton University Press.

Scimia, E. (2013, April 13). Clubs Australia forms panel on social gambling apps. *Australian Gambling* Retrieved from www.australiangambling.com.au/gambling-news/clubs-australia-forms-panel-on-social-gambling-apps/12828/

Scurry, T. (2013, December 23). Anti-gaming billboards in South Australia to be taken down. *Blackjack Champ.* Retrieved from www.blackjackchamp.com/casino-news/20609-anti-gaming-billboards-in-south-australia-to-be-taken-down

Serrels, M. (2013, December 13). South Australia's anti-gaming ads hit Photoshop with a vengeance. *Kotaku.* Retrieved from www.kotaku.com.au/2013/12/south-australias-anti-gaming-ads-hits-photoshop-with-a-vengeance

Spangler, T. (2014). Seth MacFarlane's 'Ted' Comes to Zynga Slot-Machine Game. *Variety.* Retrieved from http://variety.com/2014/digital/news/seth-macfarlanes-ted-comes-to-zynga-slot-machine-game-1201130312/

Stravopoulos, P. (2013, October 9). Provocative campaign to tackle teenage gambling. *ABCNews* (Australia). Retrieved from www.abc.net.au/news/2013-10-09/provocative-campaign-to-tackle-teenage-gambling/5012046

Streitfeld, D. (2013, February 17). Tech industry sets its sights on gambling. *The New York Times*. Retrieved from www.nytimes.com/2013/02/18/technology/ tech-industry-sets-its-sights-on-gambling.html

Stutz, H. (2014, February 14) Caesars' interactive subsidiary buys fourth social gaming business. *Las Vegas Review-Journal*. Retrieved from www.reviewjournal. com/business/caesars-interactive-subsidiary-buys-fourth-social-gaming-business

Takahashi, D. (2013, December 4). High 5 Games seeks to cash in on Asian-themed social casino games. *Venture Beat*. Retrieved from http://venturebeat. com/2013/12/04/high-5-games-announces-asian-themed-social-casino-games/

Turkle, S. (2011). *Alone together: Why we expect more from technology and less from each other*. London: Hachette UK.

Willingham, R. (2013a). Fear that gaming apps will groom young gamblers. *The Sydney Morning Herald*. Retrieved from www.smh.com.au/digital-life/ smartphone-apps/fear-that-gaming-apps-will-groom-young-gamblers-20130112-2cmre.html#ixzz2QVhYU1ns

Willingham, R. (2013b). Virtual pokie app a hit – but 'not gambling'. *The Sydney Morning Herald*. Retrieved from www.smh.com.au/digital-life/smartphone-apps/virtual-pokie-app-a-hit--but-not-gambling-20130112-2cmev.html#ixzz 2QVlsCJs1

Zynga (2014). Zynga. *company.zynga.com*. Retrieved September 2014, from https://company.zynga.com/about

7 Gambling with Markets

Stock Trading Apps and the Logic of Gamble-Play

In this book, I have argued that contemporary digital gambling and gambling-like platforms give birth to a new type of media and cultural form called gamble-play. I have mobilised this concept across different types of digital games of chance. In the current chapter, I argue that some stock trading apps follow similar procedural and cultural dynamics, highlighting the already tight connection between the spheres of gambling, play and finance (Dorn & Sengmueller, 2009; Goggin, 2012; Nicoll, 2013). I analyse the discourses surrounding the apps *Bux* (Ayondo Markets Limited) and *Robinhood* (Robinhood Markets Inc.), two products in which the cultural dynamics of casual gaming, mobile media and finance intersect. While *Bux* perpetuates the concept of finance as an aspirational, male-dominated arena, *Robinhood* rides the waves of anti-establishment entrepreneurial culture while being part of the financial status quo. Both apps are unashamedly bastions of capitalism.

Via these apps, which are part of the emerging *fintech* sector (digital technology that enables banking and financial services), lay investors can access financial markets anywhere, at any time, allowing trading to enter previously inaccessible spheres of everyday life, much like the pokie apps analysed in the previous chapter. The growth of the fintech sector is a result of a techno-historical juncture. On the one hand, the increased processing capabilities of mobile technology meant that networks were reliable and fast enough to support a high volume of financial transactions. On the other hand, big-scale market crashes led companies and people to look for alternative sources of revenue. As Annette Mackenzie points out, "It was the credit squeeze after the 2008 global financial crisis that really changed the game and suddenly made alternative sources of finance more attractive" (2015, p. 50). Among these alternatives, Mackenzie points out, are a handful of start-ups, with a structure that "combines tech-savvy whizz kids with hard-headed finance experts and entrepreneurs" who believe that technology "can make inroads into this complex, heavily regulated and most conservative of industries" (2015, p. 51). Nothing epitomises start-up culture to a greater extent than apps.

If in the early 2000s, the desktop computer allowed everyday Janes and Johns to buy and sell stock at home, mobile apps colonise the moments of respite in everyday life. The ideals of productivity and gain drive the design of these apps. Waiting is missing out on an opportunity to make money, to play the market, to achieve financial self-improvement. One can buy and sell stocks while commuting, eating or watching television. Like gambling, the de-professionalisation of finance promises a redistribution of wealth, but its mechanisms are far from being democratic.

In today's environment, finance is not only familiar to the Global North individual's daily routine but is a fundamental entangled force of their self-definition. Finance is, in fact, directly related to the sense of self and self-worth. As Randy Martin points out in the introduction to his valuable volume *Financialization of Daily Life*, "Finance, the management of money's ebbs and flows, is not simply in the service of accessible wealth, but presents itself as a merger of business and life cycles, as a means for the acquisition of self" (2002, p. 3). Finance is the prism through which transformations of self are filtered in capitalist societies. By infiltrating domestic spaces and the flows of everyday life through mobile devices, financial markets offer a promise of the sudden improvement of one's life conditions. This is strikingly similar to the mirage of success presented by gambling. In digital finance and gamble-play, a life-changing event is seemingly within reach. That moment of hesitation or decision can make or break the promise of a better future. Money becomes immaterial, a metaphor for hope and broken dreams.

Digital currency alters the dynamics of finance. In "Postscript on the Societies of Control", his much-cited essay, Gilles Deleuze presciently argues that the shift from the societies of discipline to the societies of control is tightly related to our relationship with money. Changes in this relationship are motivated as much by culture and world views as they are by reconfigurations of money as media. From coins to bits. From bags full of bills to instantaneous digital transactions. From silver and gold to shape-shifting graphics on a monitor. Deleuze contends that "discipline always referred back to minted money that locks gold in as numerical standard, while control relates to floating rates of exchange, modulated according to a rate established by a set of standard currencies" (1992, p. 5). Analogue and digital finance are two different animals. The mole and the serpent, according to Deleuze:

> The old monetary mole is the animal of the spaces of enclosure, but the serpent is that of the societies of control. We have passed from one animal to the other, from the mole to the serpent, in the system under which we live, but also in our manner of living and in our relations with others.
>
> (Ibidem)

The metaphor is effective. The serpent of volatile currency slides sinuously in the garden of forking paths that is the global financial system. Deleuze's exemplification of the new economic mode as a serpent makes us think of global financial networks, which shed skin daily, hourly, minute by minute, each second. Stock trading apps provide a window into these perpetual transformations but also a possibility for agency in a world that is hard to fully grasp. That is what makes gamble-play and digital finance so alluring: the possibility of action and transformation amidst the chaos. Or rather, perhaps, the possibility of being one with the chaos. For, as Deleuze argues, the subject of control "is undulatory, in orbit, in a continuous network" (1992, p. 6). Finance and gambling are promises of a continuous transformation.

Today, finance brings about existential questions. Finance was originally the new American dream and a neo-liberal seal of progress, and it is directly linked to the possibilities or non-possibilities of life. Finance is a way of being and becoming, a motor for change or a provider of stability. Stock trading apps are one of the many materialisations of this ethos. The recent history of finance is also a history of media change. In particular, global information networks have changed the dynamics in which trade happens, its temporality and spatial confines. As Karin Knorr Cetina and Urs Bruegger explain, a major shift happened in 1981, when Reuters launched a system that had 145 institutional subscribers in nine countries, achieving limited but relevant worldwide connection (2002, p. 931). They write,

> Before the market went on screen worldwide, dealers spent most of their time determining where the market was - that is, determining who was willing to deal and at what price, a task accomplished via phone and telex. The market stayed in territorial space, hidden in transnational banking networks of institutions that neither shared the same news and dealing prices nor knew about all interests in dealing. Any coordination of consciousness that did obtain was limited to those moments and parties involved in particular connections.
>
> (Ibidem)

Gamble-play-like financial media are one of the many ramifications of the market's move to global information systems. The stock trading apps discussed in this chapter also reveal discourses exemplary of late capitalism in Global North settings. These discourses are associated with the idea of the entrepreneurial self, hyper masculinity and what some have termed "cowboy capitalism", whereas fast, gut-inspired but possibly gutless decisions are made at the spur of the moment. The close connection between gambling and finance is also based on the ludic enjoyment that players might feel. As Christine Hurt argues, "both sports betting and stock trading have some degree of entertainment value" (2006, p. 390). Hurt goes on to discuss the similarities between sports betting and stock trading: even though success in both is ultimately defined by chance, there is a degree of perceived skill in trying to predict results. Sports bettors and stock buyers strive to make informed decisions based on statistics, team or company performance over time and affective links to particular options. Both universes are filled with titillation for the unexpected, a sense of manufactured urgency and a dose of pride fed by the labels of 'winners' and 'losers'. However, these labels are an illusion as 'defeat' or 'triumph' can only be determined through performance over a period of time. Balances generally end up being negative as the momentary sense of accomplishment after a 'big win' can blind participants to the fact that the majority of people are on the losing side.

Stock trading apps are hyper masculine in that they are marketed specifically to 'blokey blokes'. Like gambling, finance has been a historically gendered arena. In the eighteenth and nineteenth centuries, when gambling and finance were still inextricably intertwined, wagering by women was frowned upon. In Britain, "Particular concern was expressed over gambling by women; it was said that women gambled with the household money and forsook the running of the house and the care of their children" (DeGoede, 2005, p. 56). The two stock trading apps analysed here are built on a hyper masculine discourse that even led the *Daily Mail* to publish an article titled "Could you be the next Wolf of Wall Street? App turns the stock market into a game" (Woollaston, 2014), referencing the unscrupulous financier Jordan Belfort, immortalised in *The Wolf of Wall Street*, a 2013 Martin Scorsese film. Through unethical trading (he went to jail accused of crafting a fraud scheme), Belfort was able to amass a considerable fortune and lead an adrenaline-fuelled life in which debauchery and the objectification of women were the glue that held his financial 'boys' club' together. The universes of Wall Street and frat-boy culture have long commingled, a connection that is particularly relevant in the Trump era. Silicon Valley has constantly been deemed a boy's club that prides itself on being a meritocracy when, in truth, according to critics, it perpetuates gender inequalities, ableism and ethnic stereotypes. As Sallie Krawcheck argues in a piece for *The New York Times*,

> The bigger cost derives from how women's ideas are discounted and their talent ignored. I have seen it up close in the two worlds I know best: Wall Street, where I was chief executive of Smith Barney and of Merrill Lynch Wealth Management, and in Silicon Valley, where I've raised money to run my start-up, Ellevest. These places are perhaps the purest microcosms of capitalism, and their lessons are instructive for all of us. Both Wall Street and venture capital are industries whose product is money: Wall Street directs trillions of dollars to the sectors or businesses that it believes will deliver the highest returns. Likewise, Silicon Valley invests hundreds of billions of dollars in start-ups that it believes will deliver the best returns. Both pick economic winners and losers.
>
> (Krawcheck, 2017)

The discourses surrounding stock trading apps echo these two pure "microcosms of capitalism", with a particular emphasis on the 'Wall Street type'. Both Wall Street and Silicon Valley claim to be elite, innovative and accessible, when history has proved the contrary. The Wall Street heterosexual, white, macho man archetype was particularly popular in the period 1980–2000, with cinematic representations in films like Oliver Stone's 1987 *Wall Street* ("Greed is good", words famously uttered by financier Gordon Gekko) or Mary Harron's 2000 *American Psycho*, Patrick Bateman's delirious trip in which capitalist aesthetic and bodily perfection lead to a bloodbath. Both films are meant to be harsh critiques of hyper-capitalism, but both Gekko and Bateman are heroes in the finance industry, men who will stop at nothing to achieve success, to get the car, the money and the women. Currently, the Showtime show *Billions* deals with ethical questions involving hedge fund management. In all of these cases, the end (multiplying wealth) justifies the means.

Risk as the raison d'être of international markets has its advocates among Global North scholars. Caitlin Zaloom, for example, argues that complex practices, such as financial speculation, are unfairly criticised when in fact they are "exemplary acts of contemporary productivity that configure markets" (2004, p. 365). Risk, for Zaloom, is a productive force and therefore beneficial. Risk-taking is also often seen as a venerable action. As Martin (2002) argues,

> The market is treated as an ecology, as an environment obeying natural laws, and therefore welcoming to all who would come to discover it. Unlike natural disaster where exposure to danger is shared across the spectrum of participants, financial risk is a disbursement of reward that legitimates the dangers for those who are not the beneficiaries of events.
>
> (p. 104)

Stock trading apps provide a sort of exploration tour in the ecology of finance. Familiarisation with the platform by potential users is key in the expansion of mobile stock trading networks. An early Hong Kong-based study concluded that if "trial versions of mobile stock apps are available to users, investors will be willing to use it and see what it can do" (Sam et al. 2013, p. 440). Like some gamble-play platforms that offer games for play money as a lead-up to real-money gambling, stock trading app designers want to make potential players/investors feel comfortable in the platform. Woollaston (2014) describes the procedures involved in the training option in *Bux* as follows: "The app takes users through step-by-step instructions on how to search for companies to invest in, how to sell shares, and what the jargon means. They can then trade on well-known brands, using their virtual currency, to get a feel for how the system works". By allowing players to learn the ropes of the investment world, everyday stock trading apps guarantee a longer and more intense future consumption, a model consistent with gamble-play (see Chapter 3 "Gamble-play media and practices of consumption"). The sense of mastery over the procedural apparatus of an app provided by practice modalities can give false sense of control. These practice modes are not always regulated. The trial versions could potentially be rigged for higher returns, driving a kind of behaviour that benefits the house and not good investment practice. As we have seen with a variety of gamble-play platforms discussed in this book, the sense of risk can be mitigated through this false sense of undergoing a process of apprenticeship.

The stock exchange market is unpredictable, the most complex casino in the world. Historical financial upheavals have proved that stock prices are anything but fixed, and seemingly unrelated events can build up to a perfect storm of loses and uncertainty. However, there is a fundamental difference in how risk has been historically framed in gambling and in finance. While in gambling risk is a quasi-religious force, a manifestation of divine intervention, economists have defined it as the "measurable probability of an occurrence, whereas uncertainty is immeasurable" (Martin, 2002, p. 105). In finance, forecasts and predictions, the bread and butter of traders, "don't need to be right, but they do need to be quantifiable" (Ibidem). Mathematical reason tames perceived chaos. The rationalisation of uncertainty is the creed on which the financial market rests. Martin argues further that risk "is a rhetoric of the future that is really about the present; it is a means of price setting on the promise that a future is attainable" (Ibidem). Stock trading apps promise to put this future within a click's distance.

Bux and *Robinhood* are two of those apps, but they seduce users appealing to different affects and sensibilities.

Bux: Investing on the Social

Bux is an app that promises to add a social element to stock trading; ruthless but fun competition. The app was established in the Netherlands in 2014. Like most online gamble-play products, it attempts to incorporate the dynamics and affordances of social media into monetary exchanges. The app is mainly used in the United Kingdom. *Bux* is marketed as a platform that brings the social back to everyday financial transactions. In this sense, it is promoted in a similar way to some gamble-play products, exalting the ephemeral social contact that emerges through manufactured interaction. The app has two modalities: FunBux, trade in virtual money, and SeriousBux, trade in real money.

With FunBux users get a sense of the market, risking without losing, like in a practice poker table in an online casino. With the FunBux mode, users become familiarised with what I have termed procedure-images (Chapter 2), a system of symbols that contain interaction and defines what the digital platforms 'says' or 'does'. ICT's are key in mediating people's relationship with money and its flows. As Zwick reminds us when discussing an earlier form of digital stock exchange via desktop computers,

> In the process of continuous and unlimited unfolding of new communication and information technologies on the field of global financial flows and exchanges, the virtual qualities of a visual representation governed by the computer screen have come to dominate the relationship between the investor and the market. The screen brings a geographically dispersed and invisible market close to the participants as a virtual representation.
>
> (2005, p. 23)

Thus, the more familiar a user is with the visual representation of financial flows, the more knowledgeable and in control she or he will feel. For Zwick, this dynamic ends up "giving birth to the market as a site for experiencing risk as an end in itself" (Ibidem). Risk becomes a narcotic, the island of time in which investors enter and money becomes fully immaterial and malleable.

What is problematic with practice modes in financial apps, as with gamble-play media in general, is that being literate in how to use a platform does not necessarily translate in mastery over the outcomes. Procedure-images can make a user believe that they are engaged in an equal relationship with the machine. However, as black boxes, stock trading apps are just the surface of a set of relationships that resemble a rhizome – convoluted, tight, sinuous. Chains of labour, objects, intangible goods, trade routes, government policies and infrastructures converge to produce a figure as if out of thin air: such and such company's stock is worth such and such amount of money. As Osborne contended five decades ago, we can characterise the stock exchange as a black box "with an input of orders to buy and sell of various types and amounts and an output of transactions at various prices" (1965, p. 88). Stock trading apps are an oversimplification of this black box.

What the virtualisation of the market achieves, according to Zwick, is a process in which "the computer screen recodes and repackages the stock market as consumption object while enabling the individual online investor to gain a sense of (consumer) agency and self-actualization" (2005, p. 23). This agency is an illusion as the player has no control whatsoever on any of those elements – in real life finance, having privileged information is known as insider trading and constitutes a crime in most jurisdictions.

Finance is described as war by marketing teams. In its website, *Bux* invites users to "CONNECT AND BATTLE WITH FELLOW TRADERS" (sic). The framing of finance as a 'battle' further emphasises the agonistic nature of lay trading. Players do not only win; they win *against* someone else. Stock trading apps utilise social media dynamics, such as leader boards and status among 'friends', to harness people's vanity in believing that they can beat Wall Street and get the Ferrari and the mansion. As hyper masculine products, these apps encourage a capitalist survival of the fittest environment more akin to fantasy sports leagues than to wealth management.

In an animated promotional video (see Figures 7.1 and 7.2), we can see an everyday Caucasian man dressed in pants and a white shirt, happily jumping through a set of graphics and then racing a group of suited businessmen. He then falls on a pile of cash and the word BUX appears on the screen. The video then zooms out to a mobile phone where we see the app's layout, followed by a photograph of Tesla CEO Elon Musk, today's entrepreneurial archetype (corporate, masculine, heterosexual, savvy and daring). Our main character, who also sports thick glasses, then navigates through the app and invests in Tesla. He jumps on a tricycle (a metaphor for virtual money investment) and then on a bike (signifier of real money transactions) and races suited men while more money falls from the sky (Figure 7.1). He is clearly set apart from the pack: an everyday John Doe competing against the big boys, a hobbyist pedalling head-to-head with the professionals. And beating them (Figure 7.2). He crosses the finish line and raises his arms in triumph. We then see a close-up of his smartphone displaying a ranking where he is gloriously highlighted as the winner. The platforms layout is similar to gamble-play and digital games platforms where players are ranked according to their achievements.

This video is problematic for a variety of reasons. Competing against others sets up a scenario where players are making financial decisions

BUX Intro Video (English)

7,561 views   14   1   SHARE   ...

Figure 7.1 Promotional YouTube video for the app *Bux*.
Image captured on November 27, 2017 from www.youtube.com/watch?v=1NaunBuHMfo.

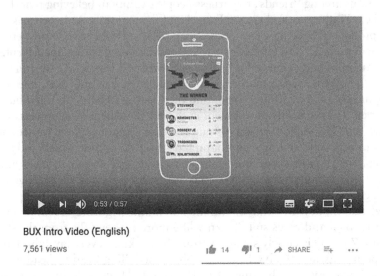

Figure 7.2 Promotional YouTube video for the app *Bux*.
Image captured on November 27, 2017 from www.youtube.com/watch?v=1NaunBuHMfo.

based on competitive forces and ego, and not necessarily on their financial position. Testosterone fuelled competition (notice that the ad only
features male investors) supersedes the cool headedness required in professional finance. The video is also clearly gendered and perpetuates the
notion that finance is a 'man's job'. Deleuze's "man of control" (1992,
p. 6) gains currency as he achieves a passing moment of self-improvement
by beating the odds. The nerdy individual beats the Gordon Gekkos and
Patrick Batemans of the world, just like the gambler takes a shortcut in
life with a big win. With the slow advances in terms of gender equality
in the Global North workforce, it is notable that *Bux* perpetuates the
representation of finance as a 'boys club'.

Robinhood: Bandit Capitalism?

Robinhood is an app that allows investors to trade stock without paying
transaction fees or commissions, a considerable variation of the prevail-
ing model of stock trading apps in which the company takes a commis-
sion (remember: the house always wins). The name is heavily loaded as
it refers to the British folk character that took money from the rich to
distribute it more fairly among the poor.

In economic theory, the term 'Robin Hood' is often used to describe
models in which the rich are taxed to redistribute wealth among the need-
iest. This model has been criticised as a failure, with authors like Parguez
arguing that the "Robin Hood welfare state" has led to an unproductive

status quo. He argues that "Redistribution is a mere illusion based on a misunderstanding of the nature of the monetary circuit: *taxes destroy income and slash aggregate demand*" (2002, p. 90). It is curious, then, that the developers of this app have chosen a name that goes counter to what the financial world considers to be an appropriate model. However, the term 'Robin Hood' does talk to recent social movements, such as #occupywallstreet, which bases its demands on the idea that 1 per cent of the population holds financial power while the other 99 per cent struggles to make ends meet. *Robinhood* discursively appropriates resistance and turns it into capitalist drive.

The app's graphic design is dominated by green hues, just like Robin Hood's iconic outfit. The app was launched in 2014 and is operated by Robinhood Financial, LCC. As part of the fintech sector, the company is based in Palo Alto, California, the epicentre of entrepreneurial culture. The company was founded by Baiju Bhatt and Vladamir Tenev, who were roommates at Stanford University, where both majored in mathematics. Bhatt and Tenev came up with the idea for *Robinhood* in 2011, after the protests in Wall Street highlighted the rampant inequality in the United States (Harris, 2017).

As of 2017 *Robinhood* can operate in the United States and Puerto Rico alone. It has been announced that in the future, *Robinhood* will be available to other markets, such as Australia. Clients can only be located in the US, a jurisdictional limitation similar to the one forced on online casinos based in the United States. In April 2017, the company was valued at USD $1.2 billion (McAlone, 2017). Its business model is based on micro transactions as it has become a "favourite among younger people looking to invest without paying USD $7 or more per trade" (McAlone, 2017). The target audience is first-time investors who are just learning the rules of the game and for whom trading could be another source of entertainment or another stream of information in their social media portfolio. *Robinhood* sits alongside YouTube, Instagram and Facebook. By making finance 'cool', they have tapped into the millennial market, long ignored by financial services (Harris, 2017).

According to its website, *Robinhood* is able to offer a free service because of the high level of automation in its processes: "Robinhood started with the idea that a technology-driven brokerage could operate with significantly less overhead. We cut out the fat that makes other brokerages costly—hundreds of storefront locations and manual account management". Through this app, Robinhood Financial is moving towards a full virtualisation of stock trading, eliminating most human interaction, which brings about questions of accountability regarding financial loss (Figure 7.3). The company states that its ultimate mission is "to democratize access to financial markets to everyone in the world" (Robinhood, 2017). However, this "democratic" drive does not

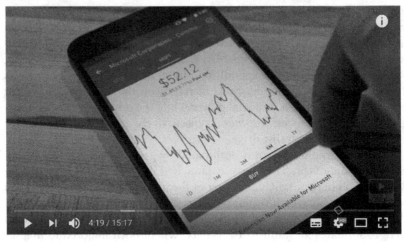

Broker Review: Robinhood Trading App

177,717 views   👍 1K   👎 83   ➔ SHARE   ☰₊   •••

Figure 7.3 Online review of the app *Robinhood* by ClayTrader.
Image captured on November 27, 2017 from www.youtube.com/watch?v=17YP6ZGmH44.

necessarily translate into fairness. Contrary to other stock trading apps that offer information on companies to support users' decisions, there is no built-in research in the *Robinhood* app, although the company will launch a web-based information service (Constine, 2017). Akin to gambling, decisions through the app are not necessarily based on facts but on hunches. Additionally, dealing in low quantities can also leave investors more vulnerable. As Constine writes in the tech blog *TechCrunch*,

> Betting on individual stocks is a serious gamble, and undiversified investors can get burned by a sudden share price drop. While *Robinhood* is democratizing trading by removing fees that can eat up the potential profit margins of smaller investors, these users may also have less net worth to protect them from investment losses.
>
> (Constine, 2017)

The company also offers a premium service, *Robinhood Gold*, which provides lines of credit and afterhours service, still with no charge for trading. About 50 per cent of the company's income comes from these paid accounts. *Robinhood Gold* reminds us of the freemium model in social games (*Words with Friends*, *Angry Birds* and such) and social casinos in which players pay to obtain heightened experiences or to hold an advantage over their competitors. The discourses of fairness, generosity and democratisation embedded in this app runs contrary to the rhetorical apparatuses of Wall Street and Silicon Valley, with as of yet unknown results.

Conclusion

As a short bookend to this monograph, this chapter expands the applicability of the conceptual framework of gamble-play and tests it in the sphere of finance. Rather than just performing a description and analysis of the gambling industry, this book looks to delve into wider issues regarding risk, entertainment and the banalisation of money in late capitalism. Gambling is an entryway into an understanding of how the worlds of entertainment, digital media and finance influence each other and generate new cultural forms, such as gamble-play.

Gambling and finance rely on risk, a jump into the abyss that, ironically, can be an optimistic respite for some in the current socio-political climate. As Martin puts it, "If modernity is a compulsive movement of presents, risk helps explain how the past is relinquished and the future embraced at any given moment" (2002, p. 106). Through platform design, gamble-play and stock trading app designers provide islands of time where the world sits still and possibilities are mischievously endless. Gambling and finance trade in vicious and often misleading vocabularies of hope. Money is lost by most and made by few. It could be argued that social stock trading apps are using the greedy mechanisms perfected by the finance industry together with the gaming techniques developed in Silicon Valley to make the market appear more accessible to casual investors. Further research needs to be done to tackle the intersection of finance, digital games and gamble-play media.

But losing is sold as a hell of a ride, an attempt to master one's own destiny.

Note

The author wishes to thank Mr Stuart Parry for his feedback on earlier versions of this chapter.

References

Constine, J. (2017, November 1). Robinhood stock trading comes to web with finance news for its 3M users, *TechCrunch*. Retrieved from https://techcrunch.com/2017/11/01/robinhood-for-web/

De Goede, M. (2005). *Virtue, fortune, and faith: A genealogy of finance* (Vol. 24). Minneapolis: University of Minnesota Press.

Deleuze, G. (1992). Postscript on the societies of control. *October, 59*, 3–7.

Dorn, D., & Sengmueller, P. (2009). Trading as entertainment? *Management Science, 55*(4), 591–603.

Goggin, J. (2012). Regulating (virtual) subjects: finance, entertainment and games. *Journal of Cultural Economy, 5*(4), 441–456.

Harris, A. (2017, August 14). How brokerage app Robinhood got millennials to love the market. *Fast Company*. Retrieved from www.fastcompany.com/40437888/how-brokerage-app-robinhood-got-millennials-to-love-the-market

Hurt, C. (2006). Regulating public morals and private markets: Online securities trading, Internet gambling, and the speculation paradox. *BUL Review, 86*, 371.

Knorr Cetina, K., & Bruegger, U. (2002). Global microstructures: The virtual societies of financial markets. *American Journal of Sociology, 107*(4), 905–950.

Krawcheck, S. (2017, December 2). The cost of devaluing women. *The New York Times*. Retrieved from www.nytimes.com/2017/12/02/opinion/sunday/the-cost-of-devaluing-women.html

Mackenzie, A. (2015). The fintech revolution. *London Business School Review, 26*(3), 50–53.

Martin, R. (2002). *Financialization of Daily Life*. Philadelphia: Temple University Press.

McAlone, N. (2017, April 27). The no-fee stock trading app Robinhood is now officially worth $1.3 billion. *Business Insider Australia*. Retrieved from www.businessinsider.com.au/robinhood-stock-trading-app-valuation-13-billion-2017-4?r=US&IR=T

Nicoll, F. (2013). Finopower: Governing intersections between gambling and finance. *Communication and Critical/Cultural Studies, 10*(4), 385–405.

Osborne, M. F. M. (1965). The dynamics of stock trading. *Econometrica: Journal of the Econometric Society*, 88–113.

Parguez, A. (2002). A monetary theory of public finance: The new fiscal orthodoxy: From plummeting deficits to planned fiscal surpluses. *International Journal of Political Economy, 32*(3), 80–97.

Sam, K. M., Chatwin, C. R., & Ma, I. C. (2013, December). Mobile stock trading (MST) and its social impact: A case study in Hong Kong. In *Industrial Engineering and Engineering Management (IEEM), 2013 IEEE International Conference on* (pp. 437–441). IEEE.

Woollaston, V. (2014, November 21). Could you be the next Wolf of Wall Street? App turns the stock market into a game. *Daily Mail Australia*. Retrieved from www.dailymail.co.uk/sciencetech/article-2842720/Could-Wolf-Wall-Street-App-turns-stock-market-game.html

Zaloom, C. (2004). The productive life of risk. *Cultural Anthropology, 19*(3), 365–391.

Zwick, D. (2005). Where the action is: Internet stock trading as edgework. *Journal of Computer-Mediated Communication, 11*(1), 22–43.

Postface
Gamble-Play in the Societies of Control

Gambling is a long-standing and persistent cultural practice that has endured through changes in social norms, regulations and attitudes towards risk-taking. Gambling has also survived and developed through media changes. Poker was first played with hand-painted cards, which were then printed and are now digital. Slot machines first produced random events with mechanical reels, which became electronic and then fully digital. The cultural logic of gambling, moreover, has influenced other spheres of contemporary life, such as stock trading, a practice that shapes global financial systems. The cultural logic of gamble-play is evident in emerging digital products, such as casual stock trading apps, discussed in the last chapter of this book.

Gamble-play cultures have also influenced the procedural dynamics and monetisation models of some digital games. Two recent bestselling games, *Star Wars: Battlefront II* and *Destiny 2*, have been heavily criticised because they accept payment for loot box features where players can win random prizes (Goodall, 2017). Critics have stated that this is basically gambling for gamers, who can potentially be underage (Kain, 2017). *Battlefront II*'s developer, digital game giant Electronic Arts, temporarily removed this microtransaction scheme to address fans' concerns (Donnelly, 2017), but this type of features makes the collision of gambling and video games even more evident and a concept like gamble-play more salient. Aaron Langille and Charles Daviau describe loot boxes in a way that eerily resembles slot machines: "Rather than paying for a guaranteed item, players are buying an inexpensive chance to receive a reward, which may turn out to be a desired item, an undesired one or one they already own" (2017). Gamble-play's tentacles stretch far.

The transformation of gambling though the appropriation of digital technologies continues humankind's enduring engagement with games of chance. After all, twenty-first-century people share similar excitement and preoccupations regarding skill and chance as people in Mesopotamia playing the Royal Game of Ur in 2600 BC; as the Castilian king Alfonso X when he commissioned his *Libro de los Juegos*, a panoply of games of skill and chance, in the thirteenth century (Cano Aguilar, 1989; Carpenter, 1998; Molina Molina, 1998); as the self-confessed problem gambler and Russian novelist Fyodor Dostoyevsky; or even as the individuals who carved dice for divination in pieces of wood, stone and ivory 10,000 years ago (Manzur, 2009).

Throughout this book I have argued, however, that gambling and gambling-like media and practices, such as stock trading apps, are experiencing a series of transformations that make us reconsider what we think of as 'gambling'. Gamble-play represents both an industry and a cultural change in which the playful aspects of gambling are exaggerated to mitigate the sensation of risk, generating and sustaining novel networks of pleasure, seduction and control. Gamble-play brings gambling closer to mass entertainment as well as audiovisual and interactive entertainment and financial technologies.

Gamble-play disrupts the spatial and temporal boundaries of gambling. Past notions of the reaches of gambling need to be reimagined. For example, as discussed in the introduction, for Gerda Reith gambling is "a ritual which is strictly demarcated from the everyday world around it", in which "chance is deliberately courted as a mechanism which governs a redistribution of wealth among players as well as a commercial interest or 'house'" (Reith, 1999, p. 1). However, in the past few years gambling practices have evolved, driven by the use of artefacts – such as computers, smartphones and tablets – that drive its normalisation as an acceptable and fun form of entertainment and even a means to earn a living. Moreover, there are new forms of wealth being traded, such as influence in social networking sites and the time invested by users to expand operators' reach in assemblages of gambling and play as well as finance. Practices such as casual betting are being reframed and institutionalised (Albarrán-Torres & Goggin, 2018).

The cultural change associated with gamble-play is motivated mainly by four factors discussed in this book. First, gamble-play platforms stage random outcomes through complex, interactive audiovisual content. Second, gamble-play becomes culturally normalised through its appropriation by the tech-savvy middle class, mainly in the Global North, which generates new practices of consumption. Third, in gamble-play, gambling undergoes material and discursive convergence with other types of media, including film, digital games, fintech products and social networking sites. In the case of film, gamble-play uses imagery from Hollywood franchises and celebrities to generate user affinity with gambling products and profit from well-established affective states. Gamble-play appropriates video game conventions in gameplay and affordances such as avatar creation. In the case of social networking sites, gamble-play allows digital media practices, such as sharing, creating an online profile and archiving one's playing history. Finally, gamble-play is experienced through devices such as smartphones, tablets and computers, which allows gambling to infiltrate the rhythms of the everyday as well as spaces previously foreign to this activity, such as domestic environments.

Gamble-play also provides a continuation of traditional casino and slot gambling practices. The graphic and audiovisual design of many gamble-play platforms preserves the 'aura' of preceding gambling cultures by incorporating icons, such as Egyptian settings, Las Vegas casino environments and even domestic spaces, in the case of platforms that aim to replicate everyday forms of gambling, such as kitchen table poker games. Gamble-play also perpetuates some of the mechanisms of control mobilised by traditional gambling industries, such as the promise of the 'big win' and the logic of 'near misses' in slot machines (Kassinove & Schare, 2001), which can lead to problematic forms of consumption. In parallel, gamble-play also institutes new media dynamics, such as social media sharing and 'push notifications' on mobile devices that promote constant play.

Throughout this monograph, I argued that changes in contemporary forms of digital gambling are a materialisation of the ideas of control discussed by Gilles Deleuze (1992). Deleuze argues that contemporary models of state and corporate management allow for forms of control that are continuous and never-ending, and that individuals are entangled in a perpetual project of self-fulfilment and realisation. Digital gambling media currently sit at a key juncture in which operators can exercise this type of control. New platforms and devices, such as online poker tables and social casino apps, help gambling infiltrate the spheres and rhythms of the everyday in new ways that encourage the perpetuity of this journey of self-realisation. They do so by provoking particular types of desire, such as the wants for unlimited fun, financial gain, class mobility and social recognition.

While traditional gambling always offers the possibility, however slim, to recuperate the money invested in a game of chance, some gamble-play media only promise what Deleuze and Guattari call an "incorporeal transformation" (2004, p. 89) – a change in how a body is classified without there being a physical change. Operators promise both enjoyment and a transformation of the player into a winner, a gambling 'friend' or a gaming expert.

Gamble-play sheds new light on other critiques of gambling's place in society. The British novelist and political thinker George Orwell, for example, offered his own indictment of gambling as a mechanism of control in his iconic novel *Nineteen Eighty-Four*, originally published in 1949, during the first years of the post-WWII era, and much discussed in the socio-political climate of the Trump presidency and the rise of the extreme right in Western Europe. The novel portrays a totalitarian regime and has also regained cultural relevance due to revelations, by whistle-blowers including Edward Snowden, Anonymous and WikiLeaks, of state and corporate surveillance through the hacking of informational networks (Coleman, 2014).

Orwell's particular indictment of gambling echoes the dynamics of control put in place by present-day digital gambling and gaming industries.

Orwell's novel also argues that gambling is a class project, a belief shared by critics of contemporary gambling industries (Markham & Young, 2014). Orwell writes about lotteries, a low stakes form of gambling, in the totalitarian state governed by the Wizard of Oz-like character of Big Brother, an archetypical embodiment of deception and control:

> The Lottery, with its weekly pay-out of enormous prizes, was the one public event to which the proles paid serious attention. It was probable that there were some millions of proles for whom the Lottery was the principal if not the only reason for remaining alive. It was their delight, their folly, their anodyne, their intellectual stimulant. Where the Lottery was concerned, even people who could barely read and write seemed capable of intricate calculations and staggering feats of memory. There was a whole tribe of men who made their living simply by selling systems, forecasts, and lucky amulets. Winston had nothing to do with the Lottery, which was managed by the Ministry of Plenty, but he was aware (indeed everyone in the party was aware) that the prizes were largely imaginary. Only small sums were actually paid out, the winners of the big prizes being nonexistent persons.
>
> (Orwell, 2011, pp. 98–99)

Orwell identified two enduring concerns involving the relationship between gambling and the state. The first concern is the existence of mechanisms of control and surveillance involved in promoting gambling among lower socio-economic sectors (Livingstone, 2001). The second concern is the persistent illusion of the 'big win' among gamblers, a logic that some scholars have identified as the "vocabularies of hope" on which the gambling industry relies (Lynch, 1990; Kassinove & Schare, 2001; Weatherly, Sauter & King, 2004). Many gamble-play technologies are also equipped with sensors that produce metadata about the user's location and patterns of consumption. Players become *de facto* market research subjects, oftentimes unknowingly.

Ubiquitous devices, such as desktop computers, smartphones and tablets, allow gamble-play operators to establish a more constant and profitable engagement with players. New products and revenue models are developed based on constant play *and* constant communication. The technical and cultural convergence present in gamble-play generates new practices and identities around the playfulness and seduction of gambling, a dynamic that I have described and analysed in this book.

References

Albarrán-Torres, C., & Goggin, G. (2018). Mobile betting apps: Odds on the social. In J. Vincent & L. Haddon (Eds.), *Smartphone cultures* (pp. 25–38). London and New York, NY: Routledge.

Cano Aguilar, R. (1989). Los prólogos alfonsíes. *Cahiers de Linguistique Hispanique Médiévale, 14*(1), 79–90.

Carpenter, D. E. (1998). Alea jacta est': at the gaming table with Alfonso the Learned. *Journal of Medieval History, 24*(4), 333–345.

Coleman, G. (2014). *Hacker, hoaxer, whistleblower, spy: The many faces of Anonymous.* London: Verso Books.

Deleuze, G. (1992). Postscript on the societies of control. *October, 59*, 3–7.

Deleuze, G., & Guattari, F. (2004). *Capitalism and schizophrenia: Anti-Oedipus.* London: Continuum.

Donnelly, J. (2017, November 20). Lucasfilm weighs in on Star Wars Battlefront 2 loot box ordeal. *PC Gamer.* Retrieved from www.pcgamer.com/lucasfilm-weighs-in-on-star-wars-battlefront-2-loot-box-ordeal/

Dostoyevsky, F. (2010). *The Gambler and other stories.* New York, NY: Penguin Classics.

Goodall, A. (2017, December 19). Are loot boxes the slot machines of video gaming? *The Spinoff.* Retrieved from https://thespinoff.co.nz/games/19-12-2017/lootboxes-slot-machines-video-gaming/

Kain, E. (2017, November 29). Loot boxes are at the heart of both 'Star Wars: Battlefront II' and 'Destiny 2' backlash. *Forbes.* Retrieved from www.forbes.com/sites/erikkain/2017/11/29/loot-boxes-are-at-the-heart-of-both-star-wars-battlefront-ii-and-destiny-2-backlash/#4fc1269c7786

Kassinove, J. I., & Schare, M. L. (2001). Effects of the "near miss" and the "big win" on persistence at slot machine gambling. *Psychology of Addictive Behaviors, 15*(2), 155–158.

Langille, A., & Daviau, C. (2017, December 15). How Star Wars battlefront 'loot boxes' & The Last Jedi change video games. *The Conversation.* Retrieved from https://theconversation.com/how-star-wars-battlefront-loot-boxes-and-the-last-jedi-change-video-games-88368

Livingstone, C. (2001). The social economy of poker machine gambling in Victoria. *International Gambling Studies, 1*(1), 46–65.

Lynch, R. (1990). Working-class luck and vocabularies of hope among regular poker-machine players. In D. Rowe & G. Lawrence (Eds.), *Sport and leisure: Trends in Australian popular culture* (pp. 189–208). Sydney, NSW: Harcourt Brace Jovanovich.

Manzur, J. (2009). *What's luck got to do with it: The history, mathematics, and psychology behind the gambler's illusion.* Princeton, NJ: Princeton University Press.

Markham, F., & Young, M. (2014). Who wins from 'Big Gambling' in Australia? *The Conversation.* Retrieved from http://theconversation.com/who-wins-from-big-gambling-in-australia-22930

Molina Molina, A. L. (1998). Los juegos de mesa en la Edad Media. *Miscelánea Medieval Murciana,* (21–22), 215–239. Retrieved from http://revistas.um.es/mimemur/article/view/j7861/7621

Orwell, G. (2011). *Nineteen eighty-four.* Melbourne: Penguin Books (Australia).

Reith, G. (1999). *The age of chance: Gambling in Western culture.* London: Routledge.

Weatherly, J. N., Sauter, J. M., & King, B. M. (2004). The 'big win' and resistance to extinction when gambling. *The Journal of Psychology: Interdisciplinary and Applied, 138*(6), 495–504.

Index

Printed in the United States
by Baker & Taylor Publisher Services

Printed in the United States
by Baker & Taylor Publisher Services